BUILDING A BUSINESS
OF POLITICS

The Delegated Welfare State: Medicare, Markets, and the Governance of Social Policy
Kimberly J. Morgan and Andrea Louise Campbell

Rule and Ruin: The Downfall of Moderation and the Destruction of the Republican Party, From Eisenhower to the Tea Party
Geoffrey Kabaservice

Engines of Change: Party Factions in American Politics, 1868–2010
Daniel DiSalvo

Follow the Money: How Foundation Dollars Change Public School Politics
Sarah Reckhow

The Allure of Order: High Hopes, Dashed Expectations, and the Troubled Quest to Remake American Schooling
Jal Mehta

Rich People's Movements: Grassroots Campaigns to Untax the One Percent
Isaac William Martin

The Outrage Industry: Political Opinion Media and the New Incivility
Jeffrey M. Berry and Sarah Sobieraj

Artists of the Possible: Governing Networks and American Policy since 1945
Matt Grossmann

Building the Federal Schoolhouse: Localism and the American Education State
Douglas S. Reed

The First Civil Right: Race and the Rise of the Carceral State
Naomi Murakawa

How Policy Shapes Politics: Rights, Courts, Litigation, and the Struggle over Injury Compensation
Jeb Barnes and Thomas F. Burke

Ideas with Consequences: The Federalist Society and the Conservative Counterrevolution
Amanda Hollis-Brusky

No Day in Court: Access to Justice and the Politics of Judicial Retrenchment
Sarah Staszak

The Business of America is Lobbying: How Corporations Became Politicized and Politics Became More Corporate
Lee Drutman

BUILDING
A BUSINESS
OF POLITICS

*THE RISE OF POLITICAL CONSULTING
AND THE TRANSFORMATION OF
AMERICAN DEMOCRACY*

ADAM SHEINGATE

OXFORD
UNIVERSITY PRESS

OXFORD
UNIVERSITY PRESS

Oxford University Press is a department of the University of
Oxford. It furthers the University's objective of excellence in research,
scholarship, and education by publishing worldwide. Oxford is a registered trademark
of Oxford University Press in the UK and in certain other countries.

Published in the United States of America by
Oxford University Press
198 Madison Avenue, New York, NY 10016, United States of America

© Oxford University Press 2016

Library of Congress Cataloging-in-Publication Data
Sheingate, Adam D., 1969– author.
Building a business of politics : the rise of political consulting and the transformation
of American democracy / Adam Sheingate.
pages cm
Includes bibliographical references and index.
ISBN 978–0–19–021719–8 (hardcover : alk. paper) — ISBN 978–0–19–021720–4
(ebook)   1. Political consultants—United States.   2. Democracy—United States.
3. United States—Politics and government.   I. Title.
JK2281.S498 2016
324.0973—dc23
2015025441

1 3 5 7 9 8 6 4 2
Printed in the United States of America
on acid-free paper

For Leo and Lila

As you wish

CONTENTS

PREFACE

———❦———

MY INTEREST IN THE POLITICAL consulting industry began in 2005 as I was writing an essay on political entrepreneurship in American politics. Political consultants, it seemed to me, were political entrepreneurs in two senses. Consultants were literally entrepreneurs in the sense that they were engaged in a speculative search for profit. After all, political consulting is a business. In a second sense, however, political consultants were entrepreneurial as they creatively combined scientific polling, artful media, and local political knowledge into winning campaign messages and strategies.

Moreover, the business of political consulting struck me as emblematic of an increasingly entrepreneurial style in American politics. Over the past century, presidents, individual members of Congress, and a myriad of organizations and interests have pursued opportunities that expand their scope for independent action. Political consultants are central to this process as well, whether helping in the pursuit of a White House agenda, nurturing a congressional career, or carving out a niche within the panoply of Washington groups. If the entrepreneurial pursuit of political advantage is now a characteristic feature of our politics, I began to wonder how political consulting became a business and how the business of consulting contributed to a broader transformation in American democracy.

In my search for answers to these questions, I found myself increasingly interested in the practitioners I discovered along the way. Well before the term "political consultant" came into use, others were attempting to sell their wares to various candidates and causes. Operating under different names, such as publicity experts or counsels on public relations, these would-be consultants developed tools and techniques during the first three quarters of the twentieth century we associate now with the modern business of politics. Connecting these early practitioners with the multi-billion-dollar industry that exists today led me to realize that political work—that is, the work people do in order to elicit the support or influence the views of the public—changed dramatically over the course of the twentieth century.

Consequently, this book is largely about the changing character of political work and the rise of a consulting industry that now controls most of that work. The business of politics is central to the media-intensive, issue-based politics we witness today, and its rise into a multi-billion-dollar industry contributes to an ongoing, almost daily search for political advantage. Through their control of political work, consultants occupy a critical position between the public and those who endeavor to represent them, profoundly shaping the character of democratic practice.

Acknowledging intellectual debts is an important element in academic work, and I have accrued many in the writing of this book. Close readers of the endnotes will be able to trace various influences, but I wish to acknowledge here (in alphabetical order) the scholarship of Andrew Abbott, Richard Bensel, Stuart Ewen, Daniel Galvin, David Greenberg, Matt Grossmann, Alexander Heard, Sarah Igo, Stanley Kelley, Daniel Kreiss, Mordecai Lee, Michael McGerr, Rasmus Kleis Nielsen, Larry Sabato, and Edward Walker, among other scholars past and present, for helping me focus my attention on the changing nature of political work and its consequences for American politics.

Parts of chapter 2 and chapter 3 appeared in "Publicity and the Progressive Era Origins of Modern Politics," *Critical Review* 19 (2007): 461–480 and "Creating Political Strategy, Controlling Political Work: Edward Bernays and the Emergence of the Political Consultant," in *Political Creativity: Reconfiguring Institutional Order and Change*, edited by Gerald Berk, Victoria Hattam, and Dennis

Galvan (Philadelphia: University of Pennsylvania Press, 2013), 146–166. I thank the publishers for permission to reprint portions of this previous work here.

Much of the research for this book relied on archival materials at the Library of Congress, the National Archives, the Eisenhower Presidential Library, and the California State Archives, among others. I am grateful to the staff at these institutions. I am also extremely grateful to Jason Bucelato at the Federal Election Commission for helping me locate the audio recordings, minutes, and agenda documents for the August 31, 1978, open meeting of the commission that discussed the rules establishing categories of legal campaign services. The material in this book also relies heavily on two sets of interviews, conducted in the 1970s and 1990s, with political consultants. I gratefully acknowledge the help of Larry Sabato, Kenneth Stroupe, and Alex Welch at the Center for Politics at the University of Virginia, as well as Jennifer Kinniff at the Special Collections Research Center of the George Washington University Libraries for making these resources available. Finally, this book makes use of figures on campaign expenditures for consulting services. Much of these data I collected and analyzed myself (as explained in the appendix). In addition, I thank Andrew Mayersohn at the Center for Responsive Politics, who provided key data on expenditures coded by function. I also thank Gregory Martin and Zachary Peskowitz for sharing their data on consulting expenditures.

Friends and colleagues have provided valuable advice on aspects of the research, as well as needed encouragement to complete the project. I especially thank Brian Balogh, Gerald Berk, Mark Blyth, Christy Ford Chapin, Jeffrey Friedman, David Greenberg, Matt Grossmann, David Karol, Robert Mickey, and Steven Teles. I also gratefully acknowledge The William and Flora Hewitt Foundation for providing critical support at the final stages of the project. I thank David McBride for his help and encouragement in bringing the book to press.

Finally, I owe an enormous debt to my family, especially Marisa Hughes Sheingate, Leo Sheingate, and Lila Sheingate, who excused my frequent absences—especially when I was at home.

BUILDING A BUSINESS
OF POLITICS

I

The Business of Politics

TEN MILES FROM BALTIMORE'S INNER HARBOR, located in a low-rise office building in Towson, Maryland, is a successful business few Americans know about. Mentzer Media Services is one of the leading political consulting firms in the country. Mentzer Media does not design or produce the ubiquitous advertisements we see on television. Instead, the company specializes in the strategic placement of campaign commercials by purchasing airtime on behalf of its many clients, deciding where and when (and how often) an ad should run. Time-buying is a critical component of modern campaign strategy. It is also a highly profitable one. According to the company's website, Mentzer Media has handled more than $1 billion in media buys.[1] Assuming an industry-standard 10 to 15 percent commission on the ads it placed, Mentzer Media has earned between $100 and $150 million over the past several election cycles. In 2012 alone, Mentzer Media placed more than $245 million worth of ads, half of which were on behalf of Mitt Romney's super PAC, Restore Our Future.[2]

Mentzer Media is just one of the many consulting firms that profited from the 2012 election. The top Democratic media firm, GMMB, handled $435 million in spending in 2012, 90 percent of which came from the Obama campaign.[3] Together, thousands of candidates, the two major parties, and a myriad of wealthy outside groups spent over $6 billion trying to win office or sway the outcome of a race. More than half of this total, around $3.6 billion, went to consulting firms specializing in media, direct mail, and digital services.[4] Although it is difficult to know precisely how much consultants earn in a given campaign cycle, the top firms in the industry appear to be doing quite well.[5] In 2012, just fifty professional firms, averaging around $50 million in expenditures, handled 75 percent of all consulting services in federal campaigns. Between 2008 and 2012, revenues and billings by the top fifty consulting firms grew in real terms by 66 percent, about seven times the rate of growth in overall political spending during the same period.[6] Much of this increase is due to the pronounced rise in independent expenditures by super PACs and other outside groups. The Supreme Court decision in *Citizens United* opened the floodgates to more than $1 billion in outside spending in 2012—most of it on television advertising produced and placed by professional consultants.[7] Even if the political consequences of the 2010 Court decision remain a matter of debate to some, the economic benefits of *Citizens United* to the consulting industry are crystal clear.

In fact, federal elections are only one potential source of revenue for political consultants. Between 2008 and 2012, for example, GMMB earned approximately $125 million in commissions from political advertisements.[8] During the same period, according to the Center for Public Integrity, GMMB received an additional $124 million in fees from the telecommunications industry, beverage companies, and several other industry groups.[9] According to one study of the political consulting business, firms typically earn less than 40 percent of revenues in an election year from federal races; the majority of income comes from a combination of state and local candidates, ballot initiatives, political parties, corporate clients, and overseas elections.[10] On this basis, the political consulting industry earned an estimated $8.9 billion during the 2012 election cycle. Politics has become a thriving commercial enterprise.

The rise of a multi-billion-dollar business of politics marks a significant change in the conduct of campaigns and the character of our democracy. Over the course of the twentieth century, the old style of political campaigns gave way to the media-intensive and candidate-focused electoral contests we know today. Whereas parties and candidates used to rely on a network of local operatives to rally the party faithful and manage the practical aspects of winning a race, most of the key decisions in contemporary campaigns are now in the hands of consultants who sell a variety of products and services such as media, polling, and direct mail to an array of causes and candidates. In the last hundred years, a modern political consulting industry took shape—and took control of American elections.

How did the consulting industry gain near-exclusive control over the provision of political services in American politics? More broadly, what are the consequences of this development for the functioning of American institutions, the role of money in politics, and the relationship between politicians and the public? This book answers these questions by examining changes in the practical work of political campaigns. Specifically, the book follows the emergence of a professional political class in the United States: the political consultants who plumb the public mind and craft the candidate's message.

The story begins in the early twentieth century when campaigns began to place greater emphasis on the qualities of the candidate as a way to get out the vote. With the spread of radio and the advent of polling in the 1930s, experts in mass communication and survey research began turning social scientific renderings of the public into carefully crafted messages. These developments continued through the 1950s and 1960s as the growth of television provided a new medium to reach the public. However, with a few exceptions in places like California, the commercial opportunities from campaign work remained limited until the 1970s, when a full-blown business of politics finally emerged. Aided in part by new campaign finance rules, the pursuit of popular support came to rely almost exclusively on products and services that consultants alone could provide. Today, the business continues to evolve as consultants incorporate new techniques of digital politics and the industry consolidates into larger firms and multinational holding companies that offer an array of services to political and corporate clients.

Changes in the practical work of campaigns have had far-reaching consequences for American politics. The rise of a business of politics keyed other important developments such as the twentieth-century growth of presidential power and the political mobilization of American business. In our own time, the consulting industry is contributing to a broader shift toward a professionally managed public sphere while serving a crucial role in the system of campaign finance that allows wealthy donors to seek power and influence through legal (if lightly regulated) political contributions. In other words, political consultants are critical intermediaries in the democratic process, standing between the voters and those who endeavor to represent them. The definition of public problems, the framing of issues, and the formation of interests all rely on the services of a professional political class. This book traces how this came to pass.

The Control of Political Work

There are those who live for politics, and there are those who live from it.[11] For some, politics offers a path toward personal fulfillment, a sense of meaning and purpose that comes from the devotion to a cause. For others, politics is mainly a source of income. The two are quite compatible, of course. Writing in the early decades of the twentieth century, the German sociologist Max Weber observed that the advent of mass democracy had given rise to a new kind of specialist whose job it was to secure popular support on behalf of a party or candidate. Weber argued that this cadre of "politically gifted people" was a defining feature of modern political life, although he hesitated to predict "what outward shape the business of politics . . . will take" in the future.[12]

The rise of the political consulting industry is part of this democratic development, although the modern business of politics represents a fundamental change in the nature of political work over the last hundred years. By "political work" I mean practices designed to elicit the support or influence the views of the public on behalf of political candidates, elected officials, or interests of various kinds. This book examines how innovations in the practical work of campaigns contributed to a shift away from the party agent who mobilized armies of partisans at the local level and toward the political consultant who crafts images and messages using mass communication and social scientific techniques.

Commentators and critics often blame consultants for much that is wrong with American politics today, particularly a media-driven, personalized style that some argue undermines the quality of public debate.[13] Others lament the rise of a permanent campaign in American politics as those skilled in the dark arts of political communication have acquired a privileged position in a White House constantly seeking public approval for presidential initiatives.[14]

Political scientists commonly take a more measured view, explaining the rise of consulting as a logical outgrowth of broader shifts in the polity such as the rise of new technology or the evolution of the national party committees into something akin to general contractors that help candidates secure campaign services like polling and media.[15] These developments were critical to be sure, but broad shifts alone cannot explain exactly how political consultants transformed the practical work of campaigns. In fact, many of the practices we associate with contemporary politics such as candidate-focused appeals and even poll-tested messages predate the rise of television or changes in party organizations. In other words, the history of the consulting industry does not fit with accounts that explain its rise solely in terms of the functional needs of parties or candidates.[16] Consequently, this book looks at the practical work of consultants themselves in order to understand how they became central figures in the American political system.

Consider the following puzzle: after decades of careful study, political scientists have found that television advertising often has minimal effects on the outcome of a race. Or, to put it more accurately, television ads are only effective at certain times and under certain conditions.[17] For instance, a study of the 2012 presidential election found that early investment in advertising by the Obama team had minimal effects on voters compared with advertisements aired at the end of the campaign. This finding is consistent with other research that shows the effects of advertising to be rather short-lived.[18] Television is also a blunt instrument for targeting supporters, particularly in large metropolitan areas that include multiple congressional districts and where viewers are regularly exposed to ads from candidates for whom they cannot vote.[19] Moreover, research suggests that door-to-door voter contact is a more effective tool than television when it comes to increasing turnout.[20] Yet, television accounts for the largest single expenditure in most campaigns, and candidates will spend as much on advertising as their fundraising prowess will allow. The 2012 election shattered records for television advertising in federal elections.[21]

If the effects of advertising are somewhat limited or only partly understood, why do campaigns devote so much of their resources to media? One answer is that candidates are always "running scared" and are therefore reluctant to cede any advantage to their opponent.[22]

Advertising can make a difference when one candidate has a big advantage in spending.[23] However, the desire to avoid being outspent on the airwaves begs another question: How did media become the core element of modern campaigns? Given the decidedly mixed evidence about the effects of television, it appears that something more is at work than candidates simply adapting to the changing conditions of twentieth-century politics. In fact, the heavy reliance on television in political campaigns makes much more sense from the perspective of a political consulting industry reliant on products and services that provide the greatest financial return.

In order to understand how techniques like polling and media became core features of American politics, it is necessary to focus on the nature of political work itself. Accordingly, this book examines how practitioners devised new methods for securing popular support, convinced would-be clients of their skills, and outcompeted other providers of political services such as party workers, journalists, and those working in allied fields like public relations and advertising.[24] Over the course of the twentieth century, consultants asserted themselves as trained experts in the provision of political advice, a claim they defended by developing a new set of political tasks that they alone were uniquely qualified to perform and, they argued, were uniquely suited to the needs of a complex modern polity. The rise of the modern business of politics hinged on the creation and eventual control over new forms of political work. As a result of these innovations, it became possible to live for and extremely well from politics in the United States.

A Brief History of Political Work

In his richly detailed account of nineteenth-century politics, Richard Bensel vividly describes how elections resembled "a kind of sorcerer's workshop in which the minions of opposing parties turned money into whiskey and whiskey into votes."[25] At the heart of this wizardry was the party agent who "ran the machinery of democracy."[26] Hired by party leaders and local bosses to secure victory at the ballot box, the party agent performed a variety of important functions during the nineteenth century, including mobilizing voters, intimidating the opposition, and even working as judges and recording clerks on Election Day. Their job, simply put, was "manipulating the returns where they could, manhandling their opponents where they must."[27]

And what a job it was. Party agents were "experienced in the customs, traditions, and techniques of party competition in and around the polling place."[28] This was a valuable set of skills that granted party agents considerable influence over the conduct of nineteenth-century campaigns. Although motivated to some extent by political beliefs, party agents "were also, in much more mundane and personal terms, rewarded by money payments, social recognition, and patronage appointments."[29] Writing at the turn of the twentieth century, political scientist Moisei Ostrogorski described the American party system in similar terms as an "immense army" of party workers "spurred by the incentive of personal interest."[30]

Financial reward has long been a feature of American politics because political work attracts individuals motivated by a mixture of partisan and pecuniary interest. This was especially the case in the nineteenth century when armies of fourth-class postmasters and customs workers owed their livelihood to partisan politics. With their jobs depending on the outcome of the presidential contest, patronage workers provided much of the labor for political campaigns and paid a portion of their salary back to the party to help cover electioneering expenses. The graft and corruption associated with some of the urban political machines that flourished through the early part of the twentieth century further illustrate how politics provided financial rewards for the privileged few.[31] Similarly today, helping one's party succeed can yield personal gains such as a political job or even a presidential appointment. Although partisanship still motivates people to work long hours on political campaigns (often for little or no money), politics has long provided a way to make a living, whether as a nineteenth-century party worker or a twenty-first-century political consultant.

Yet, a crucial difference separates the party agent from the political consultant. Unlike the party worker of the past, consultants operate under a different set of incentives. Today, the profit motive guides the conduct of political work and shapes the character of our politics in a manner and to an extent that did not exist before the rise of the political consulting industry. With the organization of political work into commercial firms, consultants can hedge political risks by working for

multiple clients and providing an array of commercial services, addressing the short-run needs of a candidate without sacrificing the long-run
interests of the business. Whereas the personal fate of the political
operative used to depend almost entirely on the electoral success of the
party, today's political consultants can lose an election without losing
their livelihood.

This book examines the consequences of this shift as the political craft of the party agent evolved into the modern business of politics. The transition begins at the turn of the twentieth century when
Progressive Era reformers embraced the idea of publicity as a way to
challenge the power of the trusts and expose back-room deals to the
light of day. Publicity subjected politics, and politicians, to careful scru-
tiny. However, the idea of publicity carried another meaning as well,
as an orchestrated campaign of persuasion that could attract public
support on behalf of a candidate, a cause, or a corporation. This dual
meaning of publicity suggested a new kind of political work, one that
depended on appeals to individual opinion rather than partisan identities or affiliations.

With the end of World War I, the progressive promise of publicity
gave way to a postwar fear of propaganda. Rather than enlightened and
informed, the experience of the war revealed a public that was easily
manipulated and even misled. Consequently, many greeted novel methods of publicity and mass persuasion with skepticism or outright hostility. In response, publicity experts and would-be consultants claimed
they were specialists in the modern science of behavior. Struggles over
the control of political work subsequently played out in attempts to
secure professional status as an expert reader and shaper of public sentiments. This professional claim dovetailed with a behavioral turn in the
social sciences and the burgeoning academic study of public opinion.
One early practitioner was Edward Bernays, a tireless promoter of public relations who worked hard to convince potential clients and the
larger public that his techniques were ideally suited to the conditions of
modern politics. To achieve his goal, Bernays cultivated close ties with
prominent social scientists in order to achieve a degree of professional
control over political work.

With the invention of radio, the ability to reach a vast broadcast
audience occasioned the need for new sources of information about the

effects of mass communication. This was especially the case in the burgeoning field of advertising as advances in market research and commercial polling gave rise to a new science of selling. The toolkit of modern business methods heavily influenced the modern business of politics. As politicians and presidents took to the airwaves, survey research offered a much-needed source of political intelligence especially suited to the radio age. In effect, as Sarah Igo explains, pollsters "transferred the techniques honed for selling soap and cereal from the buying to the voting public."[32] More than simply a way to measure public sentiment, surveys became an instrument to craft targeted appeals through a union of advertising and polling. Combining the art and science of politics was a critical innovation of the political consulting profession.

Despite these advances in polling and media, most early practitioners were unable to make a living from political work. An important exception was in California, where the team of Clem Whitaker and Leone Baxter hit upon a successful business model that overcame the uncertain and periodic nature of campaigns. Specifically, Whitaker and Baxter forged a lucrative business *of* politics by discovering new ways to organize business *in* politics. Through their firm, Campaigns, Inc., the team worked on behalf of various industry groups and trade associations to defeat candidates, ballot measures, and legislative proposals that threatened the financial interests of their clients. Their work had national implications. After Whitaker and Baxter defeated a proposal for universal health care in California, the American Medical Association (AMA) hired the pair to defeat Harry Truman's plans for national health insurance. Stoking fears of "socialized medicine," Whitaker and Baxter unleashed a media blitz that cost the AMA $3.6 million and earned Campaigns, Inc. almost $1.2 million in fees between 1949 and 1952.[33]

Despite the important advances made by Whitaker and Baxter in the 1940s, it would take several decades more before a true business of politics emerged on a national scale. This lag points to an ongoing struggle over political work as the consulting profession slowly consolidated its control over campaign services. In the 1950s, Madison Avenue advertising firms took the lead in managing the national television campaigns for presidential candidates. However, this began to change in the 1960s as advertising agencies discovered that involvement in a presidential campaign might compromise relations with their commercial clients.

Advertising firms were ill-suited to the partisan nature of political work, and their exit from campaigns provided a crucial opening for specialists in political strategy and media to build a business of their own. In the 1970s, the political consulting industry took off, aided by a new campaign finance system that required candidates to document each and every dollar spent. In effect, consultants became a legal and legitimate way for politicians to spend money. Meanwhile, technological advances in video production and computing along with lower-cost communication and transportation made it possible for consultants to service a larger number of clients across the country and even around the globe. By the end of the 1980s, a profitable business had taken hold, and the term "political consultant" began to enter wide usage as a way to designate those who provided a range of specialized products and services to political campaigns.[34]

The evolution of political work continues in our own time with the development of digital politics. The use of the Internet as a platform for raising money and the ability to leverage sophisticated data analytics to identify and mobilize armies of supporters have become staples of political campaigns in the twenty-first century. Unlike the advent of radio or the rise of television, however, recent advances in digital campaigning have occurred amid a highly commercialized market for political products and services. Rather than challenge the consultant's control over political work, digital campaign tools are just another service to sell. Meanwhile, the consulting industry is consolidating into larger firms, and the business of politics itself is increasingly part of a global communications enterprise dominated by a handful of multinational conglomerates.

Practical Innovation and Political Work

Politics is a speculative enterprise, fueling experiments in the conduct of political work. In fact, the history of consulting vividly illustrates the creative element in politics. As they devise a campaign strategy, consultants mix scientific polling and sophisticated media with local political knowledge and previous experience. In the process, consultants create the very context in which they work. As they craft the messages of the candidates, consultants define the issues of the campaign. When they interpret poll results, consultants call forth specific groups that make up an electoral coalition. In doing so, consultants recreate, reinforce, and reproduce the alignments and allegiances that inform the decisions of the candidate as well as the behavior of individual voters.

These practical responses to the shifting dynamics of a race have important consequences for the political system beyond the life of a specific campaign. As I detail throughout this book, the media-intensive, candidate-focused style of politics we witness today arose through a series of innovations that applied new methods to the old task of vote-getting. Although consultants and their forerunners exploited technological developments like radio and television as well as political opportunities that came with the decline of traditional party organizations, the industry's rise also required a willingness to experiment and a fair degree of salesmanship. It is in the successful effort to define and defend their role that political consultants transformed the conduct of campaigns and altered the character of American politics.

Changes in democratic practice reflect the shifting techniques of everyday politics, what I refer to as political work and the rise of a consulting profession that exercises almost complete control of that work. In order to understand the practical aspects of democracy, we must examine what practitioners actually do.[35] Consequently, this book follows the publicity experts, public relations specialists, pollsters, and political consultants who over the course of the twentieth century built a business of politics. To do so, I rely on a rich archive of source material that illuminates the experiments and gambits, the successes and the failures, that are part and parcel of practical innovation. Some of the figures we will encounter are well-known, like Edward Bernays, the "father of spin"; George Gallup, who broke new ground in commercial polling; or the California team of Whitaker and Baxter. Others have received much less attention, such as Gerard Lambert, who helped pioneer the use of poll results in the crafting of presidential speeches, or Jon Jonkel, a public relations man from Chicago whose unconventional tactics helped a political unknown unseat a four-term senator in Maryland. In addition to various archival sources, this book uses a series of interviews conducted with consultants in the 1970s and 1990s that provide crucial insights into the business of politics from the practitioner's perspective.[36] As we will see, consultants make politics through creative acts of campaigning, turning the practical work of elections into a thriving business that has had far-reaching implications for the American political system.

Democracy as it actually exists is more than just a set of rules, institutions, or beliefs.[37] It is also about the practical work of politics, including the consultants who collectively earn billions of dollars to craft the images of the candidate and interpret the opinions of the public. Some of the consequences of this are less than desirable, to be sure. The constant bombardment of campaign advertising and the steady stream of opinion polls contribute to the exhaustion and cynicism many Americans feel about politics today. Consultants also serve as the conduit for wealthy donors seeking political influence by turning an almost unlimited and increasingly untraceable flow of campaign contributions into various products and services. At the same time, the consulting industry illuminates how the uncertain nature of political competition spurs innovation, fueling an unending pursuit of political advantage and a continuing search for more effective instruments of persuasion. Whether we like it or not, political consultants play a crucial part in democratic practice, and the rise of a modern business of politics provides a critical window into the changing character of American democracy.

2

Publicity and the Public

THE EARLY TWENTIETH CENTURY MARKS an important turn in the history of political work. During the Progressive Era, a modern business of politics began to take shape as journalists, social reformers, and politicians embraced publicity as a distinctly modern way to communicate with the public. For many turn-of-the-century progressives, the term "publicity" evoked liberal ideals of government transparency and public deliberation considered crucial for a functioning democracy. Publicity, many believed, would hold public officials accountable to the voters and help citizens form enlightened opinions about the issues of the day. Reformers celebrated "the searchlight of publicity" as a remedy for the ills of predatory trusts, party bosses, and corrupt practices of various kinds.

But publicity had another, descriptive meaning that became more common during the first decades of the twentieth century. As a practice, publicity referred to an orchestrated campaign of persuasion designed to attract and hold public attention. Building on the growth of mass-circulation papers and magazines, publicity techniques employed modern methods of advertising and even rudimentary measures of public opinion in order to shape perceptions about an issue, a candidate, or a corporation.

These two meanings of publicity had contradictory implications. Whereas the ideal of publicity promised the discovery of objective truth, the practice of a publicity campaign conveyed a subjective rendering of the political world. Out of this very contradiction, however, government officials, corporate press agents, and even presidents of the United States devised new ways to influence or persuade the public. By invoking the ideal of publicity, figures as diverse as progressive reformer Gifford Pinchot, public relations founder Ivy Lee, and Presidents Theodore Roosevelt and Woodrow Wilson could defend their methods as a modern way to inform the public. Yet, the success of a publicity campaign hinged at least in part on the public's inability to distinguish between the objective presentation of facts and the subjective manipulation of information to appear fact-like. This ambiguity sparked important innovations in the tools of persuasion, laying the foundation for the modern consulting industry, but it also contributed to an ambivalence many Americans express toward politics that is still evident today.

Publicity Old and New

In a literal sense, publicity makes something, or someone, publicly known; it transforms what is private, or secret, into something that is public.[1] In the realm of politics, the "light of publicity" was an instrument of good government; its opposite, secrecy, was the shade that hid corruption. This view of publicity has its roots in liberal notions of popular sovereignty, a free press, and freedom of speech. According to Jeremy Bentham, "In the darkness of secrecy, sinister interest and evil in every shape, have full swing"; by contrast, "Publicity is the very soul of justice."[2] Publicity assured accountability; it put the actions of government officials before the public eye. Like his famous panopticon, Bentham believed that constant surveillance of public officials was "indispensably necessary to the maintenance of good government" by operating "as a check upon the conduct of the ruling few."[3] An independent press was critical to this process, creating the conditions for "enlightened judgment" and a well-informed electorate.[4] "Without publicity, no good is permanent," Bentham concluded, "under the auspices of publicity no evil can continue."[5]

Immanuel Kant articulated a similar view of publicity as a core feature of good government: "All actions that affect the rights of other men are wrong if their maxim is not consistent with publicity."[6] In particular, Kant emphasized the deliberative function of publicity and its role in promoting public discussion. Freedom of speech, especially the free exchange of ideas, would produce an enlightened public liberated from a tyranny that operated through secrecy and concealment. Through publicity, Kant argued, "the subterfuge of a secretive system of politics could easily be defeated."[7] In sum, publicity served as a critical component of good government and a key to active citizenship.

Many progressive reformers at the turn of the twentieth century embraced a similar ideal of publicity as a powerful weapon against those who operated in a shadowy world of political corruption, financial collusion, and social vice.[8] Like Bentham, reformers commonly celebrated the "searchlight" of investigative journalism and the "pitiless publicity" of the press.[9] As one commentator put it, "Corruption cannot exist nowadays without being discovered."[10] Albert Shaw, editor of the *American Review of Reviews*, agreed that "there is no more salutary check than the check of publicity."[11] Publicity figured prominently in discussions of the "trust question" and the problem of monopoly. Economist Henry Carter Adams described the function of publicity as a way to "let in the light and let out the facts" about the operation of large industrial combinations.[12] Wall Street financier Henry Clews insisted that publicity would end "the opportunities for business wrongdoing in secret" and force "the 'crooks,' 'grafters,' 'rebaters' and 'competition crushers' of the business world, who have schemed in darkness and shunned the light, to come out into open view."[13]

At the same time, many progressives echoed Kant in seeing publicity as a path to rational deliberation and public enlightenment. In the words of John Dewey, "Whatever obstructs and restricts publicity, limits and distorts thinking on social affairs."[14] Civic reformers viewed publicity as a way to educate the public and spur demand for efficient and accountable government. Henry Bruère, director of the Bureau of Municipal Research, advocated "greater efficiency in city administration through publicity of city affairs," arguing that "the publication of *facts* respecting the acts of government will not only prevent specific acts of misgovernment, but ensure a progressive development of governmental efficiency by providing a basis for the exercise of intelligent popular control."[15] Other reformers similarly embraced publicity, firm in the belief that "when the public fully understands any problem ... better results are sure to follow."[16] The power of publicity was in the moral outrage aroused by the exposure of social ills. Invoking "the light of publicity" was a powerful idiom of the social gospel that tapped Christian beliefs in revelation: "The hour of discovery and publicity of wrong has fully come," announced a writer for *Zion's Herald*. "We are reminded strongly of the words of [Jesus] . . . when He said: 'For there is nothing covered that shall not be revealed; neither hid, that shall not be known.' "[17]

Publicity was an important instrument of progressive reform. By evoking liberal notions of public enlightenment, press freedom, and political accountability, publicity became an important part of the vocabulary common among muckraking journalists, civic reformers, and promoters of the social gospel. Publicity formed part of what Daniel Rodgers described as "the surroundings of available rhetoric and ideas . . . within which progressives launched their crusades, recruited their partisans and did their work."[18]

However, "the searchlight of publicity" had powerful effects, prompting many reformers to experiment with the range and purpose of their methods. Gradually, a new kind of publicity took shape. More than simply a way to educate or even inspire, publicity became a technique to attract and shape public attention through an orchestrated campaign of communication. But the new publicity remained garbed in the traditional meaning of the term. Describing his campaign against child labor, *Women's Home Companion* editor Arthur T. Vance wrote that "publicity in reform is merely the application of modern business methods to reform work." Vance presented innovations in publicity as modern means to achieve the traditional end of an informed public. "Publicity has always been the active factor in the production of . . . public sentiment," Vance explained. "But nowadays we plan publicity in a more systematic, more scientific manner. . . . A modern campaign of publicity is planned precisely as a campaign of advertising."[19]

The appeal of advertising was common among reform movements of the early twentieth century.[20] Prohibitionists, for example, experimented with posters and other eye-grabbing graphics to convey the sins of alcohol.[21] Describing the campaigns of the Anti-Saloon League in 1928, Peter Odegard wrote that "publicity was the chief weapon in the arsenal of the league."[22] According to Elisabeth Clemens, leaders of the women's movement wrote practical guides for "making news."[23] In 1911, the Women's Council of Voters organized its own "publicity bureau" for its suffrage campaign.[24] Other reform groups sought expert advice on how to incorporate advertising techniques in their work. In 1910, the National Conference of Charities and Correction invited the head of the Lord and Thomas advertising agency to speak at its annual meeting about "the psychology of advertising" and how "the methods and devices of commercial advertising . . . ought to be applied to social publicity."[25] If traditional publicity let the facts, by themselves, capture the attention of an enlightened public, the newer methods of publicity embraced a belief in the psychological basis of persuasion.[26] "Advertising," advocates of the new publicity believed, could serve as "the roadway to a man's mind."[27]

These newer techniques exploited a changing media environment that expanded the opportunities for crafted communication. By 1900, party-sponsored newspapers and the independent "penny" press had given way to mass-circulation, daily newspapers and magazines supported by advertising revenue.[28] Advances in printing technology and postal subsidies such as rural free delivery helped newspaper and magazine circulation soar at the turn of the twentieth century. Between 1890 and 1904, the number and circulation of daily newspapers more than doubled, and the combined circulation of monthly periodicals more than tripled.[29] This growth accompanied an important shift in journalistic practice as reporters and editors asserted greater professional control over the "news" by claiming to present objective versions of facts and events rather than their own, partisan opinions.[30]

Ironically, the emergence of "independent" journalism also made it more difficult to establish the veracity of newspaper coverage. Advertising revenues weakened the ties between newspapers and political parties, but they also raised new concerns about business influence over press coverage. One critic described the mass-circulation dailies and the consolidated wire services like the Associated Press as "huge commercial ventures, connected by advertising and in other ways, with banks, trust companies, railway . . . and manufacturing enterprises. They reflect the system which supports them. They cannot afford to mold public opinion against the network of special interests which envelop them."[31]

More fundamentally, the journalistic ideal of "all the news that's fit to print" was at odds with the production demand to find "all the news that fits." For smaller newspapers with limited resources of their own, the production demands of regular publication left them dependent upon material prepared by others. In the late nineteenth century, political parties perfected the use of "boilerplate," shipping prepared zinc plates directly to rural editors who, by printing copies at a local press, could cheaply reproduce campaign material in the paper. As these methods became more sophisticated, however, it became increasingly difficult to discern the sources of material reproduced in newspapers or its veracity. A 1907 Interstate Commerce Commission Report found that it was a common practice of the Standard Oil Company to purchase space in newspapers that was filled not with advertisements but with prepared releases typeset to appear like a news story.[32]

In sum, the tremendous growth of newspaper circulation coupled with the rise of a journalistic profession claiming to report objective facts rather than partisan opinions increased the value of newspapers as a source of information. And with many small newspapers dependent upon wire services for content, feeding stories to the press could potentially reach large numbers of readers. Editorial discretion provided a critical opening for the production of "canned" news and the illusion that published accounts in the newspaper were written with the objective eye of the journalist rather than by a press agent on behalf of a client. As a contemporary critic of the practice complained, "The public is continually played upon by adroit and powerful forces. The average reader of the daily paper . . . does not read critically. He does not know that two or three items in a brief 'news' article presented as undoubted facts lead him to but one conclusion. He does not note the careful coloring, the skillful arrangement of parts . . . or the shrewd mis-statements."[33] Describing these developments in *Collier's*, Will Irwin wrote of "a new profession . . . the publicity manager," whose clientele included "public men, political or moral movements, even kings and nations."[34] Much like the theatrical press agent, the publicity expert made it "as hard to learn the truth about public affairs . . . as it has always been to get a just idea of the merits of a theatrical performance."[35] The *New York Times* viewed these developments more favorably, insisting that "popular government is in the ascendant and public opinion is the power behind the democratic throne. The publicity man is the attorney whose arguments may go to the nation."[36] Through the early decades of the twentieth century, these "entrepreneurs of public opinion," as the *Times* called them, found ample work in government, politics, and business, where they built support for public programs, presented candidates to the voters, and improved the public image of the corporation.

Government Publicity

The liberal ideal of publicity embraced the negative power of exposure as a check on individual behavior and a cure for the ills of corruption. Publicity would lead to a more "open" government that simultaneously weakened boss rule and energized the public in favor of efficient administration. In other words, publicity held out the promise of a modern government and a pathway to the expansion of administrative capacities. In practice, however, publicity relied on an orchestrated campaign to build public support on behalf of particular programs, policies, or institutions. The tension is evident in the work of the Bureau of Municipal Research, a forerunner of the modern think tank.[37] On the one hand, the bureau rendered "expert analytical, advisory staff services of a professional character to citizens and officers of city and other governments."[38] On the other hand, bureau staff thought carefully about how best to communicate their findings in ways that might attract maximum attention. As one of the bureau's leaders put it, "Expert government's publicity can nowhere be effective which does not act upon the same principles that private advertising has adopted for the selling of goods."[39] The key to municipal reform was the broad dissemination of information in ways that remained sensitive to the dictates of public consumption.

The creative use of publicity became especially powerful in the hands of an ambitious president on behalf of an activist government. For Theodore Roosevelt, publicity was critical to his vision and practice of executive administration. Roosevelt advocated publicity as a solution to the problem of monopoly, explaining in his first annual message to Congress that "the first essential in determining how to deal with the great industrial combinations is knowledge of the facts—publicity."[40] The value of publicity, Roosevelt argued, was that it judiciously separated the honest from the corrupt. "The corporation which is honestly and fairly organized . . . has nothing to fear from such supervision. . . . The only corporation that has cause to dread it is the corporation which shrinks from the light."[41]

As a policy tool, publicity avoided direct intervention in the economy yet still expanded the administrative capacities of the government through the collection and dissemination of facts. Publicity would protect the public interest by informing the public itself. At Roosevelt's urging, Congress created the Bureau of Corporations in 1903, an agency within the Department of Commerce, with the authority to investigate corporate conduct. Describing the origins of this new "publicity bureau," its first commissioner, James R. Garfield, wrote that "it owed its existence largely to . . . the desire for 'publicity'—in other words, the desire for information." Like Roosevelt, Garfield hailed "the power of efficient publicity for the correction of corporate abuses."[42] In fact, the Bureau of Corporations was among several government agencies that used the investigation, collection, and publication of facts—publicity—as a way to expand the administrative capacities of the federal government. In his 1906 annual report, for example, Garfield praised a strengthened Interstate Commerce Commission as "a great advance toward publicity" and the passage of the "meat-inspection and pure food laws . . . as the most recent examples of the extension of the principles of publicity."[43]

In pursuing these state-building achievements, Roosevelt skillfully combined the various meanings of publicity into a robust form of presidential leadership. As an ideal, publicity required leaders to directly engage the public rather than conduct politics in secret or behind closed doors. Writing in *The New Nationalism*, Roosevelt distinguished between "the leader [who] gets his hold by open appeal to the reason and conscience of his followers . . . in the open light of day," and the "boss" whose political machine "derives its main strength from what is done under cover of darkness."[44] As a practice, however, publicity demanded a more active form of leadership, and in Roosevelt's hands this warranted novel communication practices that could command public attention on issues the president personally deemed important. Roosevelt's embrace of these new techniques became a hallmark of his administration, one that was widely appreciated at the time. As a writer for *McClure's* remarked, "No one except old Washington newspaper men, recalls what Theodore Roosevelt, as President, accomplished in turning the operation of the national government from a dark professional secret to a matter of full-throated publicity. . . . The democracy of the printing-press had come; and Roosevelt was its founder."[45] More than simply a check against corruption, publicity became a technique to build popular support and enhance one's public image. As *Harper's* put it:

> He is the greatest publicity promoter among the sons of man today. . . . Theodore Roosevelt secured his popularity through publicity. He has retained, extended and strengthened it through publicity. . . . He even goes to the extent of advocating publicity as a sure cure for most of the ills with which the body politic is afflicted.[46]

Surrounded by aides and advisers skilled in the workings of the press, Roosevelt cultivated public support for his ambitious presidential agenda.[47]

Roosevelt's talents were particularly evident in the case of natural resource policy. With the help of Gifford Pinchot, Roosevelt's adviser and close friend, the president championed conservationism in the face of formidable political opposition. To contemporaries, Pinchot and Roosevelt were "kindred craftsmen" of publicity.[48] Together, they orchestrated unprecedented presidential media events, "great ethical and social pageants," such as the 1907 Inland Waterways Commission when the press followed Roosevelt on a steamboat down the Mississippi River, or the subsequent 1908 White House Conservation Conference, described by historian Stephen Ponder as a "benchmark . . . in the role of the executive" in leading public opinion.[49] As chief of the Forest Service, Pinchot oversaw one of the earliest and most extensive public communication campaigns on behalf of any government agency or program. Under Pinchot's leadership, the Forest Service produced "a continuous stream of publications, news releases, displays for exhibition . . . and photographs" promoting the agency's work.[50] And as documented by various biographers and historians of the period, publicity was both a critical tool for the promotion of conservation policy and a persistent source of controversy throughout Pinchot's career.[51]

Probing deeper into these innovations, Pinchot did two things very successfully. First, Pinchot organized publicity efforts on a vast scale, tailoring his communication strategies to the production demands of the press. In 1905, Pinchot established a dedicated press office, one of the first in the federal government, "to assist in the planning of all publications of the Forest Service . . . [and] expedite their passage through the press."[52] Staffed by individuals with backgrounds in journalism, the press office placed special emphasis on Forest Service activities considered "newsy" or of "general interest."[53] By 1908, the number of press releases had increased in frequency from three or four a month to one or two a day. A mailing list of nearly 700,000 names, organized by various subjects and geographic regions, helped the Forest Service target news releases and publications to particular audiences.[54] Meanwhile, the agency developed a sophisticated feedback mechanism to track the effects of publicity in the press. Using return slips attached to agency bulletins, the Forest Service asked newspaper editors to send clippings that used press office material. With the help of public circulation data on newspapers, the press office estimated that exposure to Forest Service material increased from 1 million to 42 million readers between May 1907 and October 1908.[55]

Second, Pinchot was very skillful at defending these publicity efforts against his critics, particularly those in Congress. Here, the ability to move between a newer conception of publicity as an efficient campaign of public relations and its older meaning as an instrument of public enlightenment proved crucial. Congressional opponents of conservation frequently accused Pinchot of using the Forest Service to carry out personal attacks against his critics.[56] In 1908, a proposed rider to an agricultural appropriations bill prohibited the use of funds for the preparation of newspaper or magazine material, effectively ending Forest Service publicity if passed. In response, Pinchot waged a vigorous defense of his actions. Writing to the chairman of the House Agriculture Committee, Pinchot explained that "the Forest Service is doing all it can to make its publications of wide use . . . to convert scientific information into common knowledge." Newspapers, according to Pinchot, were the most effective means to do so, but "to get information into the newspapers it is necessary to put it into newspaper form. . . . By employing men familiar with the peculiar requirements of newspaper work, and familiar with the work of this Service, it becomes possible to carry on the work of popular education on a far more extensive scale."[57] At the same time, Pinchot defended his publicity techniques by arguing that it was impossible to influence the press because the professional standards of independent journalism offered "the most effective possible barrier to any ... campaign of puffing or exaggeration." Ultimately, Pinchot argued, "The policy and method of publicity which the Forest Service has developed is to my mind the only defensible policy for any Government organization, any part of whose purpose is to collect and disseminate facts."[58] In sum, publicity was simply a tool of enlightened administration, employing modern means in the pursuit of traditional ends. Pinchot's efforts succeeded, as the Senate amended the appropriations bill so that it posed no threat to Forest Service activities.[59]

Similar controversies continued throughout Pinchot's career; in fact, publicity was at the center of the dispute that led President Taft to fire him in early 1910. The infamous Pinchot-Ballinger affair began when Overton Price and Alexander Shaw, close aides and longtime friends of Pinchot in the Forest Service, released information to *Collier's* magazine that implicated Secretary of the Interior Richard Ballinger in a corruption scandal.[60] In response, President William Howard Taft fired the pair on the grounds that Price and Shaw had violated a presidential directive that prohibited contact with the press. When Pinchot wrote a letter of protest that was read on the Senate floor by the chairman of the Senate Agriculture Committee, he too was dismissed. During the congressional investigation that followed, Pinchot's penchant for self-promotion came under fire. As John Vertrees, counsel to Secretary Ballinger, told a congressional committee, "Publicity is the breath of Mr. Pinchot's nostrils."[61]

In response, Pinchot defended his work as a mixture of traditional and modern methods. In words likely written by Pinchot himself, his counsel George Wharton Pepper explained to the committee:

The work of the Forest Service is in part an educational work, and this must be carried on through the press. In order that the people of the country may have a just view of existing conditions they must be made to understand what is being done to help them, just as they ought to be informed what is being done to hurt them. The administration of the Forest Service has proceeded upon the theory that publicity is the essential and indispensable condition of clean and effective public service.[62]

This statement nicely illustrates how Pinchot used the multiple and shifting meanings of publicity as a defense against his critics. No longer simply a means to reveal corruption, publicity had become an indispensable tool to build public support for an activist government.

Privately, however, Pinchot was acutely aware of his own public image, and he consistently monitored press coverage in his fight for conservation. Thomas R. Shipp, a former journalist who worked for Pinchot in the press office before directing publicity efforts for the 1908 White House Conservation Conference, was a key figure in this endeavor. Shipp was the first secretary of the National Conservation Association, an organization Pinchot helped found in 1909 and one that became a personal vehicle for him after he left the federal government in 1910.[63] Shipp and Pinchot maintained regular correspondence about how best to shape press coverage, not just about conservation but about Pinchot himself. Writing to Shipp in December 1910, Pinchot complained about a newspaper that had printed "a long story about a mythical break between T.R. and myself," and he suggested that Shipp "might let it get out . . . that . . . I had a delightful visit to Oyster Bay last week to talk things over and make plans for the future." Shipp replied that "it has already gone clear through the corps of correspondents that you had a good visit out at Oyster Bay. . . . I did not give this for publication . . . but as a private, personal tip."[64]

The Pinchot-Shipp correspondence offers a glimpse into the more subtle forms of publicity that accompanied the industrial-scale public relations efforts developed by the Forest Service. It also suggests a more personal form of publicity taking shape, one that cleverly fused older purposes with new techniques. Revealing another's corruption simultaneously could elevate one's own position in the public eye. In fact, whereas Ballinger resigned in 1911 under the continued taint of scandal, Pinchot's standing as a public figure only grew; he eventually served two nonconsecutive terms as governor of Pennsylvania.

As Pinchot's career continued, he remained an astute observer of publicity techniques, and he recognized the growing sophistication of its methods, whether applied to the promotion of a particular program or used in the crafting of a personal image. In an undated memo penned in advance of the 1920 presidential campaign, Pinchot wrote, "In the last ten years publicity has become near an exact science in this country. This is in a large part due to ... the organization of systematic campaigns, whether of commercial advertising or political propaganda, by publicity experts." Pinchot went on to summarize the keys to successful publicity: "(a) newspaperdom has a technique that ... must be met; (b) a news value or public interest must be achieved that is timely; and (c) it is necessary to reach the public mind under favorable conditions."[65] Pinchot was keenly aware of the importance of publicity and the role of experts in mastering a new kind of political work.

Publicity in Politics

Roosevelt and Pinchot discovered that the ability to develop favorable press coverage could be a powerful political tool. Publicity was more than just the revelation of wrongdoing; effective communication was a valuable instrument in securing popular support for government programs and an energetic national executive. However, Roosevelt and Pinchot did more than promote a specific program or policy; they also projected an image of personal virtue. Used in this way, publicity focused public attention on individual attributes—publicity revealed who was honest and qualified, as well as who was corrupt or inept. It was a short step from here to an emerging politics of personality in which candidates used publicity to cultivate a personal appeal among voters. This was especially the case for reform politicians who sought to distinguish themselves from, and often ran in opposition to, mainstream party organizations. In fact, publicity techniques were well suited to a reform climate when many viewed organized parties with some suspicion and journalistic revelations of political corruption were common. Building up one's image as the antithesis of the party politician played very well, whether campaigning for office or campaigning for policies once in office.[66]

At the same time, progressive reforms intended to root out corruption or diminish the influence of party bosses altered the terrain of political competition. The adoption of the secret ballot and the spread of the direct primary rendered traditional forms of securing votes either illegal or ineffective, leaving party managers in search of new ways to mobilize the public. As one writer noted on the eve of the 1908 presidential contest between Taft and Bryan, "The adoption of the secret ballot . . . has put an end to the ease and facility with which it used to be possible to . . . buy [votes] directly." This resulted in "the development of the spirit of independent voting among the people," and it required parties and candidates to "make the individual ballot caster everywhere see the issues of the campaign in the desired light."[67] According to historian Michael McGerr, these developments at the turn of the twentieth century marked an important shift in political campaigns toward a style of "advertised politics" that emphasized personality over partisanship.[68] By 1908, both major parties had created publicity bureaus to coordinate press communications for their presidential campaign, replacing turgid campaign literature on the tariff or monetary policy with a decidedly modern way to reach the individual voter.[69] "More and more," the *New York Times* observed that year, "campaign management has come to follow strictly the lines of publicity adopted in business."[70] According to McGerr, campaigns turned to "the tools of advertising" in order to construct a "careful packaging of the candidate . . . [and] sell him to the voters."[71]

Publicity created a new kind of campaign, one that endeavored to connect candidates with voters in a more direct fashion. This elevated the role of campaign strategists drawn from the personal circle of the candidate rather than the party. These publicity experts and press agents of the early twentieth century resemble the political consultants of our own day as they orchestrated "presidential booms" designed to generate national press coverage before the convention on behalf of hopeful nominees.[72] In what may be the first documented example of a campaign consultant suing his client for unpaid bills, one William F. Clark took the former lieutenant governor of New York, Lewis Stuyvesant Chanler, to court in 1910 in an attempt "to recover $20,000 for services as head of the Chanler Press Bureau." As the *New York Times* reported, "Clark alleges that he was engaged to give publicity to Chanler's

Presidential aspirations. The latter denies that he so employed Clark or ever employed him in any capacity."[73] By 1908, in fact, party nominees chose individuals skilled in political technique to run their national campaigns rather than simply give the honor to a Senate leader or some other party chieftain as had been the tradition in the nineteenth century. For instance, Taft chose Frank Hitchcock to run his campaign, a man the *New York Times* described as one "who believes that successful politics is mostly the practical and systematic application of business principles to the task of vote-getting."[74] Publicity altered the character of political work, and the kind of individuals hired to perform that work.

Woodrow Wilson's political career further illustrates how publicity, and the publicity expert, influenced early twentieth-century campaigns. Like other progressives, Wilson criticized party bosses and the congressional committee system for their secrecy, and he framed his own efforts to engage the public directly as a way to promote a more active citizenry—through publicity. In an unpublished essay from 1882 entitled "Government by Debate," Wilson argued that the principal defect of contemporary American politics was the secrecy with which business was conducted, and that the most effective cure was the deliberation that inevitably accompanied the publicity of public affairs. "Publicity," Wilson argued, "is more to be valued in the administration of government than wisdom which works in secret or prudence which rules in private."[75] Like Theodore Roosevelt, Wilson considered publicity to be the keystone in the construction of a more robust executive. "Pitiless publicity is the sovereign cure for ills of government which can be applied easily and effectively by men whom the people entrust temporarily with executive duties," Wilson told a reporter shortly after his election as governor of New Jersey.[76] Wilson struck a similar theme in a 1910 address: "The people are calling for open leadership . . . they are tired of the hide and seek legislation."[77]

As a candidate for governor and in his campaign for president in 1912, Wilson consistently invoked the language of publicity in calling for an active form of leadership that directly engaged the public. Speaking to an audience in Newark, Wilson declared that "there is no air so wholesome as the air of publicity, and the only promise I am going to make you, if you elect me Governor, is that I will talk about the government to you as long as I am able."[78] Similarly, the claim that "publicity is one of the purifying elements of politics" was a stock portion of Wilson's stump speech in 1910 and 1912.[79] As a candidate, Wilson called for a politics based on "Progressive methods," which included "publicity, discussion, organized opinion, the pressure of systematic agitation, and independent voting."[80]

As a practical matter, however, the "progressive method" suggested a publicity-oriented approach to campaigning that made strategic use of the press to reach voters outside of regular party channels. When he ran for governor in 1910, Wilson's accessibility to reporters earned him goodwill and good coverage—an impressive feat in a state where Republican newspapers outnumbered Democratic ones by nearly two to one.[81] In addition, Wilson enjoyed close relationships with the editors of *Harper's Weekly* and the *American Review of Reviews*, who helped him develop nationwide notice as the president of Princeton University.[82] Following his success in 1910, Wilson's close circle of advisers, many of them experienced journalists, transferred the strategy used in New Jersey to the national stage. Frank Stockbridge, who managed Wilson's press campaign for the 1912 Democratic nomination, described how "sixteen months before the Democratic convention . . . a little group of friends persuaded [Wilson] to undertake a campaign of publicity, having for its object the creation of such a strong public opinion in favor of his candidacy that the pressure could not be resisted by party leaders."[83] As Stockbridge recalled, "The experiment was a novel and audacious one in American politics. It was a repetition on a national scale of Mr. Wilson's experiment in New Jersey where he had gone over the heads of the politicians and appealed directly to the voters."[84]

Specifically, Stockbridge organized a tour of the western United States a full year before the convention where Wilson made a series of public appearances that attracted attention to his candidacy. When Wilson complained about the tedium of meetings with journalists, answering the same questions each day, Stockbridge explained to him that he was "a personality of current local interest and would have to resign himself to that fact."[85]

The 1912 campaign illustrates the publicity-driven, candidate-focused style of presidential politics taking shape. In an article in *McClure's Magazine* subtitled "The New Art of Making Presidents by Press

Bureau," George Kibbe Turner wrote that "direct popular choice of candidates had arrived ... and candidates, not parties must introduce themselves directly to voters."[86] Theodore Roosevelt's entry into the race only heightened the focus on personalities that year.

Four years later, in 1916, publicity experts were even more important in crafting campaign strategies. Wilson faced Republican challenger Charles Evans Hughes, a Supreme Court justice with a national reputation as a reformer. For both campaigns, the intentions of more than 4 million voters who had supported Teddy Roosevelt in 1912 were largely unknown, and both sides viewed these "independents" as the key to the race. As one observer put it, both candidates needed support from those "ready to vote their convictions regardless of party ties."[87] The Hughes campaign hired the leaders of a Chicago advertising agency to "give to the Republican party a permanent organization of trained publicity experts, who will ... apply to politics the same merchandising principles that are applied to successful business enterprises."[88] Although Hughes lost by a narrow margin (a shift of fewer than 4,000 votes in California would have won him the election), the lesson of the campaign appeared to be the value of publicity. As the *Wall Street Journal* concluded soon after, "If there is one thing the election has said which should sink into all men's minds, it is that we should approach the voter—not the mob—by the most modern methods of publicity."[89]

Indeed, the Democrats proved quite innovative in this regard. Under the leadership of former newspaperman Robert W. Woolley, the Democratic National Committee conducted "widespread publicity of a kind never before attempted."[90] In fact, Woolley's "bigger impact was in bringing a new class of professional communicators and ... practitioners into the world of presidential campaigning."[91] This included reform journalist George Creel, who served as Woolley's special assistant. In a campaign memo, Creel advised that "we are living in a film age. The imagination of the hour is impressed almost more by 'movies' than by the word persuasive in print."[92] To that end, Creel commissioned the production of a campaign film entitled *The President and His Cabinet in Action*.[93] Creel also recommended placing ads "systematically and extensively in newspapers, weeklies ... and magazines."[94] With Woolley's support, Creel created a successful advertising campaign that relentlessly portrayed the Republican nominee as a man reluctant to take a stand on the issues of the day. Under Creel's direction, thirty-six prominent writers and journalists signed an open letter asking Justice Hughes to state his position on ten issues. The ad copy, which read, "Yes or No Mr. Hughes?," ran in each city where Hughes appeared, often on the day he spoke. At the same time, Creel crafted an image of Wilson as a wise and principled leader, a task he accomplished with the slogan "He Kept Us Out of War" and the hiring of several advertising agencies to place the slogan in newspapers and magazines and on billboards and streetcars.[95] Creel's efforts earned him wide respect. Gifford Pinchot, a Republican, called the 1916 Democratic campaign "a masterful realization of a systematic publicity plan."[96]

In 1920, it was the Republicans who successfully used advertising techniques to portray their candidate to the voters. This job fell to Albert Lasker, owner of the Lord and Thomas agency in Chicago, one of the largest advertising firms in the country.[97] In 1918, Republican national chairman Will Hays hired Lasker to help the GOP win back control of Congress. Two years later, Lasker and Hays "carried political advertising to a new level" in the service of Warren G. Harding.[98] Lasker organized a publicity campaign around the slogan "Wiggle and Wobble," an attempt to paint Wilson and the Democrats as unprincipled and inconsistent.[99] Lasker planned for Harding to use the phrase at the end of a speech in order to make it appear as if the slogan arose extemporaneously from an offhand remark. Weeks earlier, however, Lasker had prepared signs and billboards with the slogan to be released at a strategic moment, and he instructed that no one reveal that "the publicity end of the campaign had anything to do with the expression and the thought appearing in the speech."[100]

As publicity became a central feature of presidential campaigns, its original meaning as a liberal ideal increasingly gave way to its instrumental use in coordinated campaigns of persuasion. "Pitiless publicity" no longer implied the searching gaze of an investigative press, but the incessant search for public favor. Meanwhile, there arose a new kind of specialist, the publicity expert, whose mastery of technique could shape public sentiment on behalf of a client. To many observers, the value of publicity was the ability to convey the qualities of a candidate directly to the voter. As Richard Boeckel wrote in 1920, "The overwhelming majority [of voters] are going to cast their ballots on the basis of what they know about the candidate . . . about his principles and his personality, his record and his promises." Publicity promised a modern approach to winning elections. "The first requisite to being elected President in this new age of publicity," Boeckel continued, "is to have a story of the kind that will appeal to the people, the second is to have the kind of a press organization that will get the story to them." It was the publicity expert whose skills were needed to reach voters unmoved by traditional partisan appeals. "This year the man with the best story wins. The job of telling it—telling it and re-telling it to every voter in the language he best understands—falls to the publicity agent. . . . the publicity man is this year's president maker."[101] As Lasker's subterfuge on behalf of Harding also illustrates, the 1920 election marks a culmination in the transformation of political style in which, to borrow Michael McGerr's words, "political advertisers would manipulate the voter, . . . shape his perceptions, and sell him a product." With the perfection of publicity techniques, "politics entered a new realm of contrived images and salesmanship."[102]

Corporate Publicity

Developments in electoral politics illustrate how publicity techniques departed from the original meaning of the term, giving way instead to an orchestrated campaign that used carefully crafted words and images. But the multiple meaning of publicity continued to exist side by side, generating a profound ambiguity that fueled further innovations in communication techniques. With the spread of independent journalism and the growth in print media, publicity experts found that by concealing the source of a newspaper story or its actual purpose, they could artfully present information for the benefit of a particular client. For a public increasingly unable to discern the source of information or its veracity, it became nearly impossible to distinguish the old publicity from the new.

This ambiguity is clearly evident in the area of corporate publicity. In response to the ambitious push by Roosevelt and others for government regulation, corporations abandoned an older policy of secrecy and embraced public relations. These early twentieth-century efforts to improve the public image of the corporation produced important experiments, including primitive forms of public opinion research and grassroots lobbying techniques. More important, through the work of public relations a self-conscious claim of expertise began to emerge, along with an assertion of professional control over publicity methods that would become central to the field of political consulting over the course of the twentieth century.

In 1900, a group of Boston journalists formed the first public relations firm, innocuously named the Publicity Bureau. Their first client was Harvard University president Charles Eliot, who hired the firm to write press releases for the university. Within a few years, relations with Harvard had soured, so the Publicity Bureau moved on to more lucrative corporate clients.[103] The firm's biggest undertaking came in 1905, when it organized an extensive campaign on behalf of several railroads hoping to defeat the proposed Hepburn Act, a bill supported by President Theodore Roosevelt that was designed to strengthen the Interstate Commerce Commission and regulate railroad rates. In a series of articles for *McClure's*, Ray Stannard Baker described how agents working for the Publicity Bureau designed a rudimentary instrument to track public opinion toward the railroads. Through clippings from local newspapers and extensive interviews with editors on a wide range of subjects, the Publicity Bureau developed a card file that could be used to target press releases, advertisements, and other publicity efforts. As Baker described, the system revealed "how railroad information is running high in one community and low in another."[104] Baker called the card file, which was known as "The Barometer," "as good an indicator of the atmosphere of railroad opinion in the country as could possibly be devised."[105] Like Pinchot's efforts to track Forest Service press releases, these early publicity techniques foreshadowed the development of more sophisticated efforts to measure and manage public opinion during the early twentieth century.

Although the Publicity Bureau lost its client with passage of the Hepburn Act in 1906, railroads and other industrial concerns continued to employ people who could generate favorable press coverage and shape public sentiment on behalf of a company or industry. An early innovator was William Wolff Smith, a Washington journalist who established one of the first public affairs shops in the nation's capital. In some ways, Smith was like other lobbyists whose business before

Congress had grown since the 1870s.[106] What distinguished Smith, however, was his technique, specifically a weekly column he wrote that claimed to report the news from Washington. Consisting mostly of innocuous gossip about pedestrian topics, Smith's column concluded with a paragraph written on behalf of a client that advocated a position on a particular issue or pending piece of legislation. Because few daily newspapers could afford a Washington correspondent, Smith provided a wanted source of national news; by his own account, Smith distributed his column to 300, mostly rural, papers.[107]

A *Collier's* story on "the subsidized Washington correspondent" printed excerpts of a circular Smith distributed to potential clients that advertised his skills as an expert in the effective use of publicity. According to Smith, political reforms had eradicated the more direct, if less savory, methods of influence peddling that used to pass in Washington. "The old type of legislation grafters has vanished," Smith wrote, and "in their place has risen up a more artistic tribe."[108] Smith offered a glimpse into how this worked:

> Suppose, for instance, you are the head of a big concern which will profit largely by the enactment of certain legislation. You arrive in Washington and find the situation adverse. You are seriously disturbed at the outlook. . . . At this juncture the press agent appears. You engage him, furnish him with facts and figures, and next morning in various newspapers, you are surprised and delighted to find articles that are bound to help your cause. The day following interviews are published with prominent men favoring your scheme, and the mill of publicity is thus kept going, the people educated to look upon what you propose as a good thing, and the members of Congress soon begin to reflect the sentiment of their constituents. Practically all the varied large interests that received attention at the last session of Congress sought the aid of this new brand of lobbyist.[109]

A notable example of Smith's work was his effort on behalf of the seed industry to end the congressional distribution of free seeds. Smith asked agricultural journals and dailies to print editorials denouncing the congressional seed program, and he encouraged state Granges to pass resolutions asking Congress to eliminate the seed appropriation. Smith then transmitted copies of these editorials and resolutions to Congress. Speaking to a House agriculture panel in 1906, Smith boasted that he had organized a broad coalition that included "the farmers, the agriculturalists, the seedsmen, the Department of Agriculture, and the press of the United States," all opposed to free seeds.[110]

Smith practiced what is referred to today as "outside" lobbying: using constituency pressure to influence Congress.[111] Pendleton Herring described this type of lobbying in his book *Group Representation before Congress* (1929). According to Herring, efforts to "mold public opinion" proceeded along two fronts. "In the first place, the effort is made to form a general opinion favorable to the group, and then the attempt is made to marshal this sentiment and direct its influence upon ... the members of a legislature from whom favorable action is desired." In describing this "new lobby," Herring pointed out that publicity was "the strongest weapon in the arsenal" and that "the bureau of 'information' is one of the most active of the departments in most of the national associations" he studied.[112] Smith was an important innovator of this technique and a vocal defender of his methods. In 1912, Smith sued *Collier's*, unsuccessfully, for defamation of character following an article published about him entitled "Tainted News."[113]

Smith's stridency reflected a growing self-consciousness among publicity experts who faced a skeptical press and a suspecting public about the nature of their work. One of the more articulate spokesmen in this regard was Ivy Leadbetter Lee, a founder of modern public relations. After graduating from Princeton in 1898, Lee moved to New York City to work as a journalist. Finding limited success, in 1903 Lee took a position as press representative of the Citizens Union, the same municipal reform organization that would later establish the Bureau of Municipal Research. Lee's main function for the union was to direct publicity for the re-election of New York City's reform mayor, Seth Low. Although Low lost his re-election bid, the experience brought Ivy Lee in contact with George Parker, an experienced campaigner who worked for Grover Cleveland in 1888 and 1892. In 1904, Lee and Parker joined forces designing press releases for Democratic presidential candidate Alton Parker (no relation). After the Roosevelt landslide, Parker and Lee went into business together and parlayed their political skills into publicity services for corporate clients. A key break came in 1906 when Lee issued a press release on behalf of several mining companies in advance of the anthracite coal strike. Abandoning a previous policy of secrecy, the release announced, "The anthracite coal operators, realizing the general public interest in conditions in the mining regions, have arranged to supply the press with all possible information." Lee's success during the coal strike earned him a wide reputation in the emerging field of public relations, and the client list of Parker & Lee grew accordingly. Their agency motto was "Accuracy, Authenticity, Interest."[114]

As the slogan suggests, Ivy Lee articulated a vision of corporate publicity that echoed a traditional view of objective truth even as he embraced the power of mass communication. For Lee, antipathy toward corporate power was simply the result of "misunderstandings of the public, due generally to lack of information of facts or full information." Corporate publicity would educate the public and, in so doing, defeat "the demagoguery of politicians" who demanded business regulation.[115] "We have allowed irresponsible assertions to be made for so long without denial that many people now believe them to be proven facts," Lee wrote in a press release for Bethlehem Steel. "We shall make the mistake of silence no longer. Henceforth we shall pursue a policy of publicity. Misinformation will not be permitted to go uncorrected."[116]

At the same time, Lee was keenly aware of the opportunities of modern publicity, and he readily exploited the ambiguities generated by an independent press. One of Lee's favored techniques, perfected during his work on political campaigns, was to design and typeset a press release so that it was indistinguishable from a regular newspaper column. Influenced by the later writings of Walter Lippmann on the subjectivity of reporting, Lee told an audience of advertising executives that "the effort to state an absolute fact is . . . humanly impossible; all I can do is to give you my interpretation of the facts."[117] As Michael Schudson has written, "While this perception in some hands was . . . used as criticism, for Lee it was a cynical [worldview] used to defend business's use of public relations."[118] Lee turned traditional notions of publicity on their head: "Since all opinions are suspect, all are equally entitled to a place in the democratic forum."[119] In more practical terms, Lee showed how the affirmative powers of publicity could be used for a wide variety of goals and purposes. Just as Roosevelt had toured the country to build public support for conservation policy, Lee argued that corporations must "take their story directly to the people, over the heads of the commissions, legislatures and Congress."[120]

Lee's ability to straddle these multiple meanings made him an articulate spokesperson for the publicity expert and the modern practice of public relations:

> Every company . . . should employ a publicity engineer . . . to advise with its officers and to act with them in all matters of public relationship and in the cultivation of general good will. The publicity man will know what the newspapers would send for if only they had the suggestion. He will write the matter the way the papers want it. This adviser in public relations—for such a man should be far more than a mere publicity agent—should constantly study the temper of the public mind. . . . his work, in a word, will be to interpret his company to an enlightened public opinion and to interpret an enlightened public opinion to his company.[121]

In separating himself from the theatrical press agent, Lee staked out an ambitious professional claim. He wrote, "Publicity is not a game; it is a science. The difference between the two is as wide as the discrepancy between a press agent and doctor of publicity."[122] Articulating a progressive faith in the power of expertise, Lee presented his work as part of the inevitable march of progress: "People who attempt to interfere with the progress of advertising in these borderlands of publicity are bound to encounter the same fate as those primeval men who sought to obstruct the progress of civilization in pioneer regions."[123]

Publicity and the Origins of Political Consulting

The embrace of publicity during the early twentieth century marks the beginning of a modern business of politics. Although a recognizable field of political consulting would still be several decades away, its origins are identifiable among the publicity experts who promoted their skills as a modern way to shape public sentiment in favor of government programs, in support of a candidate, or on behalf of a corporate client. In doing so, publicity contributed to the early expansion of presidential power and the turn to a more personality-driven style of politics.

Publicity helped Theodore Roosevelt forge a more robust form of executive leadership, and it allowed Woodrow Wilson to build a political career as a reform politician amid shifting partisan allegiances.[124] Publicity also figured in the emergence of the modern corporation and the recognition that, if left untreated, public opinion posed a threat to private ownership. As Ivy Lee insisted, operating a modern business "without taking the public into one's confidence, without using every legitimate means of publicity, is about as obsolete as operating street railways with horses and mules."[125] Publicity represented a new kind of political work, one that applied the tools of advertising and early measures of public opinion to address contemporary challenges such as the rise of independent voting or the growth of an activist government. Through the application of modern business methods, publicity experts contributed to the rise of a modern business of politics.

Critics complained about the early twentieth-century growth in publicity, especially journalists who saw the practice of planted news undermining the integrity of their enterprise. In defense, the publicity expert appealed to the progressive notion that an engaged public could improve the operation of government, hold elected officials accountable, and temper the excesses of unbridled capitalism. Through the free flow of information, voters would make reasoned judgments about the issues of the day. Publicity, and by extension the publicity expert, was an essential element of representative government without whom an informed, reasoning citizenry could not participate fully in public affairs.[126] However, publicity exploited an inherent ambiguity in the meaning of the term, and its practice operated on the basis of a profound contradiction. Successful publicity depended on the public's inability to discern the objective reporting of news from the contrived or manipulated event. Publicity experts promised to reveal the truth, but they did so by manipulating the facts.

The term "publicity" has largely disappeared from the political lexicon, yet the central ambiguity in its meaning and use is still evident in a certain ambivalence Americans express about politics today. Publicity was well suited to the political and social context of the Progressive Era as it justified free speech and open debate, ideals that stood in opposition to the secrecy and corruption of the period. Over time, however, the proliferation of techniques designed to attract and shape public attention has contributed to a disillusionment with politics. Political candidates and public figures may aspire to the view that the unhindered flow of information is a requirement for an enlightened public, but for many Americans the endless stream of presidential communications, interest group appeals, and campaign advertisements appear as highly contrived attempts to persuade rather than inform. As one observer lamented more than a century ago, "Truth is as elusive as ever, in spite of the multiplicity of her salaried ministers."[127] In setting the foundation stone for a modern consulting industry, the publicity expert set in motion a profound transformation in the character of American politics.

3

Professional Propaganda

IN 1917, PRESIDENT WOODROW WILSON created the Committee on Public Information (CPI), a federal agency responsible for producing an "avalanche of publicity" on behalf of the war effort.[1] The man in charge of the CPI was George Creel, the former journalist who just one year earlier had made the slogan "He Kept Us Out of War" the centerpiece of Wilson's successful re-election campaign. Now head of the CPI, Creel elevated publicity to a new level, combining the tools of journalism, advertising, and even film to build up public support for the war in part by drowning out the voices of those who disagreed.[2] Writing in 1918, Creel described his work for the government as "educational and informative," adding that public opinion "has its base in reason. . . rather than any temporary excitement of passing passion."[3] Yet, Creel also admitted that as he worked "to erect our house of truth," the purpose of the CPI was "to 'sell' America to the world."[4] Creel even titled his memoirs *How We Advertised America*, describing his efforts as "a vast enterprise in salesmanship, the world's greatest adventure in advertising."[5]

Creel's work illustrates the tension between the idea of publicity and its modern practice, a tension that became increasingly apparent in the years after the First World War. Building on a celebrated ideal of an educated citizenry, publicity experts transformed the conduct of political work by using press releases, paid advertisements, and other methods of communication to cultivate popular support for government programs, political candidates, and even corporations. However, the discovery that the U.S. government had waged a massive campaign of persuasion during the war revealed the susceptibility of the public to misinformation. Critics charged that the purpose of the CPI was not to inform, but to manipulate the public by using carefully crafted words, images, and symbols to stoke anti-German sentiment and generate support for the war.[6] If publicity described a prewar hope for a reasoned democracy, a new word, propaganda, crystallized for many the realization that such a goal was utterly unattainable.

With the taint of propaganda hanging over them, publicity experts could no longer claim the educative function of informing the public. Facing widespread criticism, publicity experts had to find new ways to promote their skills and defend their methods. One strategy was to claim the mantle of a skilled professional trained in a new science of persuasion. This assertion of professional status occurred just as a behavioral social science began to emerge, along with a set of scholars who viewed propaganda not as a scourge but as an object of scientific study. By forging links with scholars interested in the effects of propaganda, practitioners could claim that they were highly trained professionals who specialized in the practical application of social scientific knowledge.

This step in the development of the business of politics is vividly illustrated in the work and writings of Edward Bernays. At a time when the progressive faith in publicity had given way to a widespread concern about the limits of public reason, Bernays articulated a different vision about the role of propaganda in a democratic polity. For Bernays, coordinated campaigns of persuasion were a characteristic feature of modern life that required a scientific approach to the study of mass beliefs. By aligning himself with prominent social scientists, Bernays sought a measure of credibility and a degree of control over his craft. Although he never called himself a political consultant (preferring the term "counsel on public relations" instead), Bernays foreshadowed the methods and tools that would become central to the professional control of political work: poll-tested messages targeting discrete groups of voters.

The Discovery of Propaganda

The Committee on Public Information operated on a massive scale. In a little over two years, George Creel's agency issued more than six thousand press releases and produced thousands of advertisements as well as numerous photographs, motion pictures, posters, and billboards. It published material in thirty-three languages. Its daily *Official Bulletin* was disseminated widely through CPI offices around the world. And at a time when radio had yet to penetrate many households, the CPI organized 75,000 "Four Minute Men," local notables who delivered nearly 1 million prepared speeches in favor of the war at movie theaters and other public places.[7] Creel personally recruited prominent journalists and artists to the cause, including the well-known illustrator Charles Dana Gibson who designed CPI posters that graphically depicted the war effort as an epic battle between good and evil.[8] The CPI also translated its work into several languages to appeal to immigrant populations in the United States, and it established offices overseas in Europe and Latin America to monitor and shape foreign news coverage of the U.S. war effort.

After the war, commentators began to look critically at the work of the CPI as well as attempts by American allies to influence public opinion in the United States. Published reports that German atrocities had been fabricated by the British government in order to undermine American neutrality led to criticism of the CPI and the part it played in fostering anti-German sentiment at home. As one critic put it, "No effort was made to present the truth . . . This was the greatest fraud ever sold to the public in the name of patriotism."[9] Muckraking journalist Will Irwin, himself a former director of the CPI's Foreign Section, described an "age of lies," admitting that "we never told the whole truth . . . we told that part which served our national purpose."[10] America's entry into the war appeared as a fabrication secured through the manipulation of words, images, and ideas. The public had not only been misled; through the work of the CPI, the public was willfully and skillfully made to believe that the war had been waged in pursuit of a noble cause.

In a word, these postwar critics discovered propaganda. What had been a rather amorphous term used to describe the promotion of a particular doctrine or belief, propaganda took on a more precise and sinister meaning after the war. According to historian J. Michael Sproule, postwar writers understood propaganda as "the covert manipulation of news . . . and self-interested messages insinuated into a variety of ostensibly neutral channels."[11] Works entitled "The Menace of Propaganda," "The Art of Muddlement," and "Poisoned Springs of World News" appeared in popular magazines throughout the 1920s and 1930s, its authors describing "shrewd, sleepless . . . campaign[s] to educate Vox Populi to sing in various keys, major or minor, as this or that particular project requires."[12] The power of propaganda, for these writers, lay in the malleability of the public mind.

Most important, propaganda cut directly against a progressive hope in a reasoning, deliberative public. Again quoting Sproule, "the chief moral of the Great War was its demonstration that the modern public was vulnerable to dubious contrivances promoted by political leaders and institutional managers."[13] In place of the rational citizenry mobilized through the revelation of facts, postwar commentators saw an uninformed crowd easily swayed by the modern tools of mass persuasion.[14]

It was Walter Lippmann, more than any other intellectual of the period, who exploded the myth of progressive publicity. Prompted in part by his own experiences working for the CPI, Lippmann articulated a deep skepticism toward public reason. In his influential 1922 book *Public Opinion*, Lippmann questioned the assumption of a rational public, viewing the world instead through the eyes of English psychologist Graham Wallas, who wrote that "the empirical art of politics consists largely in the creation of opinion by the deliberate exploitation of [the] subconscious."[15] In similar fashion, Lippmann argued that because individuals cannot apprehend a reality that is not experienced personally, there is an unavoidable source of bias and subjectivity in news coverage. "Circumstances in all their sprawling complexity," cannot be faithfully recorded, Lippmann wrote. Consequently, there is "enormous discretion as to what facts and what impressions will be reported. . . every newspaper when it reaches the reader is the result of a whole series of selections as to what items shall be printed . . . There are no objective standards," Lippmann argued.[16]

Two important conclusions followed from the inherent subjectivity of human experience. First, editorial discretion made it possible to shape and bend the presentation of events. Impressions of the world around us were mere pictures in our head, largely painted by others. Creating this portrait of reality was the principal task of the publicity expert, whose appearance Lippmann noted "is a clear sign that the facts of modern life do not spontaneously take a shape in which they can be known. They must be given a shape by somebody."[17] Second, this subjective rendering of the world laid bare the fallacy of an omni-competent citizen who made reasoned judgments based on the evaluation of facts. As the experience of wartime propaganda made clear, public opinion was not the bottom-up articulation of popular will as many democratic theorists maintained, but instead reflected "the manufacture of consent. . . and the opportunities for manipulation open to anyone who understands the process."[18] "The creation of consent . . . has improved enormously in technic [sic]," Lippmann observed, as "persuasion has become a self-conscious art and a regular organ of popular government."[19] Lippmann anticipated a world in which skilled persuaders wielded substantial influence in public affairs. "The knowledge of how to create consent will alter every political premise," producing "a revolution . . . more significant than any shifting of economic power."[20]

The discovery of propaganda undermined the presumption of a rational public and with it the progressive justification for publicity techniques. In its place, a much more skeptical view emerged of mass society manipulated by words, images, and symbols, a public susceptible to lies and half-truths. For the publicity expert and others engaged in "the empirical art of politics," this development posed a formidable challenge. His liberal veneer stripped away, the publicity expert became the propagandist, one who employed modern techniques of persuasion in order to manipulate a largely ignorant and irrational public.

Propaganda between the Wars

Throughout the 1920s and 1930s, critics pointed to the pervasive use of propaganda in American life and its often pernicious effects on an impressionable public. Exposés described "an emerging coterie of professionalized experts" who manipulated "irrational forces for concealed purposes."[21] However, the same commentators who criticized the manufacture of consent, also marveled at the sophistication of propaganda techniques and the expanding range of opportunities for those skilled in the art of persuasion. For instance, political parties established permanent media operations, moving beyond the quadrennial publicity of a presidential campaign in order to shape news coverage between elections. With the coming of the New Deal, government agencies used a steady stream of communication in a sustained effort to build public support for the spate of newly created federal programs inaugurated during the 1930s. Propaganda between the wars attests to the ongoing transformation of political work as practitioners perfected their skills and expanded their reach.

As director of the Publicity Bureau of the Democratic Party from 1929 until 1943, Charles Michelson illustrates both the rise of the paid expert in shaping campaign messages and the still porous nature of political work. Michelson began his career in journalism, as a well-regarded Washington correspondent for the *New York World*. Reporting from the 1928 Republican Convention in Houston, Michelson described the presidential campaign that year in Lippmann-esque terms: "The American people will elect as President of the United States in November a nonexistent person—and defeat likewise a mythical identity. They will vote for and against a picture . . . that must be either a caricature or an idealization."[22] Soon, Michelson himself would play a central role in this process.

The growth in newspapers during the late nineteenth century made journalists important figures in the conduct of presidential campaigns. Newspaper experience was highly valued as the political parties placed greater emphasis on generating favorable press coverage for their presidential candidate during the election. Every four years, both parties would staff their campaigns with reporters and editors who produced a steady flow of literature, press releases, and even typeset zinc plates ready for printing. At the close of the campaign, these journalists would usually resume their employment at a newspaper, and the national party would cease operations until the next quadrennial effort.[23]

In this regard, Charles Michelson's move from the *World* to the Democratic Party appears unremarkable. However, the timing of Michelson's appointment and the methods he employed marked an important change in the conduct of political work. Stung by the defeat of New York governor Al Smith by Herbert Hoover in 1928, Democratic Party leaders resolved to put their political operations on a permanent footing. As Smith himself complained, his campaign suffered from "the habit of the Democratic party to function only six months in every four years."[24] As a remedy, the chairman of the Democratic National Committee, Jacob Raskob, formed a permanent Executive Committee with Michelson serving as director of publicity in order to create a "business-like national headquarters that will function continuously."[25]

Although Michelson himself had never worked in politics, his experience as a journalist exposed him to the "soggy bales of material" political parties routinely issued during a presidential campaign.[26] Aware that most campaign literature went unused, Michelson recast political communications with an eye toward the production demands of the press.[27] Following the October 1929 stock market crash, Michelson issued a daily stream of press releases and other statements that criticized Hoover's handling of the economy. Because Michelson knew his material would fail to reach a wide audience unless it conformed to journalistic conventions of "news," he packaged issues in a manner that would appeal to the reading public. Moreover, because official releases from party headquarters would likely be ignored as well, Michelson prepared material for Democratic senators and representatives to insert in their speeches on the floor before the galleries of the Washington press corps.

Michelson's innovation, in other words, was to create Democratic "talking points": a centralized communication operation outside the normal election cycle that could project the party message on a daily basis. Its purpose, in Michelson's own words, was to convince the public that "a man sat in the president's chair who did not fit."[28] Although this goal was not an unusual one for a party out of power, Michelson's tactics appeared novel to many, and his ability to generate negative news about Hoover illustrated the power of political propaganda. Journalist Frank Kent, a Hoover supporter, attributed to Michelson "the most elaborate, expensive, efficient, and effective political propaganda machine ever operated in the country by any party, organization, association, or league."[29] Other accounts sounded similar themes. Answering the question, "Who creates our political prejudices?," Oliver McKee explained that "trained newspaper men are an essential part of the mechanism of propaganda."[30] These commentators also detected an important change in technique as Michelson conducted party propaganda on a more sophisticated, almost scientific basis. As Will Irwin wrote in *Propaganda and the News*, "The permanent importance of the work of Michelson ... lies not in the fact that they ... helped to defeat [Hoover]. It lies rather in the contribution of a new method to American politics."[31] Whereas "political propaganda had been languishing in the hands of amateurs," Michelson "brought it up to the times and gave it a professional cast."[32]

Michelson's work for the Democratic National Committee continued through the 1940 presidential campaign, and he worked for the party in an advisory capacity until his death in 1948.[33] That he remained in politics rather than return to journalism as many did after the close of a presidential campaign is significant, for it reveals that a professional distinction had begun to emerge between journalism and political communication, a distinction driven by developments in both fields. Journalistic standards in news gathering created opportunities to shape the flow of information to the press, as Michelson's career illustrates. Ironically, concerns about the influence of propaganda prompted journalists to assert their claims of objectivity even more forcefully and eschew the active role they had taken in politics since the nineteenth century. This, in turn, opened more space for Michelson and others to specialize in crafting political speech. What had been a porous boundary, with reporters moving between partisan newspapers and campaigns, was gradually becoming two distinct occupational spheres that separated journalists from those who specialized in political communication.[34] With the election of Franklin Roosevelt, this distinction developed even further as Michelson and others like him found their skills in great demand amid the expanding activities of the New Deal state.

If Michelson's work for the Democratic Party signaled the increased sophistication of propaganda, the coming of the New Deal in 1933 brought a profound expansion in its scope. "Never before," political scientist Pendleton Herring observed, "has the federal government undertaken on so vast a scale and with such deliberate intent the task of building favorable public opinion toward its policies."[35] The New Deal opened numerous opportunities for those skilled in communication techniques as public outreach for government policies became the job of political operatives. The New Deal, in fact, offers an early example of the "permanent campaign," a term frequently used to describe the heavy reliance on political means in the pursuit of policy ends. Although the fusion of campaigning and governing is considered a late twentieth-century phenomenon, its form took shape much earlier with sustained and organized efforts to build up public support for the New Deal.[36] As one contemporary described it, "The same publicity tactics which proved so successful during the Democratic Presidential Campaign ... are being employed on an even larger scale to keep the New Deal before the public."[37]

For his part, Charles Michelson worked for several New Deal agencies following the 1932 presidential campaign, all the while maintaining his official position with the Democratic Party (which continued to pay his salary). After Roosevelt's inauguration in March 1933, Michelson helped Secretary of the Treasury William Woodin publicize the bank holiday Roosevelt declared to avert a financial panic. Once the banking crisis eased, Michelson served stints with the Civilian Conservation Corps and as press director for the US delegation to the London Economic Conference before becoming director of public relations for the National Recovery Administration (NRA), the flagship agency of the New Deal, in July 1933.[38] Working for the colorful head of the NRA, General Hugh Johnson, Michelson described his boss as "a publicity man's dream."[39]

In April 1934, advertising executive William Lawson succeeded Michelson at the NRA.[40] With help from a large staff of reporters, Lawson directed the preparation of press releases, editorials, radio addresses, and newsreels promoting the activities of the NRA. Lawson's former advertising agency created the famous "Blue Eagle" symbol and the slogan "We Do Our Part," which soon appeared "on posters, billboards, flags, movie screens, magazines, newspapers, automobile windshields, and countless products."[41] Speaking to a group of advertising executives in 1934, Johnson described the Blue Eagle campaign as an attempt to insinuate the NRA into daily American life: "Today as you drive the country's roads and glance ... toward a billboard, you see the Blue Eagle. ... It has been through advertising that the country has been gotten behind ... the NRA." This was an artful achievement, Johnson continued. As he told his audience, "The sculptor works in plastic clay ... but your material is human minds and emotions—a far more delicate and fleeting thing."[42]

Critics complained that Johnson "was dealing in propaganda on a great scale" by staging "the greatest political show ever put on in this country."[43] The loudest criticisms came from newspaper editors and journalists who saw the campaign to publicize New Deal programs as a threat to their profession. Frank Kent, a vocal opponent of the New Deal, described "an octopus of political propaganda" consisting of men and women throughout the government "who steadily and exclusively work at the job of 'selling' the administration's activities to the public."[44] Will Irwin noted a similar proliferation of New Deal propaganda, concluding that "the reporter at Washington obtained no news from the bureaus until it had filtered through the mind of an expert."[45] In 1934, the Pennsylvania Newspaper Publishers Association issued a series of pamphlets titled "Newspapers and the New Deal" that included a list of more than fifty government departments, agencies, and offices with staff dedicated to publicity or public relations functions.[46] Elisha Hanson, general counsel for the American Newspaper Publishers Association, complained that these efforts to sell administration policies constituted "the greatest danger to freedom of the press in America."[47]

Members of Congress also looked askance at these efforts to publicize New Deal programs, and they waged an ongoing congressional battle against executive branch publicity.[48] In 1936, during the struggle over executive reorganization, the Senate established the Select Committee to Investigate the Executive Agencies of Government. Chaired by Senator Harry Byrd of Virginia, the committee contracted the Brookings Institution to prepare a comprehensive report on governmental activities. Issued the following year, the Brookings report included one section that examined "official reporting, public-relations work, and other publicity activities." It found that although an appropriations rider passed in 1913 prohibited the use of funds "for the compensation of any publicity expert," executive agencies routinely evaded the letter of the law by hiring publicity personnel under a variety of titles such as "Director of Information" or "Supervisor of Information Research."[49] In total, the Brookings report found 146 "persons engaged wholly on publicity work" and 124 persons engaged part-time. During a three-month period in 1936 alone, the report continued, the government issued 7 million copies of nearly 5,000 press releases, and it maintained 3,000 distinct mailing lists containing 2.3 million names.[50]

In addition to newspapers, New Deal agencies made ample use of newer media as well, taking advantage of the rapid penetration of American society by the radio and the growing importance of visual images, rather than the printed word, to convey the desperate poverty of those in need.[51] James McCamy estimated that in 1937 the federal government aired more than 5,000 radio programs throughout the country, released 10,000 photographs, and screened 3,000 movies.[52] As the *Washington Post* editorialized, government attempts to play upon the public's emotions "convert what should be matter-of-fact statement into malappropriate [*sic*] propaganda."[53]

Congressional concern over New Deal propaganda was motivated by more than partisan difference or opposition to administration policies, although they played a part.[54] More broadly, complaints emanating from Congress reflected institutional struggles that were underway. Propaganda techniques afforded the Roosevelt administration with a more direct way to reach the public, one that did not rely on Congress or political parties.[55] Like the journalists who saw their role as arbiters of fact usurped by government publicity experts, members of Congress were similarly threatened by executive propaganda. As an observer noted, "Since our Government is increasingly a government of public opinion, politicians are naturally reluctant to authorize a system by which the President can reach the minds of the voters whom congressmen are supposed to represent."[56]

Contemporary scholars of American politics, however, saw this reliance on public outreach as an almost inevitable consequence of growing executive responsibilities. Writing in the *American Political Science Review* in 1941, Harold Stoke argued that "if the executive must take the risk of acting first and seeking the support of the people afterward, it must have—in fact, it will make sure it does have—the means of persuading people to approve its actions." Propaganda was "an indispensable instrument of government," as were "the skilled craftsmen who make programs successful by … winning popular support."[57] Moreover, as Pendleton Herring observed at the height of the New Deal, Congress was at a decided disadvantage in communicating with the public. "The deliberate and intelligently planned system for building up a favorable public opinion has developed greatly in the administrative branch." The only way to correct this imbalance, Herring concluded, was if Congress secured "the needed *expertise* in public relations management."[58]

Herring's emphasis on the need for "public relations management" is telling, for it points to an increasing reliance on experts in messaging and communication. At the time Herring wrote, in fact, the field of corporate public relations was gaining prominence as business executives increasingly saw public opinion as a vital bulwark against a perceived threat to free enterprise posed by FDR and the New Deal.[59] Along with similar developments in politics and government, the rise of public relations marks a growing sophistication in the tools of persuasion and a new kind of political work that distinguished its practitioners from journalists, party politicians, or other arbiters of popular will.

However, the status of this new occupation was far from secure. With the liberal meaning of publicity largely forgotten, attracting public attention on behalf of another carried a status akin to that of a theatrical press agent or circus promoter. The term "propaganda" had its own baggage as a form of deception and manipulation. Consequently, the paid persuader hit upon a new label, the public relations counsel, in the hopes of acquiring the professional status of a doctor or lawyer who applied specialized knowledge to the particular needs of a patient or client. Although this status remained tenuous through the 1930s, practitioners sought to portray themselves in a more favorable light as they devised new kinds of political work.

Edward Bernays: Public Relations Counsel

Edward L. Bernays was a tireless promoter of public relations, and of himself. In tracing the arc of his career, it is sometimes difficult to separate the achievements of Bernays from the residues of his own self-promotion. In spite of this, Bernays left an extensive archive of material that reveals his attempt to craft a new kind of political work while, at the same time, establishing his credentials as a professional. Bernays believed that the key to effective propaganda was to identify the distinct social, economic, and racial groups in society, their prejudices and affiliations, and the symbols, words, and emotional appeals that could attract attention and elicit support. In the 1930s and 1940s, however, this approach to political campaigns required a fair degree of salesmanship, something Bernays was well equipped to provide. To that end, Bernays worked hard to convince potential clients and the larger public that his techniques were ideally suited to the conditions of a modern society. A nephew of Sigmund Freud, Bernays drew upon his uncle's fame to build up his own reputation as an expert in mass psychology. At the same time, Bernays used advances in the social sciences to acquire a novel set of tools and a valuable set of allies as he staked out his professional claims over the conduct of political work.

Origins of a New Profession

Edward L. Bernays began his career working as a publicity man and theatrical press agent in New York City, where he developed a talent for turning social and political issues into commercial opportunities for his clients. In 1913, Bernays helped promote a play entitled *Damaged Goods* about a man with syphilis who marries and fathers a syphilitic child. The play caused something of a sensation as it challenged contemporary mores about sexually transmitted disease; promoting it was a risky enterprise at a time when Anthony Comstock was the secretary of the New York Society for the Suppression of Vice. In order to raise money for the production, Bernays established the Sociological Fund Committee, a strategy aimed at attracting reform-minded elites who saw the play as a way to break down societal taboos that inhibited social reform. With the help of Bernays, the play became a cause célèbre, gaining the support of John D. Rockefeller Jr., Franklin and Eleanor Roosevelt, and other notables whose involvement kept Comstock at bay.[60]

During the war, Bernays completed a stint with the Committee on Public Information, heading a local office in Latin America. Upon his return to the United States, Bernays orchestrated several spectacular events that established his reputation in the emerging field of public relations. Working on behalf of the American Tobacco Company during the 1920s, he devised a campaign to increase the feminine appeal of cigarettes. This was no easy task at a time when smoking by women was considered a sign of loose morals. Building on the cresting movement for voting rights, Bernays organized a march up Fifth Avenue in New York City in which women smoked Lucky Strike cigarettes and evoked the image of the Statue of Liberty by calling on their suffragette sisters to "carry the torch of freedom."[61] A few years later, Bernays helped plan "Light's Golden Jubilee," a worldwide media celebration commemorating the fiftieth anniversary of the light bulb. Organized on behalf of General Electric, these events were "meticulously staged to look like a spontaneous tribute."[62] In another public relations coup, Bernays enlisted the support of prominent doctors to recommend eating bacon for breakfast (his client, Beechnut Packing Company, was a large meatpacking concern). The success of these strategies hinged on concealing the effort behind them, prompting the author Larry Tye to dub Bernays "the father of spin."[63]

The underlying cynicism in these methods was not lost on contemporary critics, some of whom saw in Bernays evidence of a public easily manipulated by words and symbols. One profile of Bernays called him "a stern realist who operates upon the demonstrable theory that men in a democracy are sheep waiting to be led to the slaughter."[64] Another described publicity experts like Bernays as "the medicine man of the industrial tribe, whose spells and incantations work wonders which, like all religious mysteries, are either absurd or incredible when viewed by the rational mind."[65]

Bernays was well aware of these concerns, but his own experience with US propaganda efforts during the war left him deeply interested in the psychological effects of mass communication, what Bernays described as "the impact words and pictures made on the minds of men."[66] Inspired by Walter Lippmann's thinking about the ephemeral nature of public opinion, Bernays came to see his own techniques selling cigarettes or publicizing plays as manufacturing consent in ways Lippmann described. In his book *Crystallizing Public Opinion* (1923), Bernays drew frequently (and rather freely) from Lippmann's writing, describing the job of the public relations counsel as "crystallizing the obscure tendencies of the public mind." But if Lippmann explained why mass persuasion was possible in theory, Bernays sketched out how such work should be carried out in practice by "building public acceptance for an idea or product."[67]

In fact, Bernays saw his talents extending well beyond the realm of advertising. "Whether it is in cigarettes, or in a political movement, or an infant's food, it is necessary to recognize mass opinion," Bernays was quoted as saying.[68] Political campaigns, in particular, struck Bernays as "archaic and ineffective" for lacking "the expert use of propaganda" needed to "meet the conditions of the public mind."[69] To meet this need, Bernays argued for the application of modern business methods to the practice of political work. As a contemporary put it, "A political campaign ... is a selling campaign. It is a drive for votes just as Ivory Soap advertising is a drive for sales."[70] This required a "supersalesman" rather than "the old-type political manager" to "sell" the candidate "just as a problem in the marketing of toothpaste would be handled."[71]

The utility of propaganda did not end with the election. "Campaigning is only an incident in political life. The process of government is continuous," Bernays observed. Consequently, "The expert use of propaganda is more useful and fundamental ... as an aid to democratic administration, than as an aid to vote getting."[72] In a 1925 speech to the National Municipal League on "crystallizing public opinion for good government," Bernays insisted that with the right techniques, "good government can be sold to a community just as any other commodity can be sold."[73] Anticipating the future role of political consultants in the White House, Bernays told an audience at a meeting of the American Political Science Association that a special adviser, "independent of the various departments and responsible only to the President," was needed to coordinate publicity functions, "so that the public would receive a constant and integrated picture of government activities."[74]

For Bernays, Lippmann offered a response to those critics who saw propaganda as a cynical attempt to manipulate the public; instead, propaganda was an inescapable feature of contemporary life and, in the hands of trained experts, a crucial instrument of democratic practice. Seeing himself in this role, Bernays endeavored to establish himself as a new kind of professional whose skills were indispensable in a modern democratic polity. "Due to the complexity of modern life," Bernays argued, "a knowledge of the workings of public opinion and a knowledge of the media that carry ideas to the public is basic to anyone who depends on the public for success."[75] Like Lippmann, Bernays drew a very different lesson from the recent past: "The astounding success of propaganda [during the war] opened the eyes of the intelligent few in all departments of life to the possibilities of regimenting the public mind."[76] Bernays insisted that, far from a threat to democratic government, "opinion-management is one of the most vital forces today, especially in preserving democracy."[77] Accordingly, Bernays set out to explain to a wider public how "the growth and importance of this new profession" he hoped to create was in fact "the very essence of the democratic process, the freedom to persuade and suggest."[78]

Bernays staked out this professional claim against the backdrop of important developments in the social sciences and an emerging group of scholars trying to understand the sources of individual beliefs and their relation to political behavior. For those at the forefront of this behavioral turn in the study of politics, propaganda was a worthy intellectual pursuit that offered crucial insights into the nature and sources of mass opinion. This behavioral turn also brought scholars and practitioners together, forging a partnership that would play an important role in the development of political consulting. For Edward Bernays, connections with prominent academics not only furthered a search for more sophisticated techniques but also advanced a set of professional goals that were both lofty and mundane.

The New Science of Politics

Harold Lasswell stands out as an influential scholar in the study of propaganda and an intriguing figure in the development of political consulting. As a graduate student at the University of Chicago in the 1920s, Lasswell studied with the political scientist Charles Merriam, who pushed the discipline toward larger theoretical aspirations and greater scientific precision.[79] Merriam worked for the CPI in Italy during World War I, an experience that left him interested in mass psychology and the sociology of nationalism.[80] Merriam believed these subjects would form the basis for a new science of politics, and he challenged his student Lasswell to take up the study of propaganda as a topic for his doctoral research. As Lasswell later recalled, Merriam "focused my own interest on political propaganda of which the origin, effects and (particularly) the psychology were to become the subject matter of my life work."[81]

In 1927, Lasswell published his dissertation under the title *Propaganda Technique in the World War*. In it, Lasswell distanced himself from those who were "puzzled, uneasy, or vexed at the unknown cunning which seems to have duped and degraded them." By contrast, Lasswell approached the study of propaganda as a scientific enterprise: "To the somber curiosity of the discouraged democrat must be added the analytical motive of the social scientist," he wrote.[82] His purpose was to "discover and report, not to philosophize and reform."[83] Accordingly, Lasswell detailed the various ways countries on both sides of the war endeavored to shape public sentiments. Lasswell concluded that propaganda methods were an unavoidable (and indispensable) aspect of modern life, observing that "propaganda has become a profession. . . . the modern world is busy developing a corps of men who do nothing but study the ways and means of changing minds or binding minds to their convictions." In the future, Lasswell predicted that "governments will rely increasingly upon the professional propagandists for advice and aid."[84]

In other words, propaganda was simply a tool, an instrument of social control that operated through persuasion rather than coercion. In fact, it was precisely this reliance on persuasion that made propaganda an essential component of democratic government. Writing in the *American Political Science Review* in 1927, Lasswell noted how "that which could formerly be done by violence and intimidation must now be done by argument and persuasion. . . . Democracy has proclaimed the dictatorship of the palaver, and the technique of dictating to the dictator is named propaganda."[85] More precisely, propaganda was "the management of collective attitudes by the manipulation of significant symbols."[86] Walter Lippmann's influence is notable in Lasswell's work. As Lippmann wrote in *Public Opinion*, "The leader knows by experience that only when symbols have done their work is there a handle he can use to move a crowd."[87] Extending the metaphor, Lasswell insisted that this "technique of controlling attitudes . . . is no more moral or immoral than a pump handle."[88] It was the purpose to which propaganda was put that mattered; it could be used for good or for ill.

Lasswell's work was broadly influential in building a new science of politics. Scholars of interest groups in particular saw propaganda as a key feature of the political dynamics they observed. Pendleton Herring, the Harvard political scientist and future president of the Social Science Research Council (SSRC), discussed propaganda as a strategy of political influence in his study of group representation before Congress.[89]

Similarly, Peter Odegard's book *Pressure Politics* documented how the Anti-Saloon League employed propaganda "as a political weapon . . . to spur into action those voters who believed the liquor traffic to be an evil."[90] For Odegard and others, an interest in propaganda sparked broader theoretical and empirical investigations into the nature of public opinion and its susceptibility to crafted appeals. Odegard's book *The American Public Mind* (1930) asked, "What are the forces which mold our minds?" Like Lasswell, Odegard sought to disabuse his readers of the view that propaganda had a "sinister meaning." "Propaganda in itself is not bad," Odegard summed up, adding cryptically, "It never tells the whole truth, but who knows the whole truth to tell?"[91]

Propaganda remained a central scholarly focus for Lasswell and others, aided by foundations like the SSRC that provided much-needed financial support to the new science of politics. In 1931, Odegard and Herring joined Lasswell on an SSRC committee on the study of propaganda that included political scientist Harold Gosnell, sociologist Kimball Young, journalism professor Ralph Casey, and historian Merle Curti.[92] Under the committee's auspices, Lasswell compiled an annotated bibliography entitled *Propaganda and Promotional Activities* that included an introductory essay, "The Study and Practice of Propaganda," in which Lasswell reiterated many of his earlier ideas about the management of opinion through the manipulation of symbols.[93] In 1935, the *Annals of the American Academy of Political and Social Science* published an issue titled "Pressure Groups and Propaganda." As Princeton political scientist Harwood Childs wrote in the foreword, "The struggle for power, domestically and internationally, is in large part a struggle for the minds of men. The groups which excel . . . will be those most effectively implemented with the techniques and tools of opinion leadership."[94]

Lasswell also focused scholarly attention on what he saw as an emerging profession of paid persuaders, especially the criticisms they faced in a society suspicious of propaganda techniques. "The public's discovery of propaganda has led to a great deal of lamentation over it," Lasswell observed in 1928. As a result, "propagandists have sought protective coloration in such names as 'public relations counsel.'"[95] In his contribution to the *Annals* issue in 1935, Lasswell further noted how the propagandist tried to "change the name of the activity and associate it with dignified symbols" in order to raise "the prestige of a somewhat vulnerable occupation." More specifically, "The lowly press agent gives way to a profession" that further "seeks to associate itself with universities, which stand in our culture for high measures of truth and sincerity."[96] As Lasswell explained, the propagandist was both the subject and the object of propaganda.

Lasswell almost certainly had Edward Bernays in mind as he wrote about these struggles.[97] In fact, Bernays worked hard to establish his professional credentials as a public relations counsel by projecting himself as an expert trained in the science of human behavior and the "workings of public opinion."[98] As Bernays told an audience in 1934, "The development of history, sociology, psychology, social psychology, journalism, advertising and politics has made possible the work of a new type of technician, whose function it is ... to deal intelligently with the group mind."[99] Drawing upon this new "science of propaganda," Bernays described his work as "applied sociology in the broad field of influencing public opinion."[100] By linking public relations to a behavioral social science, Bernays sought credibility for his nascent profession.

To that end, Bernays cultivated a relationship with Lasswell and other academics. Bernays often wrote for academic audiences, including an essay in the 1935 *Annals* issue in which he offered "a dispassionate outline of the techniques and the media involved in the molding of public opinion."[101] A year earlier, in 1934, Bernays accepted an invitation from Pendleton Herring to sit on a panel at the annual meeting of the American Political Science Association on the topic "The Public Relations of National Administrative Agencies" along with prominent academics Marshall Dimock, John Gaus, and Louis Brownlow. Ever the promoter, Bernays wrote to Herring, "If you will let me have some further details of the meeting, I shall be glad to work out a plan to attempt to focus public attention upon it."[102] Bernays was indeed both the subject and the object of propaganda.

Bernays maintained an even closer relationship with Princeton University professor Harwood Childs, who invited Bernays to lecture his class on public opinion on multiple occasions. When Childs established the journal *Public Opinion Quarterly* in 1936, serving as its first managing editor, Bernays contributed the article "Recent Trends in Public Relations Activities" to the inaugural issue. Bernays also wrote a preface to Childs's book *A Reference Guide to the Study of Public Opinion* (1934). In the acknowledgment, Childs wrote that "Mr. Edward L. Bernays is among those whose genius enables them to bridge the chasm between laboratories of academic endeavor and the world of practice."[103] As these accolades suggest, a mutually beneficial relationship could promote the research of the scholar while furthering the professional aspirations of the practitioner.

Academic disciplines confer power and prestige, helping to legitimize professional work. Consequently, professions frequently assert their expertise as a strategy of occupational control.[104] Similarly, Bernays put forward a professional claim that public relations was the practical application of social scientific knowledge about the workings of public opinion and political behavior. To that end, Bernays surveyed prominent academics and university administrators about the study of public opinion and the possibilities for professional education in public relations. He received thirty-four replies from individuals at twenty-six universities, compiling a list of sixty-eight different courses on propaganda, public relations, and related subjects.[105] Bernays published his findings in a slim volume entitled *Universities—Pathfinders of Public Opinion* in which he detailed "the scope of academic attention to the subjects of public relations and opinion management."[106] To Bernays, the public relations counsel was a professional trained in a field of practical knowledge much like lawyers, accountants, or engineers.

In asserting his status as a professional, Bernays pursued a more immediate goal. In 1936, Bernays learned from his accountant that he faced a 4-percent tax on business income in the state of New York unless he could claim a professional exemption, defined by the state as "any occupation or vocation in which a professed knowledge of some department of science or learning is used by its practical application to the affairs of others."[107] Because the public relations counsel was not currently included in the list of recognized professions, the accountant urged Bernays to petition the state for an exemption in order to avoid paying "a substantial sum."[108] Writing to Henry Epstein, solicitor general of New York, Bernays claimed "parity with the other professions exempted under the law" by pointing to the fact that "leading universities are teaching the subject" of public relations.[109] Bernays went on to compare his work as a counsel on public relations with the counselor at law: like the attorney who stands before a court, the public relations counsel labors at "the bar of public opinion."[110]

Even if tax evasion was his principal motivation, Bernays was profoundly influenced by the behavioral turn in the social sciences, especially its insights into the nature of individual identity and the plural quality of contemporary life. Bernays frequently discussed the techniques of public relations in terms of the complex composition of society and the myriad groups to which individuals belong. In particular, he described the "interlapping" nature of group affiliation, by which he meant the composite character of identity and the various social, political, ethnic, and religious attachments of individuals.[111] For Bernays, propaganda was a tool for selectively activating or suppressing aspects of individual identity, creating and recreating group attachments as needed. The creative construction of a public was the essence of his technique.

This vision of the public and the role of the public relations counsel is illustrated in the work Bernays performed on behalf of William O'Dwyer, the Democratic candidate for mayor of New York City in 1941. Using survey research and other social scientific data, Bernays crafted a media strategy for O'Dwyer that tailored the personal qualities of the candidate to the hopes and fears of the various ethnic groups that made up the mosaic of New York City politics. This was fertile ground for Bernays, and the campaign foreshadowed the kind of political work that would characterize American elections in the years to come.

The 1941 New York Mayoral Race

With a population of almost 8 million people in 1940, campaigning in New York City was a political and logistical challenge. The electorate was spread out over 300 square miles, from the northern reaches of Manhattan and the Bronx to the boroughs of Brooklyn and Queens. Successive waves of immigration had created a rich assortment of ethnic groups, with no single element sufficient in size to control a citywide election. Instead, mayoral politics hinged on the construction of ethnic coalitions. Tammany Hall dominated the Democratic Party by attracting the support of the Irish, then Jews, and eventually the Italians. In the 1930s, however, these alliances became less stable. Jewish voters divided their loyalties between the Democrats and a succession of smaller, left-wing parties tied to the labor movement, while the city's Italian community was split between the Democratic and Republican Parties. Meanwhile, the power of the party machines diminished as the foreign-born population of the five boroughs declined and New Deal–era programs displaced the welfare functions the local machines once performed. As Chris McNickle explains in his study of New York City politics, "The implicit contract between district leader and voter, a ballot in return for bread, became harder for politicians to maintain."[112]

New York City politics was changing, making it more difficult to assemble the ethnic coalitions necessary to win citywide elections. It was in this context that William O'Dwyer entered the race for mayor against Fiorello La Guardia in 1941. La Guardia's own success illustrates the changing circumstances of city politics. First elected in 1934 on a Republican-Fusion ticket, La Guardia was a savvy politician who exploited a weakened machine in order to build a powerful if largely personal following. La Guardia's own diverse background—the son of Italian immigrants, yet born of a Jewish mother and raised an Episcopalian—embodied the diversity of his city, helping him to build a broad base of support. During more than a decade in office, La Guardia created a new kind of big-city mayor that mixed personal popularity with an expanding reach over an array of government services. As La Guardia was fond of saying, "There is no Democratic or Republican way of cleaning the streets." Much like President Franklin D. Roosevelt, with whom he forged a close political alliance, La Guardia understood the alchemy of public opinion and executive power.[113]

As a candidate for mayor, William O'Dwyer endeavored to use his own compelling biography to compete with La Guardia. Born in County Mayo, O'Dwyer could count on the support of his fellow Irish New Yorkers, but he distanced himself from Tammany Hall in an effort to attract independent and weakly affiliated voters, namely, Jews. Throughout his political rise, in fact, O'Dwyer remained in, but not entirely of, the Democratic Party. Instead, O'Dwyer used his record as Brooklyn district attorney, where he gained notoriety for his prosecution of organized crime to build a reputation as an independent-minded official untainted by corruption.[114] In early 1941, the O'Dwyer campaign asked Edward Bernays for help in devising a strategy for the race.

Five weeks before Election Day, Bernays presented the campaign with a set of recommendations that emphasized O'Dwyer's personal qualities rather than his party affiliation.

The O'Dwyer race for mayor gave Bernays an opportunity to put in practice a set of techniques he had long argued should be central to a modern political campaign. In an essay entitled "Putting Politics on the Market" (1928), Bernays insisted that "big business is conducted on the principle that it must prepare its policies carefully ... in selling an idea to the large buying public. ... The political strategist must do likewise."[115] Crafting such a strategy should begin with a survey of current opinion. "The first thing a sales manager does when he tackles a new sales problem ... is to study the public to whom he can sell." Similarly, "A survey of public desires, demands, and needs ... made as scientifically as possible ... would come to the aid of the political strategist whose business it is to make a proposed plan of the activities of the party and its elected officials."[116]

Surveys and other sources of social scientific data revealed a complex society composed of "an almost infinite number of groups whose various interests and desires overlap and interweave inextricably."[117] Consequently, Bernays argued, a modern campaign of persuasion required close study of the "group formation of society" and the various cleavages that form along "economic, social, religious, educational, cultural, [and] racial" lines.[118] "The public is not made up merely of Democrats and Republicans," Bernays noted. Instead, "the public is, in fact, many publics," and "the ordinary person is a very temporary member of a great number of groups."[119] These multiple affiliations could be "directed by conscious effort," making it the job of the modern campaign manager "to educate emotions in terms of groups" and craft political appeals that "will best serve to reach the groups he desires to influence."[120] This could be achieved through mass communication and the manipulation of "symbols which stand in the minds of the public for the abstract idea the technician wishes to convey." Accordingly, "The motion picture ... the radio, the magazines, the direct mailing piece, the word of mouth spoken thought, the parade, the mass meeting ... every method of approach to the public through the senses" may be employed.[121] Bernays described his plan for O'Dwyer as "an engineering approach" to the Democratic race, and it relied on precisely the kind of targeted media and social scientific renderings of the public that would become the essence of American political work.[122]

In preparing his plan for O'Dwyer, Bernays collected a wealth of census data, market research, election results, and interviews conducted with New York City voters in order to answer a series of questions Bernays believed were keys to the race:

> What groups and group alignments are there in New York? Where are the independent voters? What is the largest bloc of voters? How and what do the people feel about the two candidates? What lessons are there in the history of past elections? What are the underlying currents and opinions that represent the bases of public opinion and action . . .? What social, religious, economic and political blocs exist? What kind of leadership is there and what is it trying to do? What is the relationship of the great channels of communication—radio, motion pictures, newspapers—to the situation?[123]

For Bernays, effective political strategy required an understanding of the complex social structure of the electorate.

In particular, the multiethnic context of New York City politics suggested a mixture of campaign messages tailored to the concerns and prejudices of different groups. Singling out Jewish voters as the critical bloc that could swing the outcome of the race, Bernays advised using emotional appeals rather than emphasizing policy positions when addressing this segment of voters. According to Bernays:

> The analysis of attitudes from a psychological standpoint, indicates that large groups of the New York public are swayed by hate and by fear, rather than by a rational approach to the administrative functions of a Mayor. The sense of psychological insecurity . . . has created a situation where the appeals to the public, particularly to the Jewish public which represents the greatest independent vote, must be made upon other than straight municipal issues. They must rest upon gaining acceptance for the belief that the candidate is not anti-Semitic.[124]

Bernays also advised the candidate to tailor his messages to different audiences. When O'Dwyer was speaking to Italians, Bernays recommended that he should "stress complete fairness" and non-discrimination; when speaking to German Protestants, he should "stress personal qualities" such as dignity and honesty; when speaking to Irish Catholics, he should emphasize "personal qualifications" such as O'Dwyer's record on crime. Bernays articulated similar refinements along racial, economic, and geographic lines as well.[125]

Bernays also distilled a set of personal qualities of both O'Dwyer and La Guardia, what contemporary consultants call the candidate's "favorables" and "unfavorables." Bernays recommended that O'Dwyer present himself as a "powerful proponent for democracy" who was staunchly "supporting President Roosevelt" while maintaining "independence of Tammany and all bosses."[126] Bernays also advised that O'Dwyer stress his "steady, even-tempered, tactful, diplomatic character" as an alternative to what critics complained was La Guardia's crass style.[127] These qualities were to inform every activity of the candidate, "every event, every speech, every release, [and] every action."[128] In addition to speeches delivered in person and on the radio, Bernays recommended the campaign employ visual images through photographs and motion pictures that could "translate the planks of his platform into pictures."[129] Finally, a series of planned events would attract public attention for O'Dwyer, noting that "the more compelling the created circumstances ... the more likely it is to find a place in the medium." In sum, Bernays envisioned a "vigorous, strong offensive" that would result in a "building up of the candidate" and "a deflation of the opponent."[130]

Bernays projected a cost of $100,000 for the campaign: $10,000 for consulting fees, with the remainder going to media, campaign personnel, and related costs.[131] Controlling for the size of the economy, this is equivalent to around $13 million today. By comparison, Bill de Blasio spent $13.5 million in his successful race for New York City mayor in 2013, with more than half of his expenditures going through a single media firm, AKPD Message and Media, founded by the prominent Democratic consultant David Axelrod.[132]

In 1941, however, an established business of politics did not yet exist. In fact, Bernays never closed the sale, and his direct involvement with the campaign ended with a set of recommendations and an invoice for $1,750 to cover services rendered.[133] In the end, O'Dwyer lost the election by the narrowest margin in a mayoral race since 1909, a considerable feat given that FDR openly endorsed La Guardia against the wishes of New York Democrats.[134] Four years later, however, O'Dwyer won easily in a three-way contest for mayor. It was the first time in more than a decade that La Guardia was not a candidate, a fact that aided O'Dwyer's cause among the Jewish voters Bernays had identified in 1941 as the key to the election.[135]

Building a New Profession

The work of Edward Bernays offers a glimpse into American politics in the making. Although the term "political consultant" had not yet been invented, Bernays was one of the first to distinguish the role of the paid expert from other sources of political advice. Bernays would certainly be pleased to see the business of politics he helped create, but he bequeathed much more than just a profitable way to live. To describe the rise of a twentieth-century political style in the United States is to trace changes in political work, especially the reliance on polling and media to craft campaign messages. In his effort to create a new profession, Bernays laid the foundation for a new kind of campaign, one that relied on the insights of behavioral social science in order to construct coalitions out of distinct segments of the electorate. Features of society such as class, ethnicity, or religion provided the raw materials for political strategy. Rather than mobilize armies of partisans as in the nineteenth century, Bernays approached politics through the selective activation of identities and allegiances using carefully chosen symbols, images, and words.

Although claiming the mantle of science bolstered his professional claims, and furthered his financial interests, the relationship Bernays cultivated with Lasswell, Herring, and other social scientists was not simply a marriage of convenience. For those at the forefront of the behavioral turn, propaganda was an object of scientific study and an indispensable instrument of social control. More than ivory tower academics, these scholars were interested in the practical applications of their work. They envisioned a new science of persuasion at the heart of modern democratic practice.

This union between scholar and practitioner would play an important role in the continuing development of political consulting in the United States. In the 1920s, when Bernays urged campaign managers to study the attitudes of voters, sophisticated methods for doing so did not yet exist. In the 1930s and 1940s, however, advances in scientific polling provided a more reliable way to map public opinion. At the same time, the extraordinary growth of radio prompted both academics and commercial interests to study advertising and its effects. Scholars and practitioners shared much in common as they developed survey research methods to understand the influence of radio on individual behavior. This integration of polling and media techniques became the core of the political consulting profession.

Polling and media, however, are more than just tools of the trade. They also carry a distinct view of the public and the nature of politics. Increasingly, scholars and practitioners approached politics as a selling campaign, much as Bernays had envisioned. Just as one might segment the market into various demographics, political polls disaggregated the public into any number of components such as race, class, religion, or gender. Similarly, just as commercial advertising built market share by appealing to specific niches of consumers, political media used targeted messages to construct a coalition out of particular groups of voters. Political behavior and consumer behavior were one and the same; voting and buying were expressions of individual preference that could be managed through the application of technique. The result, historian Robert Westbrook notes, turned American politics into a form of commerce: campaign advertising sold candidates to voters, while the tools of survey research packaged voters for candidates.[136] Political consultants, whose services could be bought and sold as well, became crucial intermediaries in this exchange.

4

The Art and Science of Politics

FOR EDWARD BERNAYS, A CHARACTERISTIC feature of modern life was the almost universal competition for public favor. Whether in politics, government, or business, leaders "must win and obtain public approval if they are to survive in the welter of competing forces."[1] Popular support was as vital to winning an election as it was to selling a product. Yet the complexity of society and the quickened pace of communication made it difficult to know precisely what the public wanted or how to reach them effectively. This was the role of the public relations counsel: "to interpret his client to the public, and the public to his client." Communication between leaders and the led required the skills of a trained professional.[2]

As Bernays understood, technological change helped to create a vital opening for the emergence of the modern political professional. In 1921, the first licensed radio station began broadcasting in the United States. Five years later, there were more than 500 stations. Over the same period, the number of households with radio sets grew from 60,000 to 4.5 million. By the time of FDR's inauguration in 1933, 19 million homes had radio. By the time the United States entered the Second World War, this number had grown to 29 million homes, or 82 percent of all households.[3]

Radio ushered in a profound transformation in the conduct of American politics, but its influence was neither automatic nor immediate. Rather, the diffusion of radio sparked a period of trial and error as actors worked through initial experiments and failures in search of effective techniques. What counted for political skill changed for politicians as the characteristic bombast of nineteenth-century public speech confronted a new medium that favored a cool and conversational style. At the same time, mass communication replaced older forms of face-to-face contact. A political stump speech offered immediate feedback; whether in the form of catcalls or cheers, a speaker knew immediately if a particular turn of phrase had the desired effect. Broadcasting, by contrast, was a one-way relationship between the speaker and listener that provided no easy way to measure the effectiveness of political communication. Indeed, it became difficult to know even the size of an audience, something otherwise ascertained by a simple glance.[4]

In other words, radio created a new kind of distance between politicians and the public. Bernays captured this change in a 1947 essay in which he wrote how in the past, "a leader was known to his followers personally; there was a visual relationship between them."[5] The development of modern communication destroyed these personal relationships, but in a paradoxical way. "The world has grown both smaller and very much larger," Bernays observed. "Today's leaders have become more remote physically from the public; yet at the same time, the public has much greater familiarity with these leaders through the system of modern communications."[6] Radio created a different kind of political space; leaders were now closer to the public, yet also more remote. It was this space that Bernays, and others like him, sought to fill.

In particular, the mass-communicated politics of the radio age created opportunities for two new sources of expertise that would come to occupy a critical position in American politics and American political consulting: the media expert skilled in the crafting of political messages and the pollster trained in the brand new tools of survey research. In order to reach audiences over the airwaves, politicians sought help from those trained in the "techniques of radio showmanship and salesmanship."[7] Advertising and radio industry executives brought technical know-how, an appreciation of audience listening habits, and a familiarity with the business of radio to the refinement of political messages. At the same time, market researchers, commercial pollsters, and social scientists found common purpose in the development of techniques that could reliably map the opinions of the electorate. Gradually, these experts in survey research became valuable interpreters of public sentiment, lending their skills to government agencies, presidents, and political candidates.

Together, radio experts and pollsters offered a new way to craft political communication and gather information about its effects. Their work during the 1930s and 1940s was a creative blending of the art and science of politics, marrying political messages to a new science of survey research in a union that would eventually form the core of the modern business of politics.

The Promise and Perils of Radio

Radio swiftly penetrated American homes, but initial experiments in its political use demonstrated both the promise and the perils of this new technology. Traditional events such as nominating conventions fit awkwardly with the expectations and demands of a listening audience. At the same time, radio reordered political assets and liabilities as politicians adapted to the new medium.

The 1924 election marks the first time radio became widely available for a presidential campaign. Both major party conventions broadcast nearly complete coverage of their proceedings, including the dead-locked Democrats who met for sixteen days. On election night, nearly 400 stations broadcast the results across the country. However, the lack of a coast-to-coast radio network posed challenges for political broadcasts and limited the strategic possibilities of radio during the campaign.[8] Four years later, however, two national networks, CBS and NBC, greatly simplified the task of reaching a national radio audience. Meanwhile, passage of the Radio Act of 1927 established a new legal framework for political broadcasts that required radio stations to provide equal time to legally qualified candidates. And with the growing commercial reach of radio, airtime became a valuable commodity that required campaign managers to think more carefully about how to allocate resources effectively.[9]

These factors combined to make the 1928 presidential election the first true radio campaign. Both networks broadcast the major party conventions for free in order to meet their public service mandate under the 1927 Radio Act. After the convention, however, NBC and CBS charged the political parties $10,000 per hour of airtime, and both the Democrats and the Republicans spent liberally on radio during the postconvention period of the campaign. Democrats aired weekly broadcasts of speeches by nominee Al Smith and others, intensifying their frequency as the campaign wore on. Other Democratic broadcasts mixed politics and entertainment in half-hour programs that devoted ten minutes to political speeches and the remainder to performances by movie stars, musicians, and radio personalities. The Republicans organized "National Hoover Minute Men," who delivered five- or ten-minute speeches on local radio stations. Radio made it possible for campaigns to reach specific audiences; both parties, for instance, targeted women voters in 1928 by airing political broadcasts during morning hours. As historian Douglas Craig summarizes, "An electronic revolution had overtaken politics by 1928, and few aspects of campaigning escaped it."[10] Radio became the single largest campaign expenditure for both parties in 1928, as the Democrats and Republicans spent a combined $1 million on political broadcasts between July and November.[11]

Despite the growing recognition of its importance, however, party managers still lacked much practical experience in broadcasting, limiting their ability to make the most of radio during campaigns. One scholar described the 1932 party conventions as "near-disasters" in terms of programming. The Republican convention, for example, consumed large blocks of airtime and featured endless speeches. The Democratic convention was no better. On some days coverage lasted fourteen hours, including one stretch of programming consisting of an hour-long ovation for Al Smith, followed by forty-five minutes of cheering for Franklin Roosevelt.[12] Party leaders saw great potential in radio, but they were seemingly oblivious to the audience listening at home.

The same could be said for most politicians. Many candidates struggled with radio, although some adapted more easily. The normally reticent Calvin Coolidge was more comfortable speaking into a microphone than before a crowd. As Coolidge himself admitted, "I have a good radio voice, and now I can get my messages across to [the people] without acquainting them with my lack of oratorical ability."[13] The political talents of public speaking suddenly counted for a lot less in the radio age. In 1928, the Democratic nominee, Al Smith, was a gifted politician and a spellbinder on the stump, but over the radio his voice sounded "tinny." More damaging politically, Smith's Lower East Side accent and his sometimes fractured grammar aided Republican efforts to paint the New York governor as an urban bogeyman. By contrast, Herbert Hoover's businesslike demeanor, his "subdued speech patterns, his clear voice, his flat, Midwestern accent" were assets in the 1928 campaign, conjuring up "images of prairie tranquility rather than urban chaos."[14]

Four years later, the Democrats reversed the Republican radio advantage. Running against Franklin Roosevelt in 1932, Hoover faced "the first political star of the radio age."[15] Roosevelt mastered the radio address during his time as the governor of New York, sprinkling his clear patrician diction with homespun phrasing. When Roosevelt broke tradition in 1932 by accepting the Democratic nomination in person at the Chicago convention rather than await notification by a party delegation as was the custom, he did so with a 5,000-word speech that was "meant to be heard and not read." By a stroke of luck, weather delayed Roosevelt's arrival so that he went on the air at the ideal evening time of seven o'clock rather than three o'clock as originally planned. More important, Roosevelt adopted a visionary style of speech, promising "a new deal for the American people," rather than a dry recitation of policy commitments as had been past practice.[16] Richard Ellis writes that FDR "signaled a decisive turn to a modern rhetorical presidency" by crafting his 1932 acceptance speech with a radio audience in mind.[17] Indeed, the benefits of radio would redound especially to a more robust executive that took shape in the coming years.

Franklin Roosevelt was not the only political figure to exploit the power of radio or to realize its potential for mobilizing the public. Father Charles Coughlin and Senator Huey Long of Louisiana both built substantial followings for themselves with national radio broadcasts during the late 1920s and early 1930s. Their populist messages resonated with millions struggling through the economic hardships of the Great Depression. But it was the medium as much as the message that gave Coughlin and Long their power. Radio, Alan Brinkley has written, "gave both leaders direct, immediate access to millions of men and women . . . a special bond of intimacy between the speaker and his audience."[18] Coughlin began broadcasting on the radio in the late 1920s, "exploiting a system of communication whose potential conventional politicians had not yet begun to appreciate."[19] Although gifted with "extraordinary skills as a performer," Coughlin also appreciated the particular talents needed to reach a radio audience.[20] Describing his style in a *New York Times* profile in 1933, Coughlin said that "radio broadcasting, I have found, must not be high hat. It must be human, intensely human. It must be simple."[21] Coughlin's popularity was so formidable that when CBS refused to broadcast the increasingly controversial cleric, Coughlin established his own independent network that carried his sermons on more than thirty stations throughout the United States. Although the number is difficult to measure accurately, Coughlin likely reached tens of millions of listeners; some considered it the largest regular radio audience in the world.[22] Similarly, Huey Long was a gifted communicator who crafted a popular radio personality through his regular broadcasts criticizing Roosevelt and the New Deal.[23] Before his death in 1935, Long's success on the radio and the growing popularity of his Share Our Wealth movement became a serious concern of President Roosevelt and his staff, who saw the senator as a potential threat to Roosevelt's re-election chances in 1936.[24]

The Rise of the Radio Expert

Radio posed significant challenges that upset established political practices, reordered political assets, and gave a powerful voice to political outsiders. More than simply "an amplifier for traditional oratory," a loudspeaker that could reach a larger audience, radio was a novel form of political communication that offered opportunities for innovation but also posed distinct risks for those unable to adapt.[25] In facing up to these challenges, politicians and party leaders turned toward a new source of advice—the radio expert—to help craft political messages in line with the demands of the new medium.

At first, neither party possessed experienced staff that could run the radio portion of their campaigns. Although dedicated personnel handled political broadcasts as early as 1928, many lacked practical skills in radio or were unable to keep pace with the rapid developments taking place. In 1928, for example, the Democrats chose a radio novice, Josef Israels, to oversee broadcast efforts for the campaign. According to the director of political programming for NBC, Israels's only real qualification for the job was the fact that his mother, Belle Moskowitz, was Al Smith's closest adviser. Similarly, in 1932, Democratic radio strategy fell to Ewing Laporte, a longtime party loyalist with no previous radio experience. Eventually, Laporte was replaced by Herbert Pettey, who was only marginally more qualified, having formerly worked in the film industry (Pettey was rewarded for his work with an appointment as the first secretary of the Federal Communications Commission). The Republicans did not do much better. Responsibility for radio in 1928 and 1932 was in the hands of Paul Gascoigne, a former telephone company executive whose duties ranged from the coordination of national broadcasts to introducing Hoover before his speeches. One senior network official complained that Gascoigne was "utterly incapable of managing such a broadcast."[26] Overall, as one executive noted in 1932, "The political parties have not learned how to use radio to the greatest advantage."[27]

Four years later, both parties placed responsibility for the radio portions of their campaigns in the hands of experienced professionals. In 1936, the Democrats recruited a number of prominent NBC executives to supervise broadcast placement and publicity. The 1936 Democratic convention, in particular, was a "carefully conceived radio production" that reflected "a new awareness of the radio audience."[28] The convention was so meticulously scripted, in fact, that some delegates complained their only function was to "supply scenery and sound effects so that the home audience can hear the animals roar."[29] After the convention, the Democratic radio effort remained "aggressive and well-organized," adding more hands from NBC to oversee the radio campaign. Their efforts helped execute "a more efficiently run and a more commercialized campaign."[30]

Republicans also employed specialized staff in 1936, drawing heavily from the field of advertising. In a significant departure from previous years, the Republicans divided press and radio responsibilities in 1936. The Publicity Department was led by the managing editor of the *Buffalo News* and was staffed mostly by journalists. The newly established Public Relations Department, by contrast, was directed by Hill Blackett, founding partner of one of the largest advertising agencies in the country. Blackett's firm was the leading producer of radio advertising; his partner Frank Hummert created the commercially sponsored serial, or soap opera. Upon Blackett's installation, Republicans boasted of a new kind of campaign that would resemble "an intensive, subtle, highly organized salesmanship drive."[31] Accordingly, Blackett appointed staff experienced in radio time buying and program placement. Regional radio offices concentrated Republican broadcasts in areas deemed competitive, largely excluding the Democratic South. Campaign tactics conformed to what had become standard commercial practice: heavy repetition of Republican messages throughout the week and brief spot announcements that ran twice a day on the East Coast. However, the Republican division of press and radio responsibilities produced rivalries within the campaign, illustrating both the growing specialization of tasks and the competition between older and newer forms of political expertise occasioned by the new medium.[32]

Despite these difficulties, the 1936 campaign marks an important turn in American politics, as a new cadre of experts "modified the campaign to conform to radio, creating styles of political talk and amusement that were especially suited to that medium."[33] Speeches were shorter, scheduling was tailored to maximize audience size, and spot announcements became standard campaign fare. In part, the growing prominence of communication experts in campaigns and the greater sophistication of party political broadcasts reflected the continued penetration of the technology as more than 4 million additional households acquired radios between 1932 and 1936.[34] As listening audiences grew in size, so did the commercial value of airtime. In 1936, the cost of an hour-long political broadcast on CBS was more than $18,000, and a combined evening network hookup was $52,000 per hour, up from $33,000 just four years earlier.[35] As the cost of radio became dearer, presidential campaigns relied more on shorter, polished broadcasts. With considerable resources devoted to radio, both parties turned to advertising and network executives to run the broadcasting portions of their campaigns. In the hands of these radio experts, nominating conventions, spot advertisements, and other political broadcasts conformed to the tastes of the listening audience and the commercial demands of the national networks. A new, mass-mediated political style was beginning to take shape.

But the awesome power of radio also brought new challenges. Radio afforded politicians a much more intimate form of political communication to be sure, yet this new intimacy was in some ways artificial. "Radio may have brought the candidate closer to the people," historian Gil Troy notes, "but the need for careful scripting had created a new distance."[36] In part, this reflected the handiwork of the new media experts, the advertising and network executives who orchestrated an "ever more elaborate show" during presidential campaigns.[37] However, the distance to which Troy refers also reflected the challenges of a mass-mediated politics, especially the need to find new sources of information formerly derived from personal, face-to-face interactions with the voting public. Radio expanded the scale and scope of political communication, becoming a powerful instrument for political mobilization. But the effective use of radio also prompted a search for new sources of information about the effects of political communication.

Building a Business of Polling

It is in the search for political intelligence in a radio age that scientific polling first became a valued tool in American politics. As in the case of radio itself, polling was the domain of a new kind of expert: the specialist in survey research. In fact, the development of polling was the work of three overlapping sets of actors dedicated to the perfection of polling methods and their promotion across a range of activities and enterprises. The first group, market researchers, worked in business schools and advertising firms, where they developed new techniques for mapping patterns of consumer behavior. Radio was a particularly important area of focus for this group as efforts to measure audience size and listening habits spawned important innovations in survey methods. The second group, commercial pollsters, grew directly out of market research. By applying survey methods to a broad range of social questions, political issues, and election-year forecasts, pollsters built a thriving commercial business measuring the public pulse. The ability to poll a national sample quickly and relatively cheaply brought pollsters in contact with a third group, social scientists studying the effects of mass communication. Research into how radio shaped political behavior attracted the attention of these early students of public opinion who, lacking the basic infrastructure to field large-scale social surveys on their own, turned to commercial pollsters for technical expertise and support. Together, this network of scholars and practitioners found common purpose in the development and application of survey techniques that could provide a more reliable map of individual opinions, whether for the purpose of social scientific study or in the promotion of a consumer product.

Origins: Market Research

At the turn of the twentieth century, a burgeoning field of market research made a science out of selling.[38] Its early practitioners employed primitive survey methods to collect data on consumer preferences and track the effects of advertising on purchasing decisions. To the advocates of this new approach, a sophisticated understanding of the human mind was to be combined with the practical concerns of the business manager. As the psychologist Walter Dill Scott, an early proponent of market research, explained, "the principles and the methods" of modern psychology were to be "practically applied by the advertiser." Its aim, according to Scott, was to aid "that increasing number of American business men who successfully apply science where their predecessors were confined to custom."[39]

Work by Scott and others was part of a broader effort to study the distribution, sale, and use of consumer goods, a concern that eventually found an academic home in the nation's growing number of professional business schools. At the Harvard Graduate School of Business Administration, established in 1908, marketing was a required course for all students. In 1911, the school's first dean, Edwin Gay, established the Bureau of Business Research in order to develop the "scientific study of marketing."[40] Harvard soon became an influential center for market research, attracting leading figures in the field such as Paul Cherington, a former trade journalist who joined the original business school faculty in 1908 and became Harvard's first professor of marketing in 1917. Cherington promoted the idea that careful study could reveal how best to reach consumers in particular markets. The methods he devised would greatly influence the development of survey research.[41]

At the same time business schools promoted the academic study of marketing, the nation's leading advertising firms established research departments of their own devoted to the study of consumer psychology.

The J. Walter Thompson agency, then the largest advertising firm in the country, was at the forefront of so-called scientific advertising, or what company president Stanley Resor described as the search for laws of human behavior that could "guide the work of influencing the public mind."[42] In 1915, the company established a research department of its own, and in 1920 Resor hired John B. Watson, regarded as the founder of behavioral psychology, to be a member of its research staff. Watson's role at J. Walter Thompson was more symbolic than substantive; he spent much of his time lecturing on the virtues of scientific advertising to business executives, trade associations, and industry leaders in the United States and abroad. The real research work at Thompson fell to Paul Cherington, who became the company's director of research in 1922.[43]

Continuing the work he began at Harvard, Cherington perfected ways to study consumer behavior. He described the goal of his research as an attempt "to determine not only the number of actual or potential customers, but to get as good an idea as is possible of who they are, what their economic status is, what their buying habits and practices are, and what controls their purchases of the goods to be sold."[44] Such information was essential to the effective use of advertising, and it required collecting data on consumers themselves as well as their buying habits. To do so, Cherington perfected a way of drawing a representative sample of consumers for study. Specifically, Cherington segmented households into four classes, or strata, based on income: "Class A" households included what Cherington described as "homes of substantial wealth above average in culture," "Class B" consisted of middle-class homes "directed by intelligent women," "Class C" included "industrial homes" of skilled workers, and "Class D" homes consisted of unskilled laborers and immigrant stock, "where it is difficult for American ways to penetrate."[45] Under Cherington's direction, teams conducted household surveys with a representative number, or quota, of respondents in each class. The technique came to be known as the quota sampling method.[46]

The techniques developed by Cherington and others quickly became the standard for market surveys. By producing a representative sample of manageable size, quota sampling made it possible to survey the public at a reasonable cost with results that were far more reliable than simple "man-on-the-street" interviews. More broadly, quota sampling offered a way to aggregate, as well as disaggregate, the public. By selecting a set of categories or strata that the researcher deemed representative of the wider population, polls segmented the public into various categories of income or place. Looking back at Cherington's class distinctions, for example, we can see both the methodological pitfalls and the inherent biases of such an approach.[47] At the time, however, quota sampling enabled advertising and marketing experts to assemble survey results into a portrait of the mass market, or to disassemble and cross-tabulate them to reveal a particular market niche.[48]

One of the earliest and most profitable applications of the new tools of survey research was in radio. Although advertisers and broadcasters recognized radio's ability to reach a wide and diverse audience, tapping into these commercial opportunities required some understanding of its consumers. However, radio lacked the handy metric of circulation that newspapers and magazines used to estimate readership, and broadcasters struggled to fix a price for selling products over the air. Without basic data on who was listening and when, it was difficult to assign a value to radio airtime.[49]

Survey methods offered a solution to this problem, and beginning in the late 1920s, both advertisers and broadcasters turned to those skilled in market research in order to measure the radio audience. In 1927, NBC commissioned Harvard Business School psychologist Daniel Starch to conduct a national survey of listening habits. Based on a canvass of 17,000 people in twenty-four states, Starch estimated that 47 million people listened to radio, and, using the rental value of homes as a proxy for income, Starch found that radio households were generally of a higher economic status.[50] As a writer in *Commerce and Finance* observed, insights from the Starch survey extended well beyond the selling of soap: "One of the things political candidates and strategists doubtless would like to know just now is how the great invisible audience, made of many millions ... is reacting to campaign oratory."[51] Surveys revealed this "invisible audience" in ways that would make radio and other forms of mass communication a valuable political tool.

In addition to the general characteristics of radio listeners, the industry also wanted to know how many people tuned in to specific programs. In 1929, a consortium of advertisers commissioned

Archibald Crossley, a pioneer in the use of telephone surveys, to develop such a measure. Crossley established one of the first market research firms in the country, Crossley, Inc., in 1926.[52] Located in Princeton, New Jersey, Crossley's firm conducted regular telephone surveys of radio listening habits that asked respondents which programs they listened to during the previous day.[53] The resulting "Crossley Rating," as it became known, reported the percentage of radio homes that listened to a particular program, as well as a basic demographic portrait of the radio audience—something of great interest to advertisers.[54]

The great innovation of the Crossley Rating was that it offered the first ongoing audience measures for radio programs, something the popular press soon paid as much attention to as the industry for which it was designed. *Time* magazine called Crossley a "pioneer" in the measurement of "the unseen audience," noting that top radio personalities such as Jack Benny "worried more about their 'Crossleys' than their hairlines."[55] However, the method Crossley used was flawed. By relying on telephone surveys, Crossley biased his sample toward upper-income households, something that became increasingly problematic as the radio penetrated American society. These shortcomings invited competition. In the 1930s, George Gallup, whose name would become synonymous with polling, developed audience measures that supplemented telephone surveys with personal interviews. Boasting greater accuracy (and accompanied by aggressive marketing), Gallup's method replaced the Crossley Rating as the industry standard.[56]

The Development of Commercial Polling

By applying the tools of market research to a host of social and political questions, George Gallup built a successful enterprise measuring the public pulse. Although polling on social and political questions had commercial potential, as Sarah Igo reminds us, "opinion entrepreneurs" like Gallup "were first and foremost market researchers, devoted to the science of improving corporate profitability through carefully crafted advertising campaigns and public relations stratagems."[57] As Daniel Robinson has written, "Opinion polling developed conceptually and methodologically largely as an adjunct of consumer surveying itself."[58]

In fact, Gallup and other polling pioneers like Elmo Roper began their careers in advertising and market research before establishing commercial firms of their own. Gallup, for instance, first became interested in polling while helping to conduct a house-to-house survey of readers' likes and dislikes for the *St. Louis Post-Dispatch*. The experience informed Gallup's 1928 PhD dissertation in psychology, entitled "An Objective Method for Determining Reader Interest in the Content of a Newspaper." Using a quota sample of 1,000 Iowans, Gallup discovered that most people read less than 15 percent of the paper, focusing more on cartoons and photographs than on front-page news. Gallup's findings attracted attention, particularly in the field of advertising, landing him a position in New York with the Young & Rubicam advertising agency.[59]

It was while working for Young & Rubicam that Gallup perfected his methods. Fielding polls in his spare time, Gallup made his first political poll in 1932 on behalf of his mother-in-law, Ola Babcock Miller, who won a narrow victory as Iowa secretary of state. Looking back, Gallup credited Miller's candidacy with helping him become "interested in the whole possibilities of polling" and their potential use across a wide range of areas.[60] In 1935, Gallup established his own private firm, the American Institute of Public Opinion (AIPO), with offices in Princeton across the street from the main entrance to the university—a name and location that lent Gallup an air of academic credibility. Gallup began producing a syndicated feature, *America Speaks*, which reported polling results on various issues of the day. By the end of its first year in circulation, AIPO polls appeared in sixty major metropolitan newspapers across the country.[61]

The 1936 election set the cornerstone for what became a polling empire. In July, less than one month after the nominating conventions, Gallup reported the results of a nationwide survey showing a slight lead for Roosevelt over Kansas Republican Alf Landon. Gallup's prediction ran counter to the famous *Literary Digest* straw poll, which forecast a Landon victory in November. Straw polls had been widely used to gauge public sentiment since the nineteenth century, and the *Digest* poll was the largest and most accurate of its kind. In 1932, the magazine sent out nearly 20 million ballots to its readers and came within three-quarters of 1 percent of predicting Roosevelt's margin of victory.[62] However, the

Digest mailed ballots chiefly to households listed in telephone directories or with automobile registrations, a method that drew responses overwhelmingly from upper-income voters. Gallup understood that this flawed methodology overrepresented the extent of Landon support in the electorate, and he believed his quota sampling method based on a representative cross section of the voting public would yield a more accurate prediction of the race. In a rather daring gambit, Gallup backed up his claims with the offer of a money-back guarantee to the more than seventy newspapers subscribing to his column if his prediction turned out to be incorrect.[63]

As the campaign unfolded, Gallup issued a steady stream of poll results that tracked the overall state of the race as well as the constituent parts of each party's coalition.[64] The AIPO polls gave a new look to the "horse race" of the campaign by emphasizing the battleground states where the Electoral College would be won or lost. Tracking polls followed FDR's support over time, offering what Gallup boasted was "the first graphic picture of the ups and downs in a President's majority ever available in history."[65]

Gallup also explained the procedures he used in an effort to convince the reader of the accuracy of his methods.[66] More was at stake for Gallup in 1936 than the outcome of the race. As the *Washington Post* observed, "When American voters give their verdict on Election Day, it will not be political questions alone that are decided. At least one scientific question will be decided too. . . . 'How far can science go in predicting the outcome of an election?' "[67] On November 1, in his final column before Election Day, Gallup wrote that "Tuesday's election will show which procedures for polling public opinion can be relied up [*sic*] with greatest faith in the future—the mass-balloting method or the scientific sampling method."[68] Although Gallup's prediction of a Roosevelt victory with 54 percent of the popular vote and 477 electoral votes was off by a fairly wide margin, it was far more accurate than the *Digest* poll, which called the election for Landon. The following week, the *Post* reported that the election result "vindicates the scientific sampling technique."[69] Meanwhile, Gallup triumphantly announced an expansion of AIPO polling in the coming year on a wider range of subjects, adding that "if public opinion is to rule in a democracy, there must exist the mechanics for reporting it."[70]

The 1936 election offered a very public demonstration of the reliability of scientific sampling, as well as the commercial potential of polling. However, Gallup was not the only one to recognize these opportunities. Elmo Roper also built a successful polling business out of a career in market research, although he began somewhat by chance. Crisscrossing the country as a traveling salesman for a jewelry manufacturer, Roper concluded that the product line he sold fell between two market segments: too fancy for farmers, yet not fancy enough for an urban clientele. Roper later described his analysis to Richardson Wood, a friend and advertising executive at J. Walter Thompson, who encouraged Roper to consider a career in market research. When Roper moved to New York a short time later, Wood introduced him to Paul Cherington, who had recently left Thompson to work as an independent consultant. In 1934, the three established their own market research firm, Cherington, Roper, and Wood (CRW). The firm's promotional materials offered "to supply to management significant facts ... from a representative sampling of consumers."[71]

Much of the early work of CRW used the tools of market research to inform corporate public relations. With the rising activism of the New Deal, the threat of government regulation made selling the corporation to the public just as important from a business standpoint as selling the product itself.[72] Power companies in particular sought out CRW's services as they battled against proposals for public ownership of utilities. For instance, facing a referendum on municipal control of the water supply, one utility company hired CRW to study its public image. When the survey revealed that most consumers were happy with their service, the utility company launched a campaign touting the benefits of private ownership and eventually defeated the referendum. Roper described the survey as "our first piece of political research," and it illustrates how the tools of market research could be used to measure public sentiments on a range of political and social matters their corporate clients deemed important.[73]

Seeing this potential, in 1934 Wood secured a major new client when *Fortune* magazine, the country's leading business weekly, commissioned CRW to produce a quarterly report on the beliefs, preferences, and opinions of the American public.[74] Introducing the first column in the July 1935 issue, *Fortune* proudly announced "a new technique in journalism," one that used "the technique of the commercial survey" to provide "a sampling of public opinion" on various issues.[75] The *Fortune* survey quickly became one of the most popular features of the magazine, reporting on a wide range of subjects, from vital issues of the day to the seemingly trivial. The January 1936 report, for example, described the extent of anti-Semitism in various regions of the country and included a fairly sophisticated discussion about the challenges of question wording on matters such as "racial antagonism" that most people were reluctant to discuss openly with an interviewer. Yet, the same issue of *Fortune* (on the very same page) reported the results of a survey that asked people whether they preferred their beer in bottles or cans.[76] Undoubtedly, both kinds of questions were of concern to *Fortune* readers. By 1938, the survey had become a monthly feature, and Roper, who had formed his own firm after parting ways with Wood and Cherington, was a recognized authority on public opinion.[77]

Yet unlike Gallup, Roper was reluctant to delve too deeply into the business of election forecasting. In 1936, the *Fortune* survey reported public sentiments toward Roosevelt on the eve of the election but did not venture an outright prediction.[78] When Gallup privately suggested four years later that "those of us who are interested in this job of measuring public opinion . . . set up rules by which we could stake our claims for the championship," Roper politely declined.[79] However, the commercial pull was too great, forcing Roper to make predictions, albeit reluctantly. Although motivated by a desire "to protect from harm this infant science of marketing and public opinion research," Roper wrote to his friend Jay Darling in 1944, "I think the prediction of elections is a socially useless function. . . . But apparently those of us who have stuck our necks out in election predictions are expected to keep on doing so."[80] Roper feared that one miscalled election would do irreparable harm to the polling business, a reality he and others would confront four years later in the fiasco of 1948 when the major polling companies incorrectly predicted that Dewey would defeat Truman in the race for president.[81] The difficulty, as Roper explained, was that election forecasting required knowledge not only of voter preferences but also of the composition of the electorate on Election Day. Differential turnout rates among various groups made it difficult to draw an accurate sample of likely voters—a challenge pollsters still face today.

However, polling on political questions faced more than just technical hurdles. For commercial pollsters like Roper, elections offered little in the way of financial rewards, particularly when compared with the corporate clients that were the mainstay of the polling business. Roper did accept political clients from time to time. In 1946, he conducted polls in his home state of Connecticut on behalf of Chester Bowles, who was eyeing a run for governor.[82] However, political work paid poorly—the fees Roper received from his political clients was less than 1 percent of his income in 1946—when it paid at all.[83] Trying to secure payment from a candidate in the 1942 Louisville mayoral race, Roper pleaded, "please, pretty please, and for god sake to send us some money."[84] In fact, Roper was still chasing up $500 from Chester Bowles one year after his election as governor in 1948.[85] In other instances, Roper simply offered his services for free. A lifelong Democrat, Roper worked for the Democratic Senatorial Campaign Committee in 1957 as an unpaid adviser, helping raise $100,000 to underwrite polling efforts in every state with a competitive Democratic candidate.[86]

For these early pollsters, politics was something of a sideshow. Election forecasts could publicly demonstrate the validity of survey methods, as they did for Gallup, or allow one to privately pursue a cause, as was the case for Roper. However, the vast majority of income from polling still came from corporate clients. Despite this fact, commercial pollsters did lay the groundwork for the wide use of polling as a political tool. As Sarah Igo has shown, Gallup and Roper made polls a part of popular culture; the AIPO and *Fortune* surveys offered a new way to portray the public to itself. In time, survey results would supplant older measures of public sentiments such as letters from constituents, editorials in newspapers, or even the reports of precinct captains and ward heelers as the voice of the people.[87] Pollsters, Igo concludes, became, "crucial middlemen in deciphering popular views and determining what public policy stances candidates and organizations should take."[88] However, this way of looking at politics and the public did not go unchallenged. Instead, polling met with skepticism, fueled by a general misunderstanding about the nature of statistical sampling techniques. Many wondered how anyone could divine meaningful information from a survey of only a few hundred people. Pollsters would have to overcome these suspicions before they could establish their supremacy as interpreters of public sentiment.

Social science would play an important part in this development. For an enterprising group of academic researchers, commercial polling offered a way to study mass publics. In particular, academic interest in the effects of radio on political behavior brought scholars in contact with commercial pollsters skilled in survey methods. During the 1930s and 1940s, George Gallup and Elmo Roper offered technical support and advice to leading scholars of public opinion such as Hadley Cantril and Paul Lazarsfeld. United by their belief in the benefits of these techniques, a partnership between social scientists and commercial pollsters simultaneously furthered the academic study of public opinion even as it enhanced the scientific credibility of commercial polling. And when the pollsters failed to predict the outcome of the 1948 election, it was the academy that came to the rescue.

Social Science and the Promise of Polling

In 1935, the *New York Times* observed that "professors who revel in a study of the unknown have the listening habits of the unseen radio audience as something . . . new to analyze."[89] The occasion for the article was the publication of a new book, *The Psychology of Radio*, written by social psychologists Hadley Cantril and Gordon Allport. As the authors described in the preface, their goal was "to map out . . . the new mental world created by radio."[90] In particular, Cantril and Allport believed that radio "interposes a serious psychological barrier between the broadcaster and his audience," resulting in "a marked distance between the listener and the speaker."[91] This new distance created challenges for those who wished to communicate with the public, but it also presented opportunities. Someone like Father Coughlin or Huey Long, Cantril and Allport noted, uses "less bombast and more artistry, less brute force and more cunning. He [directs] his attention to the invisible audience and [makes] each listener feel welcome as a member of the circle."[92] These radio spellbinders developed new ways to communicate, and understanding their appeal to the public required new ways of knowing. "Radio is a *novel* means of communication . . . requiring *novel* methods of investigation," Cantril and Allport insisted.[93] Combining surveys, census data, and the results of psycho-logical experiments, Cantril and Allport offered, as the *Times* put it, key insights into "the psychology of the invisible multitude."[94]

Cantril's interest in the effects of mass communication drew him to the study of survey research just as George Gallup and Elmo Roper began popularizing their poll results in syndicated columns and in *Fortune* magazine. As Cantril later recalled, the work of Gallup and Roper convinced him that "here was a new instrument the social scientist . . . had better look into."[95] Cantril got his chance in 1936 when the *New York Times* asked him to write about the use of polling to predict the upcoming presidential election.[96] Cantril traveled to Princeton, New Jersey, where he met with George Gallup. Recounting the meet-ing, Cantril wrote that Gallup "was delighted to have a social scientist take his work seriously, and offered his facilities at cost for any research I might want to do."[97] The meeting would begin a long friendship. For Cantril, the opportunity to make use of Gallup's facilities was so attractive—the pollster employed a staff of thirty and nearly a thou-sand part-time interviewers across the country—that Cantril accepted a position in the Princeton psychology department the following year.[98] For Gallup, on the other hand, forging ties with an academic social scientist boosted his status as a public opinion professional.[99]

At Princeton, Cantril advanced the academic study of public opin-ion even as he solidified his ties with a budding polling industry.[100] In 1937, Cantril joined Princeton political scientist Harwood Childs in launching *Public Opinion Quarterly*. In its initial incarnation, the journal served as a forum for both the academic and the commer-cial side of survey research. As the editors described their mission in the first issue published in January 1937, "The understanding of what public opinion is, how it generates, and how it acts becomes a vital need touching both public and private interest."[101] The *Public Opinion Quarterly* was a big tent indeed. Its first issue included contributions from editorial board members Harold Lasswell and Pendleton Herring as well as pollster Archibald Crossly and public relations counsel Edward Bernays. In its first year of publication, in fact, a third of all articles in the journal were written by authors with a business rather than academic affiliation.[102]

Cantril was also a central figure in a scholarly network formed under the auspices of the Rockefeller Foundation that examined the effects of radio on public opinion. In 1937, a Rockefeller grant established the Princeton Radio Research Project. Its goal was to apply commercial survey research methods to the study of radio and its psychological effects.[103] One of Cantril's first efforts for the project used Gallup surveys to study the panic that ensued following the radio broadcast of "War of the Worlds" by Orson Welles.[104] In 1939, Cantril secured another grant from Rockefeller, this time to establish the Princeton Office of Public Opinion Research, the first university institute of its kind solely devoted to survey research. Its purpose was to examine "the development of opinion, the changes which opinion undergoes under varying conditions, and the reasons for change."[105] Specifically, Cantril proposed taking interview data collected by Gallup so he could study the influence of radio, print, and film on public attitudes toward the war in Europe.

Although public opinion research would eventually enter the social science mainstream, survey methods raised eyebrows in the 1930s and 1940s. To its critics, polling was a commercial tool better suited to marketing studies or crude election forecasts than to meaningful investigation into public thinking on important matters.[106] In fact, many of the scholars who first embraced the study of public opinion were closer to commercial pollsters than their academic colleagues in the social sciences. Lacking the basic infrastructure to conduct their own surveys, scholars like Cantril depended on commercial pollsters like Gallup and Roper, who provided access to their national network of interviewers scattered across the country. More fundamentally, academic survey research rested on a set of assumptions about human behavior that differed little from their commercial counterparts. Just as advertisers wanted to know why consumers bought certain products, students of political behavior wanted to know why voters supported certain candidates. As Cantril noted in a 1940 article, all forms of strategic communication employed emotive symbols such as "justice, beauty, [and] liberty" whether it was intended to promote "cigarettes, political campaigns, [or] appeals to join the army."[107] The purpose of a survey, in other words, was to understand the architecture of individual choice. As the sociologist Paul Lazarsfeld explained, surveys assumed "the methodological equivalence of . . . voting and buying soap."[108]

Lazarsfeld's career illustrates this overlap, in both substance and method, between consumer research and political behavior. As a young scholar in Vienna, Lazarsfeld became interested in social stratification, its psychological effects on individuals, and, above all, the kinds of methods one could employ to study them. It was at this time that Lazarsfeld first came across marketing studies that employed survey methods, and he quickly incorporated them into his own research on social psychology. In 1934, Lazarsfeld arrived in the United States on a fellowship from the Rockefeller Foundation, and in 1937 he became the director of the Rockefeller-funded Princeton Radio Research Project. In 1940, Lazarsfeld moved to Columbia University, where he began work on his landmark study of voting behavior, *The People's Choice*.[109] Lazarsfeld's interest in voting was part of his broader research on mass communication, using the effects of campaign messages to study "how and why people decided to vote as they did."[110] Focusing on Erie County, Ohio, Lazarsfeld used a sample of 600 respondents who were interviewed seven times over the course of the 1940 presidential campaign. Thus, the election panel study was born. In fact, the panel method was already a common tool of market research used to save time and money by reinterviewing the same people. Lazarsfeld's insight was to use the panel method to study the "psychology of choice" and how the decision-making process unfolded over time.[111] Writing several years earlier in the *Harvard Business Review*, Lazarsfeld described consumer behavior as a sequence of steps that culminated in the purchase of goods. Survey research disaggregated the "structure of the purchase" and rendered it intelligible by revealing the psychological influences behind the decision of what to buy.[112] Lazarsfeld saw voting much the same way. Moreover, elections offered methodological advantages over consumer research because the sequence leading up to the "purchase" culminated on the same day for each individual and under a relatively controlled environment of media and other stimuli thought to influence the vote. Elections, in other words, offered a chance to study "a large-scale experiment in political propaganda and public opinion."[113]

As it turned out, the results of the Erie study provided very little evidence that radio or other forms of political communication influenced the vote. Most of those surveyed made up their minds early in the campaign, and only very few, 8 percent, switched their support from one party to the other. Lazarsfeld and his colleagues also found that socioeconomic status, religion, and rural or urban residence explained a great deal more of the variance in voting behavior than exposure to radio or other political messages. In fact, many respondents paid relatively little attention to the campaign. Of those who were exposed to political propaganda through the newspaper or radio, most had already made up their minds. Voters whose support vacillated or remained undecided until the end—so-called independent voters—were the least politically engaged of those in the study. At best, Lazarsfeld and his coauthors concluded, the campaign reinforced political predispositions or activated latent partisan sentiments. Summarizing his findings in a 1944 article in *Public Opinion Quarterly*, Lazarsfeld wrote, "Modern Presidential campaigns are over before they begin."[114]

Lazarsfeld's conclusion about campaign effects had important consequences, especially for the polling industry. The mistaken prediction of a Dewey victory in 1948 had a number of causes; however, a critical source of pollster error was the acceptance of Lazarsfeld's main findings about minimal campaign effects. When Republican candidate Thomas Dewey opened a sizable lead over President Harry Truman after the conventions, Gallup and Roper effectively pronounced the election to be over. Writing in his nationally syndicated column on September 9, Roper, who partially funded Lazarsfeld's research, explained that "past elections . . . have shown us that normally there is little change in the final standings between early September and Election Day." Convinced that "Thomas E. Dewey is almost as good as elected," Roper decided to cease all polling on the presidential contest, adding that he would rather "devote my time and effort to other things" than act "like a sports announcer who feels he must pretend he is witnessing a neck and neck race."[115] Although their own recent experiences of presidential elections certainly influenced the decision, Gallup and Roper adopted the position of leading social scientists in their decision to cease polling and incorrectly call the race for Dewey.

Indeed, the debacle of the 1948 election showed just how much the commercial polling industry and academic survey research shared a common fate. Writing in *Public Opinion Quarterly* in 1949, Robert K. Merton—a close friend and colleague of Lazarsfeld—discussed the "traumatic November episode" and whether it might adversely affect the "public images of social science."[116] That same year, the *International Journal of Opinion and Attitude Research* published the proceedings of an extended symposium in 1949 on "The Opinion Polls and the 1948 U.S. Presidential Election."[117] Meanwhile, the Social Science Research Council (SSRC) conducted its own investigation, establishing the Committee on the Analysis of Pre-election Polls and Forecasts eight days after the election to discover what went wrong. In its report issued just weeks later, SSRC President Pendleton Herring noted that "extended controversy regarding the pre-election polls among lay and professional groups might have extensive and unjustified repercussion upon all types of opinion and attitude studies and perhaps upon social science research generally." The report concluded that the decision by commercial pollsters to end operations weeks before the election was a considerable source of error; however, the committee was quick to emphasize that "the public should draw no inferences from pre-election forecasts that would disparage the accuracy or usefulness of properly conducted sampling surveys."[118] If anything, the errors of 1948 illustrated the need for more polling, not less. With the status of commercial survey research basically intact, the crisis proved to be a fleeting one. Roper himself noted approvingly a year after the election that his business had barely registered a blip after the unfortunate events of the previous November.[119]

As it developed in the 1930s and 1940s, polling combined market research with academic social science to produce a new and powerful instrument of opinion measurement. Such a tool was particularly valuable at a time when the tremendous potential of radio seemed limitless, yet a precise way to reach (and influence) such a vast audience remained elusive. Whether in marketing, commercial polling, or the academy, it was the search for an invisible or unseen public that sparked innovation. Unified by a common goal, academic and commercial concerns overlapped in a diverse network of actors who worked together to perfect their methods and popularize their techniques.

Indeed, with backgrounds that spanned advertising, marketing, and the social sciences, survey researchers held a particular view of politics and the public. The measurement of mass opinion often assumed a rough equivalence in the motivations guiding behavior, political or economic. Scholars such as Lazarsfeld approached the question of how a political campaign shaped the decisions of voters the same way as market researchers studied the effects of an advertising campaign. Attachments to particular products or brands were the methodological equivalents of attachments to particular candidates or parties. As Lazarsfeld and his coauthors wrote in an important summary of the literature in 1954, "The decisions that a modern Western man makes every few years in the political arena are similar to those he makes every day as a consumer of goods and services."[120] Building on these analogies with market share and product loyalties, pollsters brought both the language and the tools of business into the conduct of politics.

More fundamentally, public opinion polls offered a way of "selling" candidates and issues to the public, trimming political messages so that they aligned with the preferences of a particular audience. This was an important step in the commercialization of political advice. In time, polling became inseparable from media as those who mastered the technical demands of survey research would join the experts in mass communication to occupy a privileged role in the conduct of campaigns.

This union did not occur right away. Pollsters and media experts would have to work hard to establish a niche for themselves in a market for political intelligence still dominated by journalists and party workers. In the meantime, the marriage of media and polling found a home in a presidency increasingly dependent on the mobilization of the public to achieve its policy goals. The use of poll-tested messages by the Roosevelt administration demonstrated the promise of combining modern survey methods with crafted communication, as well as the opportunities for a new kind of practitioner to establish a position of influence in political affairs.

FDR and the Political Use of Polling

In the spring of 1935, the Democratic National Committee (DNC) conducted a public opinion poll in order to assess whether Huey Long's massive radio appeal posed a threat to Roosevelt's re-election chances the following year. Using a national sample of nearly 31,000 voters, the DNC poll asked respondents to indicate a preference for Roosevelt, an unnamed Republican, or Huey Long, for president. Although a majority favored Roosevelt, 11 percent of respondents preferred Long in the hypothetical three-way contest. The survey also revealed Long's broad appeal, one that extended well beyond his native South into the urban centers of the Northeast and Midwest. Seeing the results of the poll, DNC chairman James Farley feared that Long might hold the balance of power in 1936.[121]

The 1935 poll was the work of Emil Hurja, a deputy director of the DNC whose knowledge of statistics and deep interest in voting produced important innovations in the political use of survey methods.[122] In 1928, while working as a mining stock analyst on Wall Street, Hurja tried to convince then DNC chair Jacob Raskob that he could forecast election results using the same principles of sampling he used to test mineral assays. As Hurja later explained:

"You apply the same test to public opinion that you do to ore. In mining you take several samples from the face of the ore, pulverize them, and find out what the average pay per ton will be. In politics you take sections of voters, check new trends against past performances, establish percentage shift among different voting strata, supplement this information from competent observers in the field, and you can accurately predict an election result."[123]

In other words, Hurja proposed the same kind of sampling techniques that were then gaining prominence in market research and eventually in commercial polling and other areas of survey research. Raskob, however, dismissed Hurja as a crank.

Undeterred, Hurja offered his services to the DNC again four years later. In 1932, he drafted a memorandum that promised to give the DNC a moving "picture of sentiment" as it evolved over the course of the campaign. By combining all manner of political information—straw polls, census data, historic voting patterns, and newspaper editorials—Hurja claimed he could provide a statistically accurate portrait of Roosevelt's strength in different parts of the country. Because Hurja recognized the shortcomings of any single source of information, he supplemented traditional straw polls with census data and voting records in order to weight the results and correct for any bias. Armed with a multidimensional picture of the electorate, Hurja promised to "save needless expenditure of campaign funds in districts where [they were] not needed."[124] With the help of publicity director Charles Michelson, Hurja convinced DNC chairman James Farley to hire him as a special consultant for the 1932 campaign.[125]

Over the next several months, Hurja wrote weekly memos summarizing Roosevelt's strengths in various parts of the country and among different segments of voters. In what sounds commonplace today but was innovative for its time, Hurja produced a map with red and blue counties in progressively lighter shadings to differentiate those states in play from the ones safely in the hands of the two parties. Displaying tremendous resourcefulness in acquiring information—including house-to-house polls conducted by local bookmakers wagering on the election—Hurja accurately predicted a broad-based shift of urban voters to Roosevelt in 1932.[126]

Hurja continued to work closely with Farley after the election, employing his statistical skills to direct the distribution of federal patronage and, later, guiding party strategy during the 1934 congressional midterm elections. Again, Hurja used a combination of election results and polling data to develop a more reliable map of Democratic Party strength in various parts of the country. Hurja even polled Works Progress Administration workers to assess public opinion toward the New Deal.[127] Hurja's ability to pinpoint areas of Democratic strength and weakness and to focus campaign resources accordingly helped the Democrats in 1934 pick up nine seats in the House and ten in the Senate.

Hurja showed that poll results could inform political strategy. At a time when his contemporaries such as Roper or Gallup mainly produced election forecasts for public consumption and only dabbled in political polling, Hurja worked within the Roosevelt administration as an adviser and strategist. His ability to translate polls into political action pointed toward a "newly developing science of public opinion . . . and the political consulting business that would later grow from it."[128] In the meantime, Hurja's success attracted the attention of *Time*, *Collier's*, and other popular magazines that described him as a "political soothsayer" and "prophet extraordinary of the Democratic Party."[129] A 1936 profile in the *Saturday Evening Post* titled "Prof. Hurja, The

New Deal's Political Doctor" described him as "a great political diag-
nostician" equipped with "political stethoscopes, popularity meters,
and mass-mind indicators."[130] In fact, Hurja's skills were much more
than a campaign tool; they were also a critical device for the promotion
of presidential initiatives. "The function of Hurja is to discover what
the people are talking about," the *Post* explained. "If the conversation
is harmful to the New Deal, the next step is to change the conversation."[131] The blending of scientific surveys with White House communications would become a powerful tool for modern presidents.[132]

Radio, of course, was a key instrument for promoting the New
Deal as the refinement of communications techniques increased considerably during Roosevelt's time in office. The sheer volume of press
releases, radio shows, newsreels, and press conferences reflected a belief
by Roosevelt and his closest advisers that the success of New Deal programs depended on building public support through a coordinated
communications strategy. Stephen Early, Roosevelt's press secretary,
oversaw many of these efforts, including the appointment of more than
100 former journalists to staff press offices in every executive agency.[133]
However, it was in the use of radio that Early's influence on the future
of political work was most keenly felt.

Radio offered distinct advantages over newspapers for communicating administration policies. By 1933, for example, the estimated number
of radio listeners surpassed the combined circulation of the largest daily
newspapers.[134] In addition, the radio offered a way to circumvent hostile newspaper coverage; radio afforded a more direct form of public
communication. As Early explained, newspapers "cannot misrepresent
nor misquote."[135] Finally, and most important, the government enjoyed
privileged access to valuable airtime. Although broadcasters operated
under a relatively lax regulatory environment, they still depended on
government licenses to operate. The Radio Act of 1927 stipulated that
broadcast licenses be granted for reasons of "public interest, convenience,
or necessity." However, as historian Douglas Craig has noted, actual federal oversight of radio was minimal. The 1927 act established a system
of self-regulation later codified in the Communications Act of 1934 and
the creation of the Federal Communications Commission. Fearful of
further regulation, most broadcasters obliged government requests for
free airtime as a way to fulfill their public service mandate.[136]

Capitalizing on these advantages, the administration issued a steady stream of radio broadcasts, including 20 talks by the president, 17 by Eleanor Roosevelt, and 107 by members of the cabinet in the first ten months of the New Deal alone.[137] Many federal agencies produced their own weekly radio programs for the national networks or distributed recordings for use by local and independent stations. By 1936, a total of 5,000 government recordings were in circulation.[138] Stephen Early coordinated many of these efforts, securing airtime for administration broadcasts and tailoring programs to meet the interests and expectations of radio listeners.[139] Easy access to network airtime became a valuable resource for Roosevelt as he headed into the 1936 election. Much to the consternation of the Republican Party, the networks deemed many of the president's speeches that year as nonpartisan in nature and therefore aired them free of charge. As Douglas Craig summarizes, radio "added a powerful new advantage to incumbency."[140]

Of course, the centerpiece of Early's radio strategy was Roosevelt himself, notably the "fireside chats" and other radio addresses he delivered while in office. The president possessed an appealing radio persona that created a personal relationship with the public, but it is important to emphasize how hard Early and those around him worked to make the most out of the president's gifts. Broadcasts were timed to maximize audience and effect, often scheduled between nine and eleven in the evening, when East Coast listeners were not yet in bed and those on the West Coast were returning home from work. Care was given so that a broadcast would not conflict with popular radio programs. Content was carefully considered to fit within both current events and larger administration goals. Advance publicity and press releases built up audience anticipation. In the case of the first fireside chat on March 12, 1933, Early even arranged for spot advertisements throughout the day promoting the speech. Words were painstakingly chosen and drafts endlessly rehearsed by Roosevelt in order to perfect the rhythm and pace of his speech. During recording, special paper was used to dampen the sound of rustling pages, and Roosevelt even wore a bridge to cover a missing tooth so he would not whistle when he spoke.[141]

In the days after a fireside chat, Early would make a careful study of its effects, noting editorial and newspaper coverage of the speech as well as telegrams and letters from listeners themselves.[142] In addition, Early tracked the size of Roosevelt's radio audience using available surveys and audience measures. In a span of fourteen radio addresses between June 1936 and February 1942, the number tuning in to hear the president grew from 6 to 60 million homes. Audience surveys also showed that the fireside chats attracted the occasional radio listener as well as those who regularly tuned in, helping Early appreciate the distinctive nature of this format and prompting him to reserve its use for special issues or important administration goals.[143]

Surveys and other instruments of audience measurement offered a new way to gauge the president's popularity: through his radio appeal. More broadly, innovations in the political use of radio illustrate how the development of media and polling went hand in hand. As radio expanded the reach of political communication, survey methods offered a way to measure its effects. Developing a portrait of the listening audience, who was tuning into the president and when, was an important first step in assessing the political value of radio. However, reliable measures of audience size merely begged the question about the *influence* of radio communication on listeners. This, after all, was the question that motivated market researchers and social scientists alike, whether radio was used as a tool of advertising or as an instrument of political propaganda. For the Roosevelt administration, in particular, tracking the size of the radio audience was part of a deeper concern about whether the president and his staff could shape public opinion through crafted communication.[144] In seeking an answer to this very question, the Roosevelt administration turned to a variety of experts who straddled the commercial and academic worlds of public opinion research.

As noted previously, Princeton was an important locus of activity where academic and commercial survey researchers worked in close proximity to one another. Princeton was home to the first university research center on public opinion established by Hadley Cantril as well as the journal *Public Opinion Quarterly* he cofounded. Princeton was also the center of the commercial polling business, including the American Institute of Public Opinion founded by George Gallup in 1935. Within the confines of this one university town, a network of academic and commercial pollsters interacted regularly, perfecting their methods and promoting their infant industry.

These connections helped spawn early experiments in the use of poll-tested messages by the Roosevelt administration. Hadley Cantril, in particular, was a key figure in this regard. "Perhaps more than any other social scientist," Jean Converse has noted, "[Cantril] bridged the gap between commercial polling and social science."[145] With a foot in both worlds, Cantril understood that polls had to be deciphered in politically useful ways for them to be of any use to politicians. During his work on behalf of the Roosevelt administration throughout the 1940s, Cantril interpreted poll results with an eye toward the political needs and communication strategies of the president, translating the scholarly insights of the social scientist into the digestible format of the pollster's memo.

Cantril began work for the Roosevelt administration in 1940, when his former college roommate, Nelson A. Rockefeller, asked him for help surveying public opinion in several South American countries. Rockefeller was then head of the Office of Inter-American Affairs (OIAA), a somewhat shadowy agency the United States established to check Axis influence in South America. Propaganda was an important part of this strategy, and it was here that Cantril's expertise on radio and its effects proved valuable.[146] In cooperation with George Gallup, Cantril set up a nonprofit research institute, American Social Surveys, to conduct polling operations abroad. With funding from the newly established Executive Office of the President, Gallup and Cantril sent a crew of twenty interviewers to Brazil to collect information on radio listening habits. Jean Converse described the effort as "an intelligence operation disguised as market research," enabling Cantril to gauge the extent of Nazi sympathies and the potential reach of US propaganda.[147]

Cantril's research in South America led to more work for FDR.[148] With the conflict in Europe raising debates at home about US neutrality, Cantril supplied the president with memos explaining the results of Gallup surveys about potential American involvement in the war. Roosevelt took particular interest in the results of a July 1940 poll in which 37 percent of respondents thought the United States should help Britain, while 59 percent responded that the United States should avoid war altogether. At Roosevelt's request, Cantril included the same question in subsequent polls, eventually developing a trend report for the president that he updated as new polls became available. As Cantril later recalled, "Nothing interested [Roosevelt] more than the trend charts," especially those that showed a growing sense among Americans that involvement in the war was inevitable.[149] By the time the United States entered the war in December 1941, White House requests for polling data had exceeded the resources available to Cantril either through the Rockefeller-funded Office of Public Opinion Research or through the continued generosity of George Gallup.[150]

Providence intervened in the form of a financial angel named Gerard Lambert. A Princeton graduate himself, Lambert made his fortune building his family's business, which produced the popular mouthwash Listerine. In fact, it was Gerard's talent for marketing, pitching Listerine as a cure for "chronic halitosis" (a term he invented), that transformed the brand into a mass-market phenomenon. By the 1920s, Lambert had amassed a vast fortune and retired to the stately mansion he built for himself and his family in Princeton, two miles from the university gates. It was there that Lambert met George Gallup, who in turn introduced Lambert to Hadley Cantril.[151] Shortly after the Japanese attack on Pearl Harbor, Lambert and Cantril met to discuss the growing need for survey work on behalf of the president, and they agreed to establish a polling operation of their own, independent from the funding limitations of the Rockefeller Foundation or the field staff and facilities of the Gallup Organization. Their creation, the Research Council, Inc., operated out of Cantril's Office of Public Opinion Research at Princeton on punch card equipment on loan from IBM. Within months, interviewers began polling a nationwide sample of 1,200 respondents. Lambert covered the costs. "At the end of each month," Cantril recalled, "I sent Lambert's New York office a report of the amount of money spent during the month, and a check was returned to the Research Council immediately."[152]

In fact, Gerard Lambert was much more than just a benefactor. He also brought considerable experience in marketing and advertising, as well as early attempts to use public opinion data in the conduct of campaigns. After a disappointing tour in Washington working for the Federal Housing Administration, Lambert returned to Princeton, where he devoted his energies to defeating Roosevelt in the 1940 election. As Lambert recounted in his memoir, "My first step was to go to Dr. George Gallup. . . . From him I borrowed some men and began to run small public-opinion polls of my own."[153] Specifically, Lambert tested different versions of political speeches to see how slight changes in their substance would affect their public appeal, much as he had done when perfecting advertising copy for Listerine. Sometime in 1939, Gallup introduced Lambert to Thomas Dewey, then the New York City district attorney, who asked Lambert to conduct opinion surveys in his bid for the 1940 Republican presidential nomination. Lambert agreed. Again with help from some of Gallup's top assistants, Lambert set up polling operations for Dewey. After Dewey failed to garner the nomination, Lambert continued his public opinion work for the Republican nominee, Wendell Willkie, but he found the candidate to be uninterested in his advice. Lambert claimed that his pre-election polls predicted Willkie's loss to Roosevelt by two percentage points.[154]

A little over a year later, with the United States at war, Lambert found himself back in Washington. Dedicating himself to the war effort, Lambert helped Cantril establish a polling operation that reported regularly to members of Roosevelt's inner circle. According to historian Richard Steele, "The relationship [with the White House] grew as the war progressed, and although it was never Roosevelt's only source of public opinion, it was probably his most important."[155] Their work ranged widely, including memoranda on public views toward lend-lease, governmental secrecy, and the progress of Allied forces on the Italian front. Cantril and Lambert probed domestic issues as well, such as what the public thought of full employment policies. Their services could be called upon at a moment's notice, as when the White House wanted to gauge the reaction among Catholics to the possible bombing of Rome.[156]

Across the range of issues they examined, Cantril and Lambert often emphasized how public opinion polls recommended particular communication strategies by the president. In a December 1942 memorandum on production targets for war materiel, Cantril and Lambert advised "a policy of understatement and overperformance" when FDR communicated to the public.[157] At the request of Sam Rosenman, FDR's speechwriter, Cantril and Lambert poll-tested different versions of a radio address designed to explain federal subsidy programs to farmers. On other occasions, Cantril and Lambert used poll results to recommend a particular rhetorical style or tone. A February 1944 memorandum suggested that FDR would achieve greater support from the public if he used an upcoming radio address to ask for cooperation with his aims rather than criticize those who opposed him. Another time, Lambert and Cantril reported that "our studies show a wide desire on the part of the people to have the President admit a few human failings and to minimize sarcasm in his speeches."[158] In a message to Congress on the war's progress shortly thereafter, Roosevelt acknowledged that "mistakes have been made," but he also noted that, on the whole, the country had met its wartime challenges successfully.[159] *Time* magazine cheered the speech, adding caustically that such admissions of fallibility from FDR "have the rarity of pearls in a restaurant oyster."[160]

Cantril and Lambert took great care crafting their memos to the president. Both understood that the style in which they presented their findings would influence how their recommendations would be received. As Cantril himself noted, "A great deal of valuable material social scientists uncover or create is presented in so academic or slipshod a fashion that no busy person is going to waste time digging out what may be of significance."[161] As they prepared a report for the president, Lambert and Cantril reviewed and revised, paring down their memos to at most two or three pages. Major findings and conclusions were highlighted, and poll results were summarized with a graph or chart. Cantril recalled that "we always tried to remember that the President . . . would completely lose interest if we became verbose or technical."[162] It was here that Lambert's experience in business and advertising contributed to the collaboration by helping to convey detailed findings of various surveys in a simple, easily understood fashion. There was an art as well as a science to polling, especially when interpreting technical findings in politically meaningful ways.

In sum, polling offered a new source of information and a new kind of expert who could distill social scientific information in politically useful ways. Both challenged older sources of political intelligence. As Gerard Lambert reflected on his experiences as a political adviser, "This technique of discovering people's attitude by public-opinion surveys is a controversial subject. In general those who are vociferous in opposing it have one thing in common. They derive their prestige or their living by expressing their own opinions." Lambert focused much of his scorn on newspaper editors, columnists, and other "high priests of opinion."

For these traditional interpreters of public sentiment, "a survey robs them of their oracular authority." Polling, Lambert concluded, "is an encroachment upon their own domain."[163]

An Emergent Profession of Political Advice

The radio experts and pollsters of the 1930s and 1940s represent an emergent profession of political advice whose ability to craft messages and plumb the public mind would grow in value over the course of the twentieth century. Radio, and later television, changed the relationship between leaders and led, opening a space for a new kind of specialist to emerge who could interpret a public that was often "invisible" or "unseen." In the first part of the twentieth century, newspaper publicity was a rather straightforward affair that sought to shape opinions by influencing the content of what people read. The discovery of propaganda raised the spectre of a public that was manipulated rather than informed, but it shared with publicity a simplistic notion of influence. Commentators, whether critical of propaganda or not, overstated the susceptibility of the public to mass persuasion.

Radio, however, posed new challenges and a new view of the public. Rather than a straightforward task of publicity or an undifferentiated public easily swayed, mass communication encountered an audience that could choose not to listen. Considerations such as the timing, format, and content of political broadcasts became important. Surveys offered a way to track the appeal of the new medium to particular groups or demographics, or even the individual listener.

Together, sophisticated media and scientific polling had far-reaching effects on American politics, contributing to a shift in the institutional balance of power between the executive branch and the rest of the political system. Through the instrument of public speech, modern presidents developed a new and powerful instrument of executive power.[164] Radio was crucial to this development because it allowed presidents to speak directly to the people without the mediating influence of a potentially hostile press. Beginning as a powerful tool of the presidency, the use of poll-tested messages eventually spread throughout the political system, helping give rise to a consulting industry that today exercises almost complete control over the conduct of political work.

5

A Business Takes Shape

CHANGES IN THE CHARACTER OF American democracy placed a premium on the ability to solicit popular support, providing opportunities for those promoting their skills as a new kind of political professional. As aspirants for office took greater responsibility for their own political fortunes, candidates sought advice from experts who could help them communicate with voters. With the invention of radio and the accompanying advances in survey research, specialists in polling challenged the ward heelers and precinct workers as a valued source of political intelligence. And, with the growth of presidential power, those skilled in the use of media and crafted communication became key participants in building an energetic executive.

However, it remained difficult for the forerunners of the modern consulting industry to reap many financial rewards from the conduct of political work. Although the collaboration of Hadley Cantril and Gerard Lambert, pollster and media man, foreshadowed the lucrative business of politics that would eventually emerge, neither made any attempt to capitalize on their innovations. Emil Hurja similarly contributed to advances in presidential polling, but he retired from politics into relative obscurity. Elmo Roper dabbled in political polling, but it could not pay the bills for him either. Even such an enterprising figure as Edward Bernays found corporate public relations a much more lucrative enterprise. Motivated by personal political goals or a sense of civic duty, these early practitioners lived for politics more than they lived from it.[1]

In California, however, a true business of politics was taking shape. In 1933, Clement Whitaker joined forces with Leone Baxter to manage a campaign against a statewide ballot initiative. Following their success defeating the measure, the former journalist and director of a local chamber of commerce established Campaigns, Inc., the first dedicated political consulting firm in the United States. Over the next twenty-five years, the team of Whitaker and Baxter managed scores of campaigns on behalf of the state's leading industries, interest groups, and candidates. Through their work, Whitaker and Baxter crafted evocative messages and served as an important conduit between their clients and the media, realizing to a degree previously unknown the opportunities and rewards of professional campaign management.

In some ways, California was an environment rich in opportunities to develop a business of politics. Progressive Era reforms left political parties organizationally weak. Cross-filing allowed candidates to run in primaries for either party, while a penchant for direct democracy placed numerous ballot initiatives regularly before the public. The sheer scale of the state, almost 800 miles from end to end, coupled with the extraordinary mobility of the population, meant candidates and campaigns in California leaned heavily on mass media to reach the voters. As the economy and population of California grew during World War II, conflicts emerged between the government in Sacramento and powerful business interests in the state. For Whitaker and Baxter, these corporate clients provided them with a steady flow of work aimed at limiting the scope of government regulations.

In fact, Whitaker and Baxter did more than create a lucrative business; they forged a new kind of interest group politics as well. In the capable hands of Whitaker and Baxter, business groups and trade associations used sophisticated campaign tools to defeat candidates, ballot measures, and legislative proposals that threatened their financial interests. Indeed, Whitaker and Baxter's methods provided a powerful and effective means for business groups and professional associations to engage in political action to a much greater degree than was previously possible. Their discovery had national implications. After perfecting their model of political action in California, Whitaker and Baxter replicated their efforts at the national level as they led the American Medical Association campaign to defeat Harry Truman's plans for national health insurance. California did offer distinct opportunities for a political consulting profession to take shape, but the Golden State also served as a laboratory for innovations in political practice that eventually spread throughout the country.[2]

Campaigns, Inc.

That Whitaker and Baxter had hit upon a novel, and lucrative, business of campaign management was clearly evident to scholars and journalists of the day. In 1951, Carey McWilliams, an astute observer of California politics, provided a detailed account of Campaigns, Inc. in a three-part series for the *Nation*. According to McWilliams, "The firm has evolved a style of operation which makes the old-fashioned boss and lobbyist completely obsolete. Whitaker and Baxter has ushered in a new era in American politics—government by public relations."[3] Five years later, Campaigns, Inc. figured prominently in the first scholarly treatment of the consultant-for-hire, *Professional Public Relations and Political Power* by political scientist Stanley Kelley. According to Kelley, "It was a Whitaker and Baxter inspiration to conceive of political campaigning as a business."[4] Similarly, Robert Pitchell, writing in the *Western Political Quarterly* in 1958, called Whitaker and Baxter "the giants of the industry, the most successful practitioners of the art of campaign management and the model by which all other firms may be measured."[5]

Several key features contributed to Whitaker and Baxter's success. First, Campaigns, Inc. attracted a diverse set of clients who provided the firm with a steady stream of revenue. Second, Whitaker and Baxter developed close relations with state and local media, and they understood well the economic incentives of newspapers and radio broadcasters. Third, the firm created a financing model that enabled clients to afford their services, frequently becoming the conduit through which firms and trade associations pooled their resources for political action. Fourth, although the Whitaker and Baxter model was well adapted to the particular conditions of California politics, their methods were easily replicated for a range of clients and campaigns at the local, state, and even national levels. In particular, Whitaker and Baxter demonstrated the power of issue-based appeals, speaking to voters in terms of individual interests and beliefs rather than partisan identities and attachments.

California provided fertile ground for Whitaker and Baxter to perfect their methods. In their first campaign together in 1933, the pair defeated a referendum supported by the powerful Pacific Gas and Electric Company that, if passed, would have blocked an ambitious public works program that threatened private utilities in the state. Working on a budget of less than $40,000, Whitaker and Baxter won by focusing their efforts strategically on the few counties that stood to gain the most from state spending. Their political savvy attracted notice throughout California, not least among the leaders of Pacific Gas and Electric, who put their erstwhile opponents on an annual retainer. Soon, the firm was handling as many as five or six initiatives and referendum campaigns in a single year, usually on behalf of the state's most powerful industries.[6]

Ballot measures were only one important source of revenue for Campaigns, Inc. In addition, Whitaker and Baxter worked on statewide political campaigns and several municipal races as well. The firm orchestrated the opposition to Upton Sinclair's bid for governor in 1934, managed George Hatfield's successful run for lieutenant governor the same year, and helped elect two governors: Earl Warren in 1942 and Goodwin Knight in 1954. In addition, Campaigns, Inc. coordinated Northern California efforts for Eisenhower's presidential campaign in 1952 and Nixon's 1960 White House run. Finally, Whitaker and Baxter also served the public affairs and advocacy needs of corporate clients, trade associations, and interest groups seeking to influence the passage of legislation. Most notably, Campaigns, Inc. managed a statewide effort on behalf of the California Medical Association against Earl Warren's proposal to create a public system of health insurance in the state. Their success in that campaign brought Whitaker and Baxter to the attention of the American Medical Association, which hired the team in 1949 to help defeat Truman's plan for national health insurance, an effort that earned the firm almost $1.6 million in fees over a period of four years.[7] In sum, Whitaker and Baxter devised a successful model of political consulting that generated a steady stream of revenue from a diverse array of clients and campaigns that included ballot initiatives, elections, and advocacy work.

This steady cash flow enabled the firm to spend freely on statewide media, a necessity given the scale and cost of California campaigns.

However, effective communication required more than well-crafted messages; it also required understanding how the media worked as a business. Whitaker and Baxter grasped the production demands of the press. Operating as a link between newspapers in need of advertising revenue and various interests in search of influence, Campaigns, Inc. secured favorable press coverage for the causes and candidates it represented. Savvy media relations also brought in more revenue for the firm as Whitaker and Baxter received commissions on the campaign advertising they sold their clients on top of the fees they charged for providing political advice. Here was a crucial innovation in the history of campaign management: by charging for individual products and services, media-intensive campaigns afforded consultants with multiple and varied opportunities to make money.

If the geographic scale of California politics required a heavy reliance on mass communication to reach a widely dispersed electorate, it was Whitaker and Baxter who discovered how to leverage the purchasing power of a statewide media campaign into a form of political influence. Early in their career together, Whitaker and Baxter combined the publicity functions of a press agent with the eye of an advertising account executive. This enabled the pair to work both the "buy" and the "sell" side of newspaper content: Campaigns, Inc. purchased advertising space in newspapers on behalf of their clients in order to ease the way for press releases and other forms of publicity designed to shape the content of news coverage.

In order to carry out these functions, Whitaker and Baxter created several business entities within Campaigns, Inc. that, together, gave them greater control over the conduct of political work (while also providing multiple streams of revenue for the firm). Whereas Campaigns, Inc. managed overall strategy and client relations, the Clem Whitaker Advertising Agency produced all of the firm's advertising work. The California Feature Service, also under their direction, distributed a free, weekly compendium of news items written to promote the interests of Whitaker and Baxter's clients but written to appear as objective reporting of political events. Many rural and small-town editors in need of content simply reprinted portions of the California Feature Service in local papers or reworked the material into their own editorials.[8]

In fact, the pair made no secret of their desire to translate massive advertising buys into favorable press coverage for their clients. Whitaker and Baxter routinely sent letters to editors throughout the state informing them of their campaign efforts and, especially, their intention to purchase advertising on behalf of their clients. A 1936 letter was typical: "We recognize that newspapers cannot pay bills with publicity! We accept the management of campaigns only after a general advertising schedule has been approved. *If you receive publicity from Campaigns, Inc., you will also receive paid advertising!*"[9] These advertising announcements often included an explanation of the issue and an explicit plea for support. Working to defeat a proposal for state pensions for the elderly (also known as the "Ham and Eggs" Plan), Whitaker and Baxter ran advertisements in 400 Northern California papers. In a letter to editors that accompanied the ad copy and payment, Whitaker and Baxter wrote, "We sincerely believe that the Ham and Eggs pension scheme . . . would bring bitter disillusionment to elderly citizens who are now supporting it," adding that, "If you can make use of the news material inclosed [*sic*] with this letter, or lend us support during the weeks to come, we shall be deeply grateful."[10] To ingratiate themselves further, Whitaker and Baxter never deducted commissions from their advertising buys, as was common practice at the time. Instead, they earned their return from the fees they charged their clients. In sum, Campaigns, Inc. sought influence by providing the newspaper business with a steady source of advertising revenue.

Whitaker and Baxter's emphasis on paid media had another advantage: it was much easier to document expenditures for newspaper advertisements and radio spots than it was for lobbying and other traditional forms of political spending. Whitaker and Baxter used this fact to sell their services, especially to business clients accustomed to careful accounting practices. This businesslike approach distinguished professional campaign management from the old-style politics it sought to replace. "Managing campaigns is no longer a hit-or-miss business, directed by broken-down politicians," Clem Whitaker wrote. Instead, "It is rapidly emerging . . . to become a mature, well-managed business, *founded on sound public relations principles.*"[11] Rather than "hundred-dollar bills floating around campaign headquarters like pennies raining down from heaven," Campaigns, Inc. provided each client with an item-by-item breakdown of its expenditures.[12] This was important given the scale of a statewide advertising campaign. According to Whitaker, a typical media effort designed to reach the 4 million voters in California required 10 million pamphlets, 2 million postcards, and 500,000 letters, as well as radio spots and movie trailers throughout the state. Whatever the expense, however, Campaigns, Inc. promised that "in every campaign, we do our utmost to get a dollar's value for every dollar spent, just as we would if we were merchandising commodities instead of selling men and measures."[13] By operating according to "sound public relations principles," Whitaker and Baxter could calculate for their clients the return on investment for services rendered.

This businesslike approach to campaign management extended to fundraising efforts as well. Typically, Campaigns Inc. solicited funds directly from business groups and trade associations in order to cover the firm's expenses and fees during the course of the campaign. For example, in 1938, Whitaker and Baxter managed the opposition campaign against the Garrison Bond Act, a measure that would have made it easier for cities and counties to finance the construction of public utilities. In order to deny local governments this new source of revenue, private utilities in the state organized the California Debt Relief Association to defeat the measure in a legislative referendum.[14] Essentially a shell organization meant to conceal the political efforts of the power industry, the California Debt Relief Association amassed a $100,000 war chest to fund a barrage of newspaper advertising, radio spots, and direct mail. Campaigns Inc. handled everything, including raising money from power companies that were instructed to send "all remittances ... immediately on receipt," with checks made payable to "the California Debt Relief Association, c/o Clem Whitaker, 111 Sutter Street, San Francisco."[15] Throughout the campaign, Whitaker and Baxter provided the power companies with "a finance statement, covering all income received ... and an analysis of all expenditures," including "a check-by-check accounting of all disbursements."[16] Handling fundraising efforts also made it easier for Campaigns, Inc. to collect the $15,000 fee the firm was owed by the state's power companies, as Whitaker and Baxter simply deducted payment from the contributions they collected.

In sum, Whitaker and Baxter developed a successful and self-sustaining model of campaign management. Media-intensive campaigns cost more money than traditional forms of vote-getting, but the money used to purchase advertisements and radio could be spread throughout the state, earning goodwill from newspaper editors and station managers. Whitaker and Baxter needed to help them convey their clients' message. At the same time, expenditures on media could be easily accounted for, allowing Whitaker and Baxter to present themselves as competent professionals rather than political hacks. This endeared them to the California business community, which provided Campaigns, Inc. with much of its work. In some cases, Whitaker and Baxter helped create the organized groups they served, effectively underwriting the costs of collective action through their fundraising efforts. For a fee, Campaigns, Inc. could turn a disparate collection of interests into a potent political force.

Whitaker and Baxter at Work

The expression of common purpose required the articulation of a message that could unite diverse interests under a single banner. Whitaker and Baxter were particularly talented in this regard, and it was their effective use of media as a tool of public persuasion that made the pair so valuable to their clients and distinguished them from other political operatives working in California at the time. As Stanley Kelley put it, "Whitaker and Baxter are interested in building public attitudes and in standardizing opinions about particular political issues. Success . . . requires study and selection of political 'markets,' alternative ways of framing appeals, and methods of distributing ideas."[17] Clem Whitaker put it this way, "Words still mold the minds of men—and still direct the ebb and flow of their emotions."[18] Distinguishing his methods from the old-style politics of the past, Whitaker wrote that "machine politics never could stand the light of a hard-hitting, modern day public relations and advertising campaign."[19] For Leone Baxter, the essence of their innovation was "building specific public opinion—on highly-contested issues—within set time limits." This modern business of politics consisted of "trained personnel, paid in prideful fees, not patronage," whose expertise was essential to securing popular support whether on behalf of a ballot measure, a legislative initiative, or an individual candidate.[20]

To that end, Whitaker and Baxter developed a keen sense of messaging, selecting campaign themes that drew stark contrasts between their position and the opposition. Frequently, this meant offering a positive alternative or proposal to the measure under consideration. As Leone Baxter put it, "You can't beat something with nothing ... a negative, wholly attacking campaign isn't sound."[21] In addition, Whitaker and Baxter understood the difficulty of holding public attention; they developed concise messages and slogans that could be communicated easily through a variety of media. Working on behalf of the California Teachers Association, for example, Whitaker and Baxter cleverly reframed the issue of teachers' salaries as a matter of educational quality: "We are not championing the teachers, primarily; we are championing the right of the children of California to have competent instruction—and they can't continue to have that, if we permit teaching to become a cast-off profession, starved by our failure to recognize the crisis which confronts us."[22]

Finally, Whitaker and Baxter saw the electorate as composed of a diverse mix of interests. In order to reach these different audiences, the firm targeted messages at specific groups considered to be strategically important for the campaign. As Stanley Kelley explained, "[Whitaker and Baxter] are acutely aware ... of the individual's multi-group affiliation." Consequently, a practitioner like Whitaker or Baxter "must *activate* the group loyalties that he wants to operate," as well as "approach the voter through a variety of media and with a variety of arguments aimed at different sides of his political personality."[23] According to Baxter, "The masses are also individuals ... classifying people too categorically is dangerous. ... A Democrat is not solely a Democrat; he may also be a farmer, a truck driver, a salesman, teacher—or even a Dixiecrat."[24] As we have seen with other practitioners, such as Edward Bernays, the mid-century professional imagined ways to activate certain dimensions of political identification deemed strategic for a particular goal or purpose. In Stanley Kelley's estimation, Whitaker and Baxter possessed "an intuitive feel for political marketing conditions."[25]

Whitaker and Baxter's work on behalf of the Pacific Gas and Electric Company is illustrative in this regard. The powerful utility company owned exclusive rights to sell water and power from the Hetch Hetchy dam and reservoir to the City of San Francisco. Seeking to break the company's monopoly, public utility advocates put a series of bond measures before the voters of San Francisco that would have allowed the construction of a public system of power generation. In order to defeat the measure, Whitaker and Baxter developed a strategy to undermine support by shifting discussion away from the merits of public ownership and toward an ongoing struggle between the City of San Francisco and the federal government over water rights in California, reframing the issue as one of federal interference in state and local affairs.[26] "This campaign will require smart boxing as well as some two-fisted slugging," the pair wrote. "We strongly recommend a positive, constructive campaign to marshal public opinion, hammering away constantly at the fact that San Francisco has been viciously discriminated against [by the federal government]."[27] The benefit of this strategy was clear. By turning the question of public ownership of utilities into a battle with Washington, DC, Whitaker and Baxter drew attention away from the efforts of the Pacific Gas and Electric Company to defeat the bond measure and protect its profits.

Whitaker and Baxter also recognized that the bond issue touched on a variety of interests and concerns among San Francisco residents. The struggle over federal power and local control was just one of "many different aspects of the issue which can be interpreted and used most effectively with special groups."[28] Building coalitions was critical, and by emphasizing the cost of the Hetch Hetchy bonds, Whitaker and Baxter could appeal to a range of groups fearful of the effects a debt-burdened city government might have on their particular interests. "Every special group in San Francisco ... can be made an active, crusading campaign group against Hetch Hetchy bonds," Whitaker and Baxter concluded.[29] This included public sector workers concerned about salary cuts, as well as homeowners and taxpayers opposed to a "deluge of debt."[30] In addition, business interests of all kinds would rally around the larger issue of government power as "every business man who fears eventual government invasion of his field of work can be reached with the message that it is time to stop political encroachment on private enterprise."[31]

Throughout their career, Whitaker and Baxter frequently conjured similar fears of government run amok.

Whitaker and Baxter often targeted their campaign messages to specific audiences. As the team explained in a campaign memorandum, "With so many special groups . . . interested for their own special reasons, we should have highly specialized literature," including "special direct-mail campaigns . . . conducted to reach the rank and file."[32] Whitaker and Baxter understood that reaching an audience was not easy. Effective communication required the right media as well as the right message. Whitaker and Baxter campaigns typically used billboards, direct mail, newspaper advertisements, and, of course, radio. In the case of the latter, Whitaker and Baxter advised "spending a large portion of the radio budget in short, dramatized skits, spot announcements, and news broadcasts, with our campaign material worked into the news." For the Hetch Hetchy bond measure, Campaigns, Inc., purchased airtime on five San Francisco stations, running a mixture of spots and longer broadcasts almost every day leading up to the vote.[33]

In order to track the efficacy of their efforts, Whitaker and Baxter gathered information about the voters whom they sought to influence. Again, the particular features of California politics offered distinct advantages in this regard. Because of the preponderance of direct legislation, a lucrative business developed in collecting the needed signatures to place a measure on the ballot. During the Hetch Hetchy campaign, Whitaker and Baxter hired Robinson & Company, which enjoyed a near monopoly on the signature collection business, to circulate a petition calling for congressional repeal of the federal legislation that governed water rights in the Hetch Hetchy Valley. However, the immediate purpose of the petition was not to lobby Congress but rather to provide precinct-level assessments of public opinion. Writing to Clem Whitaker a week before the vote, the principal of the firm, Joe Robinson, reported that his company interviewed more than 300,000 people. Based on the reports of his staff, Robinson confidently predicted that "you will defeat the bond issue by not less than twenty thousand votes." In fact, the bond measure was defeated by almost a two-to-one margin, 67,214 for and 114,879 against.[34]

As the Hetch Hetchy campaign illustrates, Whitaker and Baxter tailored their methods to the needs of California business, especially the threat posed by ballot initiatives that placed economic policy in the hands of the voting public. These same techniques proved highly effective on behalf of political candidates as well, an advantage that also stemmed from California's unique politics. At the turn of the twentieth century, powerful railroads dominated the Republican Party and enjoyed unparalleled control over state politics until a series of reforms hobbled party organizations. In addition to the initiative, referendum, and recall, California Progressives instituted a unique system of cross-filing that allowed candidates for state and federal office to run in multiple party primaries without any party identification on the ballot. By the 1940s, when Whitaker and Baxter reached the height of their influence in California politics, 80 percent of the state's assembly districts and a majority of US congressional seats were held by candidates who had captured the nomination of the two main parties, rendering the general election a mere formality.[35] In addition to California's unique electoral rules, exceptionally high rates of in-migration and geographically dispersed communities throughout the state made it difficult to establish the kind of local party organizations more commonly found in urban centers of the East.[36]

These factors produced a weakly affiliated electorate. A 1942 analysis of national politics by political scientist Harold Gosnell concluded that "the most striking fact" of voting behavior in California "is the almost complete absence . . . of any party discipline." Instead, Gosnell observed, voters "changed their party allegiances from election to election in accordance with changing issues and personalities."[37] Carey McWilliams, perhaps the most astute observer of California politics of his day, placed much of the blame on the state's "notorious cross-filing procedure," which had "made a shambles of party regularity and party discipline in California."[38] A more recent analysis confirms these earlier conclusions, adding that "it is difficult to overstate the destructive effect cross-filing had on local party organizations."[39] In sum, Whitaker and Baxter worked in a political climate where parties failed to provide meaningful cues to voters or operate as effective organizations for the conduct of elections.

As one might expect, weak party organizations and fickle partisan attachments had important consequences for the conduct of political campaigns. According to McWilliams, "Candidates think in terms of personal machines, personal followings, individual campaigns, and not in terms of party organization."[40] The result was a "freewheeling style of politics," in which "candidates must depend on individual political merchandising" in order to win office.[41] In other words, McWilliams concluded, "They must 'sell' themselves as candidates."[42] Accordingly, Whitaker and Baxter tailored their services to the needs of individual candidates by focusing on the personalities and issue positions of their clients rather than their party affiliation. This included tactics designed to build up support for their candidate by diminishing the stature of their opponent in the eyes of the electorate. Although the practice is commonplace today, Whitaker and Baxter perfected an early form of the negative campaign.

This highly personal and occasionally nasty style of electoral politics began early in Whitaker and Baxter's career. In 1934, only a year after forming Campaigns, Inc., Whitaker and Baxter landed their first state-wide race when George Hatfield hired them to manage his bid for lieu-tenant governor. Although Hatfield ran on the Republican ticket with gubernatorial candidate Frank Merriam, voters would cast separate ballots for the top two offices in the state. However, a strong showing by social activist and writer Upton Sinclair in the Democratic primary left Merriam looking vulnerable and Hatfield's camp unsure if or how California voters might split their tickets. Although the Republican Hatfield might position himself as a balance to Sinclair, voters might prefer Merriam for the top spot and choose the Democrat for lieu-tenant governor instead. In short, Hatfield had to wage his own cam-paign, and he turned to Whitaker and Baxter to do it. The strategy they employed, and one they would reproduce in many subsequent campaigns, was to build up the positive qualities of their candidate even as they sought every opportunity to undercut the credibility of their opponent.[43]

The challenge for Whitaker and Baxter in 1934 was that both Hatfield and the Democratic candidate, Sheridan Downey, were relative new-comers to politics with little record to run on or past controversy to exploit. However, what Hatfield and Downey lacked in excitement was made up for by the presence in the race of Upton Sinclair. A former member of the Socialist Party, Sinclair attracted broad support from the state's poor and working class as he promised to turn idle factories and farmland into cooperatives for the unemployed. As Sinclair's popularity grew, Whitaker and Baxter waged a bitter campaign against him, mining the author's many books for controversial quotes that when taken out of context portrayed Sinclair as a dangerous radical.[44] Operating through a front organization, the California League Against Sinclairism (CLAS), Whitaker and Baxter flooded the state's newspapers with editorials and canned news items warning of the dangers of "Sinclairism." According to historian Greg Mitchell, CLAS was funded by "big-money interests" and led by "hard-knuckled politicos" in the California Republican Party. However, Whitaker and Baxter's media campaign carefully avoided partisanship or party labels in order to convince Democratic voters to support the GOP candidates Merriam and Hatfield.[45] In words likely written by Clem Whitaker, George Hatfield told an audience of veterans, "This campaign is not between Republicans and Democrats, but between believers in American institutions and those that wish to implant State socialism." Hatfield even called Sinclair "an adroit propagandist who . . . has advocated everything from nudism and free love to Bolshevism."[46] Earl Warren, chair of the California Republican Central Committee, hit upon similar themes: "This is no longer a campaign between the Republican and Democratic Party in California. . . . It is a crusade of Americans and Californians against Radicalism and Socialism."[47] In order to stoke fears of social upheaval, Metro-Goldwyn-Mayer Studios produced a short film in the style of a newsreel that purported to show hobos streaming into California from across the country in anticipation of a Sinclair victory.[48]

Frank Merriam soundly defeated Upton Sinclair, and George Hatfield won his race for lieutenant governor. The following year, Sinclair penned a book entitled *I, Candidate for Governor, and How I Got Licked*, in which he described his defeat at the hands of "the biggest business men in California," whose "staff of political chemists" prepared "poisons to be let loose in the California Atmosphere."[49] Sinclair called it "The Lie Factory." In fact, Sinclair had encountered a new kind of campaign that combined modern media with highly personalized negative attacks. As Greg Mitchell documents, the campaign against Sinclair was a harbinger of things to come.[50]

Although few races matched the vitriol of the 1934 campaign, or attracted as much national attention, the methods Whitaker and Baxter employed became stock-in-trade for subsequent clients. During their career together, Whitaker and Baxter ran a number of prominent California campaigns, including those of Mayor Elmer Robinson of San Francisco and Governors Earl Warren and Goodwin Knight. The 1954 gubernatorial race, in particular, repeated many of the same tactics that Whitaker and Baxter first employed in 1934. Although Knight's opponent, Richard Graves, had been a registered Republican before switching to the Democratic Party, Whitaker and Baxter portrayed Graves as a captive of the extreme left and launched attacks on Graves and other Democratic candidates through a shadowy organization called the Democratic Conference against Radical Party Leadership.[51] Meanwhile, Whitaker and Baxter exploited divisions in the state's labor movement to secure support from the California American Federation of Labor, including the "Labor for Knight" committee that distributed campaign literature attacking Graves's Republican past. All the while, Knight stayed above the fray, his campaign speeches made up of trite remarks as he traveled around the state telling voters, "You are a smiling, happy, prosperous people."[52] As historian Jonathan Bell explains, Whitaker and Baxter perfected a strategy that portrayed Knight "as representative of all of California," and anyone who opposed him as "an extremist or someone alien to the political culture of the state."[53]

By the 1940s, Whitaker and Baxter were well-known figures in California politics, offering an array of services to various causes and candidates. Their work on campaigns and ballot initiatives paid handsomely in fees, particularly from clients in the business community eager to preserve their power and influence in the Golden State. For their part, Whitaker and Baxter sold their services well, combining a proficiency with words and symbols and a sophisticated understanding of the press to become a highly sought after source of expertise and advice. Within a decade of joining forces, Whitaker and Baxter developed a successful model of professional campaign management that transformed their clients' money into a powerful form of political influence.

A New Kind of Issue Advocacy

Although rewarded generously for their efforts, Whitaker and Baxter were not simply guns for hire. The business model they developed fit comfortably with their broader ideological commitments. Whether working on behalf of a ballot measure or a candidate, Whitaker and Baxter saw themselves as defenders of free enterprise against the steady encroachments of an overreaching state. Nowhere is this more evident than in their work to defeat proposals for government-provided health insurance, first in California and then on the national stage. Without Whitaker and Baxter, "socialized medicine" might not have become the politically loaded phrase it is today. However, the pair contributed more than a mere slogan to American politics. Whitaker and Baxter's work mobilizing doctors represented a new kind of issue advocacy, and their success promoting the virtues of private insurance shaped the trajectory of US health policy for decades to come.

Whitaker and Baxter's first battle in the health care wars began with the campaign to defeat Governor Earl Warren's plan for universal health coverage in California. Although Warren himself was a former client—Campaigns, Inc. managed his successful run for governor in 1942—Warren's national aspirations and liberal inclinations increasingly put him at odds with Whitaker and Baxter's conservative views. Preparing for a re-election campaign in 1946 and eyeing a possible presidential run in 1948, Warren embraced universal health care as an issue that could secure a record of accomplishment and raise his profile before a national electorate. With these goals in mind, Warren submitted a bill to the California Assembly in January 1945 to provide health care to Californians through a system of public insurance financed by a new payroll tax.[54] Although Warren anticipated some opposition to the plan from doctors, the medical profession in the state was poorly organized. In Carey McWilliams's words, doctors had "little political influence and a notoriously inept sense of public relations."[55] This was about to change dramatically.

Soon after Warren announced his health insurance plan, the California Medical Association (CMA) hired Campaigns, Inc. on a $25,000 annual retainer to coordinate opposition against the governor's bill.[56] As they had done in other campaigns, Whitaker and Baxter sought to mobilize opposition to the Warren Plan while building up public support for a well-defined alternative. More precisely, Whitaker and Baxter recommended that doctors embrace and promote voluntary private health insurance as an alternative to the public provision of care. Outlining their strategy in April 1945, Clem Whitaker warned the CMA that defeating the Warren Plan "will require more than just defensive action. . . . It will require affirmative action to make pre-paid medical and hospital service available to all the people on a voluntary basis . . . so that the proponents of government medicine will be stripped of all effective argument for their program of compulsion."[57] With widespread adoption of private insurance in California, Whitaker predicted that "compulsory health insurance will be dead as a legislative issue—and neither Governor Warren nor any other Governor will have the effrontery to disinter the remains."[58]

Whitaker and Baxter's plan required a fair bit of salesmanship, not least among doctors themselves. In the early 1940s, private health insurance covering hospitalization and medical services was still in its infancy. In 1939, the CMA created the nation's first Blue Shield plan, offering prepaid medical care through the California Physicians' Service (CPS). Public reception of prepaid care was fairly tepid, and many doctors remained opposed to any form of insurance, private or public, for fear that it would lead to negotiated prices and lower fees.[59] Whitaker and Baxter sought to change doctors' perception of private insurance, arguing that "we can think of no better protection the medical profession can have against . . . government regimentation than a strong, successful CPS."[60] Consequently, Whitaker and Baxter advised the CMA that the best way to defeat public health insurance was "to overcome all opposition to [private insurance] in the medical fraternity, so that the system can function effectively in every section of the State."[61] Their goal, in short, was "to develop and expand California Physicians Service, and all other acceptable voluntary medical and hospital systems, . . . [so] that the majority of the people, who need pre-paid health coverage, will have it before our campaign is ended."[62]

For the adoption of private health insurance to succeed, Whitaker and Baxter conceived a massive public relations campaign guided by a simple message: "The Voluntary Way Is the American Way."[63] As Whitaker and Baxter put it in their campaign literature, "There is nothing that Government can do for citizens in the field of health insurance which they cannot do better themselves—and do at less cost!"[64] But voluntary health insurance did more than protect against the costs of unexpected illness; it provided a vital bulwark against "a rigid system of government regimentation, conceived in goose-stepping Germany, [that is] utterly foreign to our American way of life."[65]

Whitaker and Baxter's portrayal of the Warren Plan as both a threat to the American health care system and a violation of deeply held American values tapped into the sentiments of a postwar public weary of price controls and wary, perhaps, of the growing reach of the modern state. Sensing these concerns, Whitaker and Baxter sought to convince doctors that their struggle against the Warren Plan had implications that reached beyond the borders of California. Outlining their strategy for the California Medical Society in 1946, Whitaker and Baxter wrote that the debate over health policy was "a crusade which will echo throughout the United States," adding that "California has been the testing ground for a great many visionary schemes and phony movements—but it has also become the burial ground for most of them," an oblique reference to their success in defeating Upton Sinclair's campaign for governor and, later, a statewide plan for old-age pensions.[66] In fact, California was a laboratory for a conservative message that would go on to shape national health care debates, from President Truman's campaign for universal coverage in 1948 to the contentious struggle over the Affordable Care Act in 2010. Whitaker and Baxter's extended influence over health policy attests to their skills in crafting messages, as well as their ability to intuit the preferences and prejudices of the public.

Whitaker and Baxter were guided by more than feel: their reading of opinion also relied on the latest techniques in survey research. In 1945, Campaigns, Inc. contracted a market research company, Knight and Parker Associates, to carry out a statewide survey of opinion about health insurance. As Whitaker and Baxter explained, the results of the survey provided "a preliminary test of some of the arguments which are effective in influencing public sentiment on this question."[67] In particular, Whitaker and Baxter discovered fairly wide support for public health insurance in principle but a widespread concern that "state medicine" would result in lower-quality care. According to Whitaker and Baxter, "This fear of incompetent doctors, inferior service and assembly-line medical methods undoubtedly represents the No. 1 argument against compulsory health insurance with rank and file voters."[68] At the same time, the Knight and Parker survey revealed that among respondents whose families were covered by private insurance, more than 70 percent were satisfied with their private plan.[69] As Whitaker and Baxter told the CMA, "The general public satisfaction with the service being rendered . . . would seem to indicate that a stepped-up drive to expand [private insurance] would be highly successful and would help spike the guns of those advocating compulsory [public insurance]."[70] In addition, the survey reported that women were more suspicious of public insurance than men, leading Whitaker and Baxter to conclude that "doctors' wives should play a vital part in lining up the leading women in their communities to . . . work against the [Warren Plan]."[71]

Bolstered by the survey results, Whitaker and Baxter used public concerns about the quality of care as the basis for a massive campaign to promote sales of private health insurance policies in California. Over a period of three years, Campaigns, Inc. spent $367,470 on pamphlets, newspaper advertisements, and even a dedicated weekly radio program extolling the virtues of private insurance.[72] The centerpiece of the publicity effort was Voluntary Health Insurance Week, a series of carefully planned events, public meetings, and advertising efforts designed to "dramatize the crusade" and attract "enthusiastic news and editorial support" for private health insurance.[73] Using a system of county campaign committees led by "an able, aggressive doctor," Voluntary Health Insurance Weeks transmitted a carefully crafted set of messages formulated by Whitaker and Baxter at their headquarters in San Francisco.[74] By 1948, fifty-three of fifty-eight counties held insurance weeks throughout the state.[75]

With meticulous precision, Whitaker and Baxter reported multiple measures of their success: more than 400 newspapers opposing public health insurance compared with only 20 in favor; 200 civic organizations and 100 chambers of commerce on record against public insurance; 120 mayors enrolled to serve as chairmen of Health Insurance Weeks; and tens of thousands of inches of newspaper space in advertising, news coverage, and editorials all opposed to the Warren Plan. Moreover, Whitaker and Baxter pointed out that since the Warren Plan nearly passed the California Assembly by a single vote in 1946, no bill on behalf of public insurance had even made it out of committee. Finally, Whitaker and Baxter took partial credit for the fact that membership in the California Physicians' Service had quadrupled since their publicity campaign began, while enrollment in private insurance schemes had doubled to more than 5 million people throughout the state.[76]

In spite of these developments, some members of the California Medical Association expressed concern that a public relations campaign diminished the professional standing of doctors. Others wondered if the extraordinary cost of these efforts was worth it. Rankled by such complaints, Whitaker and Baxter reiterated the high stakes involved. Responding to their critics in the CMA, Whitaker and Baxter wrote, "Your profession is in the front lines in one of the most critical struggles in the history of this Nation—a basic struggle between . . . socialism and capitalism. . . . Call it what you like, it is a war to the death."[77] Hyperbole aside, the continued skepticism toward Campaigns, Inc. and its methods testifies both to the novelty of their practices and the challenges Whitaker and Baxter faced in creating a powerful medical lobby in the United States. Drawing parallels between the medical profession and their own status as trained experts, Whitaker and Baxter informed their clients that "in public relations, as in medicine, it is of first importance that you have confidence in your doctor. And if at any time you lack that confidence, then you should change doctors."[78] At the same time, Whitaker and Baxter insisted that their methods were a critical weapon in the fight for free enterprise, upbraiding those physicians who held on to "the specious dogma that doctors shouldn't muddy their togas in the field of politics."[79] Instead, doctors needed to see themselves in common cause with other business interests fighting against the encroachments of the modern state. A sustained campaign of public relations waged through modern channels of communication was simply "the price of liberty" to maintain "the dignity of a free profession, [and] of men."[80]

If doctors had some doubts about their methods, others recognized the importance of Whitaker and Baxter's achievement. As Carey McWilliams put it, "Whitaker and Baxter [wrote] a political script in which doctors, originally cast as special-interest heavies, emerge[d] as crusaders for the people's health. This is expert political management; this is government by Whitaker and Baxter."[81] In fact, doctors around the country took notice; several directors of state medical societies requested material and advice from Campaigns, Inc. in waging their own fights against public health insurance.[82] And in 1949, when

President Truman staked his presidency on the enactment of a national health insurance plan, the American Medical Association came calling.

Whitaker and Baxter's work on behalf of the American Medical Association in many ways represents the apotheosis of all they had learned and accomplished in California. In both form and content, the campaign to defeat Truman's push for national health insurance reproduced many of the same themes and tactics the team successfully employed against Governor Warren several years earlier, only on a larger scale. Scholars have rightly viewed the AMA campaign as a pivotal moment in the history of American health policy.[83] In addition, the AMA fight against national health insurance marks a broader development in American politics: the rise of professionally managed issue advocacy campaigns. Although such tactics look familiar today, the AMA effort was remarkable for its time in both sophistication and scope.[84]

Whitaker and Baxter came to the attention of the AMA in 1948 as the prospects for a political breakthrough in national health insurance brightened. In May, Truman convened the National Health Assembly, at which he reiterated his commitment to improving the health and health care of all Americans. In September, Oscar Ewing, chairman of the Federal Security Administration, presented Truman with a report, *The Nation's Health—A Ten Year Program*, that outlined plans for a federal system of compulsory health insurance. With Truman's unexpected election victory in November and Democratic majorities in both chambers of Congress, the goal of national health insurance seemed within reach.[85]

Three weeks after the election, Clem Whitaker traveled to St. Louis, where he appeared before the National Medical Public Relations Conference. Organized under the auspices of the AMA, the meeting promoted the value of public relations techniques to the medical profession and included workshop sessions titled "Using Public Relations to Promote Medical Prepayment Plans" and "Selling the Need for Public Relations to State Medical Society Members."[86] Whitaker, who McWilliams described as "a masterful speaker and a superb salesman," used his appearance in St. Louis to convince the AMA leadership in attendance that Campaigns, Inc. should lead the effort against Truman's health plan.[87] A few weeks later, an AMA press release announced it had retained the firm "to direct the organization's forthcoming campaign against the threat of socialized medicine."[88] In February 1949, Whitaker and Baxter set up shop in Chicago, Illinois, home to AMA headquarters, and established the National Education Campaign. As their practice had been in California, Whitaker and Baxter demanded complete control over the campaign and its finances. To that end, the AMA levied a $25 assessment on each member. Although a minority withheld dues in opposition to the outright politicking of the AMA leadership, the organization quickly amassed an ample war chest of $2.25 million for the campaign.[89] For their part, Whitaker and Baxter received an annual fee of $100,000.[90]

As they had done in California, Whitaker and Baxter framed the issue as a choice between private health insurance and a compulsory, government-run program, the first step toward a creeping and dangerous socialism. Whitaker and Baxter even recycled some of the same language from the California campaign, using slogans such as "The Voluntary Way Is the American Way" to extol the virtues of private insurance as an alternative to public provision.[91] As before, the goal was to conjure images of government bureaucrats deciding who was to receive health care and when. "The challenging and tremendous task we have undertaken," Clem Whitaker told the AMA House of Delegates in 1949, "[is] to alert and awaken the American people to the danger which threatens them; to crystallize and mobilize public opinion, so that the people's mandate on this issue shall be unmistakable."[92]

In outlining their strategy, Whitaker and Baxter realized not only that health care touched upon very personal connections between patients and their doctor but that physicians themselves constituted a national network of highly respected "opinion leaders" who could carry the AMA message directly to the public.[93] To capitalize on this potential, Whitaker and Baxter directed much of their effort toward engaging doctors in the fight against national health insurance. As Leone Baxter put it, "The medical profession has a vitally important story to tell, and who in the world is to tell it ... with more truth or with more sincerity than doctors themselves?"[94] From campaign headquarters in Chicago, Whitaker and Baxter sent pamphlets to doctors throughout the country for distribution to their patients. Posters of the well-known painting by Luke Fildes of a doctor carefully attending to a sick child in his home as his grateful parents looked on hung in more than 40,000 physician waiting rooms, accompanied by the caption, "Keep Politics Out of This Picture!" As Baxter explained, "The painting of the doctor may be old fashioned in some respects. . . . But there is something in that picture which represents one of the most priceless possessions you men of medicine have in your whole fight against assembly line medicine . . . compassion."[95] It was this ability to craft compelling, impassioned appeals that made Whitaker and Baxter so effective. As Stanley Kelley put it, "They tried to present their case in a way that would have meaning to the individual citizen, to translate public issues into private emotions."[96]

In addition, Whitaker and Baxter understood how to convey their core message through all variety of media so as "to effect maximum reiteration . . . from as many apparently independent sources as possible."[97] Scores of pamphlets, press releases, and other literature were issued from the National Education Campaign to doctors, state medical societies, and women's auxiliaries made up of physicians' wives. As in California, Whitaker and Baxter paid particular attention to women as an influential group who were receptive to the message about the perils of national health insurance. As Whitaker explained, "Women are realizing they will not only pay their doctor bill under socialized medicine; but they will pay a double bill—for hordes of bookkeepers, clerks, bureaucrats, and personnel."[98] In addition, women feared "there would be a general deterioration of care" as a result of an "assembly-line type" of state medicine. Federations of Women's Clubs in nine states went on record against the Truman Plan.[99] Similarly, other groups believed to be receptive to Whitaker and Baxter's message received special appeals from the AMA. By the end of 1949, more than 1,800 allied organizations announced their opposition to national health insurance, with thousands more joining the ranks over the next three years. Newspaper editors received regular correspondence from the national campaign, while a publicity firm in Portland, Oregon, distributed canned editorials for reprint in rural newspapers.[100] A massive advertising buy attacking "socialized medicine" appeared in full-page display in 11,000 newspapers, while spot radio announcements ran on 1,000 stations across the country.[101] Explaining his strategy, Clem Whitaker wrote, "We want the terrific impact of all the media hitting at once," so that "medicine's story can be hammered home by repetition."[102] All of this was designed to convey the impression of massive, widespread support for the AMA position and the virtues of private health insurance.

According to Whitaker, such a broad-gauge effort was essential to counteract "the tremendous power of the government propaganda machine ... beating the drums for socialized medicine."[103] In truth, the AMA effort exceeded anything the Truman administration accomplished or even contemplated on its behalf. In 1949, the National Education Campaign distributed more than 54 million pieces of mail at a cost of over $1 million, with another 43 million pamphlets sent out the following year. In 1950, the AMA Board of Trustees approved an advertising budget of $1.1 million for newspapers, radio, and national magazines, most of it spent over a two-week period in advance of the midterm election.[104] According to *Congressional Quarterly*, the AMA spent a total of $3.6 million on the National Education Campaign between 1949 and 1952. During the first two years of the campaign alone, the AMA accounted for more than 15 percent of all reported lobbying expenditures, making doctors the best-financed and arguably the most formidable lobby of the day.[105]

In their work for the AMA, Whitaker and Baxter helped develop a new kind of advocacy in which a coalition of like-minded actors came together under the banner of a single issue. Success required, first and foremost, convincing physicians that their personal and economic interests could only be advanced through political organization. Speaking to an audience of doctors in 1949, Baxter underscored the "need to give a demonstration throughout the nation at this time of the unanimity of the medical profession."[106] The fate of doctors overseas under the National Health Service offered a cautionary tale. "The final force that crumpled British medicine," Baxter told the AMA in 1949, "was simply the inability to get together and stay together."[107] Complementing this strategy was the promotion of private insurance as an alternative not only to make public insurance less desirable but also to bring the insurance industry along in the effort. Health and accident insurance groups, sensing their stake in the issue, contributed significantly to the advertising campaign against the Truman Plan.[108]

As the pair learned in California, health care motivated a broader set of ideological concerns perfectly attuned to the growing postwar debate over the nature and scope of American government. The struggle against national health insurance concerned more than just doctors or the insurance industry. As Whitaker put it, "The concentration of power in Washington is frightening, and the constant reach for more power is unending. It is only a short step from the 'Welfare State' as our Washington planners envision to the 'Total State,' which taxes the wage earner into government enslavement, . . . stamps out incentive and soon crushes individual liberty."[109] This was a message with potentially broad appeal, and Whitaker and Baxter used the threat of national health insurance to enlist the support of a range of allied groups, including the American Farm Bureau Federation, the American Bar Association, and the National Association of Small Business.[110]

Emboldened by their success in defeating Truman's goals for national health insurance, Whitaker and Baxter sought to use health care as an electoral issue in congressional contests and as a way to organize groups on behalf of the Republican Party. According to Stanley Kelley, Whitaker prepared a campaign plan entitled "The Power of a Single Issue Aggressively Sold to the Voters" in which he outlined strategies to enlist doctors to work on behalf of Republican candidates.[111] This included examples of form letters doctors should send their patients encouraging them to vote for candidates who "consistently and firmly opposed compulsory sickness insurance," explaining that "you and your family will be far better off under voluntary plans . . . with complete freedom to choose your own doctor."[112] Other letters struck a more ominous tone: "Your doctor's service is being threatened by both the outside invasion of socialists who are trying to tell us how to vote in Tuesday's election and by the ideology of socialized medicine which the invaders are trying to force upon us."[113] In a special election in New York for the US Senate in 1949, doctors sent 2.4 million letters to patients urging them to vote against Democrat Herbert Lehman. Although Lehman won that race, Democratic candidates in Utah, Nebraska, and Wisconsin lost their seats in part due to the involvement of doctors.[114] These efforts on behalf of congressional candidates became a template for the 1952 Republican presidential election. With the National Education Campaign winding down, Whitaker and Baxter joined the former chairman of the AMA Coordinating Committee, Dr. Elmer Henderson, to form the National Professional Committee for Eisenhower and Nixon. Its goal, the *New York Times* reported, was to "enlist medical, dental, legal, engineering and other professional men and women" in support of the Republican ticket.[115]

More than sixty years later, the same strategies and tactics Whitaker and Baxter employed in the fight against national health insurance are evident in the ongoing struggle over health care reform. During debates over passage of the Affordable Care Act, the bugaboo of socialized medicine and government bureaucrats run amok resurfaced in the rumors of federal death panels that would supposedly dictate who among the elderly would receive care. In fact, the long shadow of Whitaker and Baxter extends beyond the rhetoric over health policy. Emboldened by their success against Truman, the AMA leadership embarked on an ambitious and at times arrogant political agenda that diminished support for the organization among doctors and led to declining political influence for the profession. As historian Christy Ford Chapin documents, AMA missteps would later haunt physicians as the insurance industry gained in strength, both politically and economically, at the expense of doctors who saw their power over the provision of care steadily erode.[116]

In fact, Whitaker and Baxter's influence over American politics extends even further. Unrealized at the time, Whitaker and Baxter foreshadowed the rise of the modern conservative movement in American politics.[117] By turning policy debates over health insurance into a Manichean struggle over personal freedom, Whitaker and Baxter at once set the outer limits of the New Deal state and developed a powerful message that would, in time, pay rich political dividends for the Republican Party. In what would become a core conservative strategy, Whitaker and Baxter leveraged the vast financial resources of American business to foster an antigovernment skepticism among the American people.

California: The Great Exception?

Whitaker and Baxter's work on behalf of the AMA showed that professional campaign management, first perfected in California, could be used effectively on the national stage. Yet it was not until the 1970s that political consulting spread fully throughout the country.

What, then, set Whitaker and Baxter apart? What explains the rise of Campaigns, Inc.? Without ascribing to a crude California exceptionalism, the Golden State did provide a rather conducive environment for the rise of a professional political class, as several astute observers have noted.[118] Understanding these unique features of California politics not only sheds light on the rise of political consulting but also illuminates a broader transformation underway in the style and substance of American politics.

First and foremost, there was an abundance of political work in California. Whitaker and Baxter fully capitalized on these opportunities, particularly the many ballot initiatives that regularly came before California voters. Between their first campaign together in 1933 and the election of Goodwin Knight in 1954 (arguably the zenith of Whitaker and Baxter's political influence), Campaigns, Inc. handled nearly half of all ballot measures in California, twenty-nine in all. Combined with candidate races and issue advocacy campaigns, Whitaker and Baxter secured a steady stream of clients that enabled them to overcome the feast-or-famine nature of political work.[119] Direct legislation also gave professional campaign managers like Whitaker and Baxter the opportunity to perfect their craft. Unlike candidate races, ballot measures afforded an extraordinary degree of control over the contours of a campaign. Issue framing, media strategy, and even fundraising all came under the direction of Campaigns, Inc. Moreover, ballot initiatives generally avoided the risk of scandal or unscripted moments that often accompanied electoral campaigns. As one California consultant put it, "I would much rather have a nice, clean proposition than a candidate anytime ... no proposition ever made an ass of itself on national television."[120] Ballot initiatives enabled consultants to conduct campaigns largely as they saw fit and without the approval of a candidate or his circle of close supporters.

Another distinctive feature of California politics was the weakness of party organizations and the geographic scale of statewide races. These factors combined to encourage the early development, and dependence on, media-intensive campaigns using newspapers, radio, and direct mail to reach loosely organized voters dispersed across the state. In particular, California served as a testing ground for the use of television in political communication. Like the advent of radio in the

1930s, television prompted a series of adjustments in campaign practices. During Goodwin Knight's 1954 race for governor, Whitaker and Baxter asked one of their associates to research the value of television as a campaign medium. His conclusion, based on media surveys, audience measurement studies, and interviews with station managers and advertising representatives, was that television held great promise as a way to project "the candidate's personal characteristics and personality . . . into the living rooms of the voters."[121] Television, in other words, was an ideal medium for candidate-focused campaigns, but it competed with other demands on the attention of the audience. Consequently, to be effective television required high-frequency advertising to reach the voter. In the Knight campaign for governor, Whitaker and Baxter invested heavily in TV advertising, running a total of 1,329 one-minute spots on each of California's twenty-eight stations.[122]

Mass communication, including television, did not come cheaply. In fact, an important element of Whitaker and Baxter's success was the large sums of money they controlled through the conduct of media-intensive campaigns. Earl Warren's successful 1942 campaign for governor cost in excess of $1 million; Whitaker and Baxter's budget for Goodwin Knight's 1954 primary race alone was $600,000. Ballot initiatives were expensive as well. A single mailing to each of California's 6 million registered voters might cost $360,000, while an effective campaign for one of the lesser statewide campaigns might cost upwards of $300,000.[123] The high cost of California campaigns enabled Whitaker and Baxter to occupy a critical position between their clients and various media outlets in search of advertising revenue. As a result, Whitaker and Baxter became the conduit through which powerful interests sought influence in California politics.

The cost of campaigns points to a third important feature of California politics: the existence of a wealthy business community willing to engage in political action to promote and defend its economic interests. In mid-century California, electoral politics became a vital instrument of business influence. Although traditional forms of lobbying continued, various business groups depended on the ballot box to defeat direct legislation that threatened their interests or to elect candidates friendly to their cause. Understanding this, Whitaker and Baxter became adept at organizing campaigns on behalf of trade associations or industry groups, using the fear of an encroaching state to secure the financial backing necessary to spread their message about the dangers of a government unchecked. Whitaker and Baxter's approach, especially the heavy emphasis on media, likely appealed a great deal to their clients, many of whom had grown accustomed to marketing and advertising techniques as an essential component of modern business methods. This made it easier for Whitaker and Baxter to convince their clients that a carefully planned political campaign offered a better return on investment than indiscriminately showering elected officials with cash and favors.

Together, the preponderance of direct legislation, media-intensive campaigns, and an array of politically active business interests made it possible to earn a great deal of money in California politics. In fact, Whitaker and Baxter were not the only ones to reap such rewards, even if they were the first to realize its possibilities. In Southern California, Herbert Baus, a former publicity director for the Los Angeles Chamber of Commerce, formed his own consulting shop in 1946. Recalling his start in the business, Baus remarked how an associate told him, "There's a lot of gold out there in political campaigns," referring in particular to Whitaker and Baxter's success up north. Several years later, Baus joined with William Ross, the owner of a small advertising business, to form Baus and Ross Campaigns.[124] Like Whitaker and Baxter, Baus and Ross supplemented even-year elections with off-year mayoral races, city council elections, and other local political campaigns. In fact, there was enough business in California, and the politics sufficiently distinct, that the two firms effectively split the state in two: Baus and Ross handled the southland while Campaigns, Inc. managed affairs up north. On occasion, the two firms worked together, dividing responsibilities for statewide campaigns as they did for Richard Nixon's 1960 presidential campaign.[125] However, the campaign business was not always so amicable.[126] William Ross recalled that after working a few campaigns with Whitaker and Baxter, "they began to fear us, and we went our separate ways."[127] California may have been a land rich in opportunities, but these early consultants were keen to defend their slice of the pie.

In other words, a market for political services developed earlier and to a greater degree in California than in other parts of the country. Alongside full-service firms like Campaigns, Inc., the state also supported several small polling firms, as well as a lucrative business that specialized in acquiring and certifying signatures for ballot initiatives.[128] Moreover, the success of firms like Campaigns, Inc. attracted others seeking a fortune in politics. In the 1960s, the duo of Stuart Spencer and William Roberts achieved prominence for their work on behalf of Nelson Rockefeller in the 1964 California primary and their management of Ronald Reagan's successful campaign for governor in 1966. As Spencer put it, "Bill [Roberts] and I decided that we'd watch Whitaker and Baxter [and] we'd watch Baus and Ross. . . . [W]e assumed those guys made money and we thought that's a much better way to go into politics."[129] The financial rewards notwithstanding, early consultants were not simply political mercenaries lacking in partisan commitment. According to William Roberts, "We stayed with Republican campaigns because that was what we believed." Yet Roberts also acknowledged that "you can't be a political whore to the extent that you go both ways [working for both parties]. If you do, who trusts you?"[130] Ideological consistency was good politics and good business.

The partisan nature of political work meant that even in California the opportunities to make a living depended on what side of the street you worked. Before the 1960s, political consulting flourished more on the political right than on the left. With few exceptions, the leading consulting firms like Campaigns, Inc., Baus and Ross Campaigns, and Spencer-Roberts were all closely associated with Republican issues, interests, and candidates.[131] Democratic-affiliated consultants such as Joe Cerrell became important figures in California politics after the 1958 election, when Pat Brown's victory in the gubernatorial race that year ushered in a new era for California Democrats and, simultaneously, opened up opportunities for party operatives like Cerrell and others to create consulting businesses of their own.[132]

The Republican-tilting character of professional campaign management suggests that consulting grew out of a distinct political economy in California. Absent a formal party organization at the grass roots and with a powerful business community seeking to preserve its hold on state government, individual firms, local chambers of commerce, and trade and professional associations assumed an important role in political campaigns. In fact, business groups provided the earliest opportunities for professional campaign managers. Both Leone Baxter and

Herbert Baus began their careers managing publicity for local chambers of commerce before specializing in political campaigns. Baus used his connections promoting commercial development in Southern California to secure campaign work on bond issues and ballot initiatives that concerned the business community in Los Angeles.[133] Much of Whitaker and Baxter's work was on behalf of California business interests as well, whether it was stopping Upton Sinclair's insurgent campaign in 1934, blocking ballot initiatives that would have weakened private utilities' control over electricity, or promoting private insurance as an alternative to Governor Earl Warren's health care plan. In sum, the booming postwar economy in California coupled with the organizational weakness of the Republican Party created ample amounts of political work largely managed outside of a regular party structure.

Constituting Interests

In a career together that spanned the middle third of the twentieth century, Clem Whitaker and Leone Baxter showed one could live exclusively from politics as well as for it. In doing so, Whitaker and Baxter built considerably on the innovations that preceded them. Like Edward Bernays, for example, Whitaker and Baxter communicated to their clients the professional nature of political work as they nurtured public relations' "precocious baby."[134] Like Charles Michelson, Whitaker and Baxter exploited the political advantages of attacking an opponent at a time when the personal qualities of candidates were increasingly important. And like Hadley Cantril and Gerard Lambert, Whitaker and Baxter understood that polls afforded much more than a simple barometer of public sentiment; survey research offered a way to target and trim their message, enabling one to construct majorities out of a highly differentiated public. What truly set Whitaker and Baxter apart from these early innovators was their ability to place professional campaign management on a sounder financial footing.

California presented distinct opportunities in this regard, but the state also foreshadowed the kind of issue-focused campaigns and the partisan networks of candidates, activists, and allied groups that characterize American politics today. Whitaker and Baxter illustrate how the professional control of political work contributed to these changes in the character of American politics. For-profit firms like Campaigns, Inc. performed the critical task of building electoral coalitions out of groups motivated by discrete issues and demands, turning diffuse and inchoate interests into organized blocs of support for a particular policy goal or on behalf of a specific candidate. Whitaker and Baxter anticipated this new form of issue-driven politics in which professional consultants play a central role in the constitution of political interests.[135]

Whitaker and Baxter reveal another critical component in the rise of political consulting. Money matters. The early appearance of a consulting industry in California depended in part on the extraordinary financial resources available, especially from a business community anxious about the encroachments of an activist government. Absent this ability to tap into a rich and largely unregulated vein of campaign spending, it is unlikely that Whitaker and Baxter or those who emulated them could have stayed in business for long. In the words of the California pol Jesse Unruh, "Money is the mother's milk of politics."[136] Consulting became a viable enterprise, first in California and eventually elsewhere throughout the country, once two conditions held: a steady demand for professional campaign services and a large supply of cash to acquire them.

6

Advertising Politics

THE SUCCESS OF CAMPAIGNS, INC. in California pointed to the financial and political promise of consulting. Exploiting a mix of frequent ballot initiatives, a politically engaged business sector, and a widely dispersed population, Whitaker and Baxter perfected a model of issue-focused, media-savvy campaigns. By the late 1950s, in fact, a number of other full-time firms had set up shop in California, seeking to emulate Whitaker and Baxter's success. Although California provided a conducive environment for the business of politics to take shape, practitioners still had to convince their clients of their worth. Hard work and salesmanship were required at every step.

This hard work is especially evident when we look beyond California to the gradual professionalization of political campaigns across the country. As careful observers noted at the time, paid experts were beginning to play a greater role in elections during the 1950s and 1960s. However, professional involvement varied in different states and regions, at different levels of government, and in some respects even between the two main political parties. In addition, multiple sources of expertise were active in the political marketplace. Alongside a few specialized consulting firms like Campaigns, Inc., commercial public relations and advertising firms also frequently took on political clients.

This variation illustrates how the control of political work remained up for grabs in the 1950s and 1960s. Although political and technological changes combined to create new commercial opportunities for those skilled in the practical work of campaigns, it remained unclear exactly who should provide these services and how. In the case of television, for example, national advertising firms initially took the lead in adapting the medium to the needs of the candidate. As they did with commercial clients, ad agencies secured contracts with presidential campaigns to produce and place political advertisements on television. However, the growing prominence of commercial firms in presidential politics sparked criticism, renewing concerns about a mass public that could be easily misled. Candidates were eager to avoid appearing too close to Madison Avenue, while the advertising industry itself began to question the commercial value of political campaigns. Ill-suited to the partisan nature of political work, commercial advertising firms eventually turned away from campaigns altogether, setting the stage for the growth of the political consulting industry in the 1970s and 1980s.

Political Public Relations

Few political scientists writing in the 1950s and 1960s paid much attention to the actual conduct of political work. Advances in survey research had revealed that individuals held rather durable attachments to one party or the other, leading many prominent scholars of the time to conclude that efforts to sway opinions during the course of a campaign had marginal effects at best.[1] If elections mostly reflected voters' partisan identities, there seemed to be little point in studying the practical side of politics.

However, scholars who cared to look discovered an important transformation underway as politicians and political parties incorporated new technologies, such as television, and experimented with new techniques intended to bring voters out to the polls. Even if most citizens made up their minds weeks, or even months, before the first Tuesday in November, candidates and their campaigns pressed hard up until the very end to make sure their supporters turned out to vote. Political scientists who studied the strategies and resources deployed during a campaign found paid professionals taking an increasingly important role in the American political system.

One such scholar was Stanley Kelley, who wrote an early assessment of this shift in his book *Professional Public Relations and Political Power* (1956). An outgrowth of his PhD dissertation, Kelley's book described the growing use of public relations and advertising in political campaigns, from Whitaker and Baxter's rise in California through the innovative use of television in the 1952 presidential election. However, it is Kelley's retelling of the 1950 Maryland Senate race that perhaps best illustrates the changing character of political work.[2]

The 1950 election pitted four-term incumbent Democrat Millard Tydings against a political newcomer, John Marshall Butler, a Baltimore lawyer, in his first campaign for elected office. Tydings appeared to be a safe bet to win a fifth term: serving in the Senate since 1927, Tydings won his previous election by a margin of more than 130,000 votes in a state that was 70 percent registered Democrats.[3] In 1950, however, Tydings chaired a Senate subcommittee that investigated Senator Joseph McCarthy's allegations of Communists in the State Department. When the Tydings Committee concluded that McCarthy's claims of Communist infiltration were "a fraud and a hoax," the Republican senator from Wisconsin and his conservative allies targeted Tydings in his bid for re-election.[4] Four months later, Butler defeated the incumbent senator by more than 40,000 votes.[5]

Stung by defeat, Tydings claimed he was the victim of smear tactics and dirty tricks, a charge that prompted a Senate investigation into the alleged use of "scurrilous and untrue printed matter designed to deceive the electorate."[6] At issue was a photo distributed by the Butler campaign that purported to show Tydings in conversation with a former Communist leader.[7] The picture was a fake: separate images had been joined in a composite made to look as if Tydings and the man were together. In the Senate investigation that followed, attention turned to Jon Jonkel, a public relations man from Chicago hired to run the Butler campaign for a fee of $1,250 a month.[8] Jonkel denied authorizing the photo, or even recalling paying for it, but his work on Butler's Senate race drew attention to the role of paid outsiders in the conduct of campaigns.

Jonkel joined Butler's staff on the recommendation of Ruth McCormick Miller, editor of the conservative *Washington Times-Herald* and a supporter of Joseph McCarthy. Although Jonkel lacked any previous campaign experience, he astutely perceived that Tydings had failed to appreciate how his actions against McCarthy played back home. This weakness formed the basis of Jonkel's campaign strategy. As Jonkel explained during testimony before a Senate subcommittee, "Senator Tydings may have conducted the loyalty hearings in a way that would satisfy a reviewing judge. . . . But there was another place that he was working and that was in the court of public opinion, and there he very obviously did not satisfy the people."[9] Maryland voters may have doubted whether Communists really infiltrated the State Department, but McCarthy's accusation that Tydings had "whitewashed" his committee's report raised questions as well. Jonkel turned this lingering doubt into the central theme of the campaign: "We worked with the fact that a very, very big doubt existed in the minds of the people of Maryland. . . . I said, 'Let's not get into the business of proving whether or not it was a whitewash, let's stay in the business that a doubt does exist.' "[10]

Stanley Kelley described Jonkel as "an able public relations man" whose strategy of "merchandising doubt" about the incumbent's integrity helped to peel away supporters of Tydings, especially African American voters, who overwhelmingly supported the Republican Butler in 1950.[11] Working on behalf of an unknown challenger with limited resources, Jonkel made the most of what he had by drawing upon a range of techniques and technologies. Jonkel even conducted rudimentary surveys in order to identify his opponent's chief weakness and craft his candidate's messages accordingly. When Tydings bombarded the radio airwaves with lengthy five- and ten-minute programs in the closing days of the race, Jonkel ran cheaper thirty-second spots just before and after each broadcast that raised questions about the senator's record.[12]

These were the tools of modern public relations, and they proved to be more effective than the traditional methods of a political machine. In fact, Kelley argued that Tydings's reliance on local party operatives led him to overlook how precarious his position was with the voters until it was too late.[13] As Kelley put it, a machine politician like Tydings was reluctant "to give central authority to a man who did not have intimate knowledge of, and involvement in," local politics.[14] In the end, however, it was the outsider Jonkel who had the edge, an experienced public relations professional accustomed to "stepping from a train or a plane and organizing . . . a campaign to crystallize public attitudes."[15] With Jonkel's help, Butler was "better prepared to meet the problems of mass communication politics than ... Tydings and the Democrats," despite lacking a viable party organization from which to draw support.[16] In Jonkel, Kelley saw how "the old methods of the political machine are superseded by the newer ones of the mass media specialist."[17] The lesson, Kelley concluded, is that "the politician whose thinking has been dominated by the logic of the boss ... [is] guilty of idolizing an ephemeral technique."[18]

The Senate report issued in August 1951 denounced the involvement of "outside influences" in the race, including Jonkel and several of McCarthy's aides who took part in the effort to defeat Tydings. Criticizing what it called "a big doubt campaign," the Senate report went on to describe the use of tactics designed to "undermine and destroy the public faith and confidence in the basic American loyalty of a well-known figure."[19] In effect, Jonkel ran a successful negative campaign. This, by itself, was not illegal; however, the Senate investigation also revealed that Jonkel deposited campaign contributions directly in his personal bank account on more than one occasion. Moreover, Jonkel's outsider status ran afoul of Maryland's Corrupt Practices Act that barred nonresidents from running a political campaign in the state. Following the Senate investigation, Jonkel pleaded guilty to six violations of state election law and paid a fine of $5,000.[20] Jonkel never worked in politics again, an unwitting pawn in the larger battle over McCarthyism, but his controversial tactics would eventually become commonplace in the conduct of American campaigns.[21]

Uneven Development

If Jon Jonkel represented the future of American politics, the degree to which candidates hired paid experts or embraced new technologies like television varied considerably during the 1950s. At the national level, for example, the Republican Party had a fairly sophisticated communications operation by the mid-1950s, prompting Stanley Kelley to observe that the publicity arm of the Republican National Committee operated, in effect, like "commercial public relations agencies performing political functions."[22] The Democratic Party, in contrast, lacked the same in-house capacity, and party leaders encouraged candidates "to retain professional advertising and publicity experts" on their own.[23]

If both parties recognized the value of professional advice, Republicans were a bit more adept in meeting this new reality, a view supported by recent work showing how Eisenhower's victory in 1952 commenced an active period of Republican party building.[24]

Things looked much different at the state and local levels. According to Kelley, an informal survey of state party chairmen revealed that in seventeen states "the use of public relations men in campaigns is increasing," mostly in statewide races for the US Senate, governor, and the occasional presidential campaign.[25] State and local races, on the other hand, remained largely amateur affairs. As an informant from Washington state put it, "Frankly, the kind of assistance given in most political campaigns, other than top level, are second rate practitioners picking up an odd dollar and usually contributing very little."[26] This suggests that a great deal of political work still rested in the hands of individuals whose professional claims were more of an aspiration than a reality.

We gain a more complete picture from political scientist Alexander Heard, whose landmark study of campaign finance, *The Costs of Democracy* (1960), offers key insights into broad changes in American politics during the 1950s.[27] Working as a consultant to the Senate Subcommittee on Privileges and Elections, Heard had access to thousands of pages of documents detailing political contributions and expenditures made during the 1952 and 1956 campaign cycles.[28] Heard also gathered his own data on the changing character of political campaigns and the growing influence of professional staff to run them.

In 1957, for example, Heard surveyed members of the Public Relations Society of America, sending questionnaires to 200 firms around the country asking them about the extent of their involvement in political campaigns. Of the 130 firms that replied, 60 percent responded that they had conducted some kind of political work during the previous five years. Services ranged from purchasing advertising space or airtime to preparation of publicity material, fundraising, and general campaign strategy. A third of the firms reported that they offered complete campaign management services, as Whitaker and Baxter did in California.[29] Heard also found that firms were active at all levels of government, from mayor all the way up to president of the United States. In fact, two-thirds of the campaigns that involved public relations firms took place at the state and local levels. Heard also found a great deal of regional variation: 70 percent of active firms worked in just seven states and the District of Columbia.[30] In a separate survey of state party chairmen, Heard found that around one-third of state party committees employed a public relations firm at some point in 1956 or 1957.[31] Advertising firms also found ample work in several states, working in thirteen states during the 1952 campaign cycle, where they accounted for 40 percent of disbursements by state and local committees.[32]

In discerning some pattern from these findings, Heard concluded that "public relations firms seem to play their most important organizational roles in states of weak party organization." California was emblematic of this trend as its "lush, chaotic politics ... afforded enormous opportunities for anyone who could provide a sensible and economical way to run a political campaign."[33] However, Heard cautioned against the view that somehow professional campaign services and robust state party organizations were mutually exclusive. Instead, he found that "no wholesale displacement of party functionaries has occurred sufficient to convert political campaigns into contests between advertising firms."[34] In fact, both Heard and Kelley found a number of state party committees that worked closely with public relations and advertising firms. In some places, in fact, the Republican Party used public relations firms to circumvent state campaign finance laws that banned corporate contributions to political candidates. According to one Republican state finance chairman, the party regularly used public relations firms on corporate retainer to provide services directly to GOP candidates. As Heard explained, this practice exploited a loophole in state campaign finance law by enabling public relations firms to "do political campaign work as part of their responsibility to their employer."[35] Rather than being antithetical to party organizations, political professionals provided a vital connection between parties, candidates, and allied groups—especially business interests.

However, it is important to remember that the use of professional services like media and polling was rather uneven and quite limited in the 1950s, especially compared with the present day. This was particularly the case for congressional campaigns, as illustrated by the results of a survey conducted in 1958 by University of Michigan political scientists Warren Miller and Donald Stokes.[36] Although most House candidates reported using at least some radio and television in their campaign, only 13 percent considered it to be of primary importance in reaching voters. Polling was even less common. Only 40 percent of candidates used surveys at all, and less than 5 percent considered polls to be the chief way of finding out about district opinion.[37] Overall, less than 10 percent of candidates were heavy users of polls, radio, or television, while more than a third of candidates ran for Congress with little or no polling or media at all.[38] To put this in perspective, in the 2014 campaign more than 75 percent of House candidates spent at least $100,000 on media, polls, and direct mail; among incumbents running for re-election, more than 90 percent of candidates spent $100,000 or more on the services of professional consultants.[39]

Televising Politics

Despite this uneven growth, paid professionals were occupying a larger role in the conduct of political campaigns. In the 1950s, television provided another avenue for paid political work. In 1956, according to Alexander Heard, television surpassed radio in overall campaign spending.[40] Between 1952 and 1956, in fact, Heard found that total spending on television in political campaigns increased from $2.9 to $6.5 million, more than twice what was spent on radio that year. This growth is even more remarkable when compared with the trend in overall campaign spending during the same four-year period. Whereas spending on television increased by 80 percent in real terms, overall campaign costs actually declined by 10 percent between Eisenhower's two elections.[41]

As was the case with radio, the political use of television created new opportunities for those able to sell products and services over the airwaves. In particular, the growing reliance on political spots gave a more prominent role to advertising agencies, especially in the conduct of presidential campaigns. Stanley Kelley described this process in detail in his account of the 1952 Eisenhower campaign. Under the guidance of Robert Humphreys, public relations director for the Republican National Committee, the Eisenhower campaign made television the centerpiece of its communication strategy. As Humphreys put it in a strategy memo written in August 1952, "TV offers the best, if the most expensive medium to carry the personalities of the candidates to the firesides of America."[42] In particular, Humphreys believed television was the best way to reach the "stay-at-home" voter who, if mobilized, could turn the tide for the GOP. In addition to covering the candidates as they traveled across the country, Humphreys advocated "informal, intimate television productions addressed directly to the individual American and his family" using "the best directional and technical facilities ... to achieve maximum utilization of the assets" of the Republican ticket.[43] Humphreys placed special emphasis on televised "spots" during the closing days of the campaign.

To that end, Humphreys secured the services of three prominent firms to handle the campaign's television needs: the Kudner Agency; Batten, Barton, Durstine and Osborn (BBD&O); and Ted Bates and Company. As Kelley described it, "The Republicans bought political experience as well as advertising skills."[44] Several of these firms boasted veteran campaigners among their ranks; BBD&O, in particular, helped create political television on behalf of Thomas E. Dewey in 1948 and had worked on the Senate races of Republicans Robert A. Taft and John Foster Dulles.[45] In 1952, BBD&O's work for Eisenhower included time buying, outreach to local media, and ad production. The Kudner Agency provided a number of television advance men to cover rallies and produce studio shows as Eisenhower and Nixon toured the country.[46] Meanwhile, the creation of a series of spot advertisements was the work of Rosser Reeves, a partner in Ted Bates and Company. It was Reeves who argued that spot advertisements would be more effective than a lengthy speech at garnering voters' attention and therefore would better serve Eisenhower in the closing weeks of the campaign.[47]

Experts in public opinion and audience measurement also figured prominently in campaign decisions about television strategy. For example, George Gallup's polling firm tested several possible campaign themes to gauge which ones resonated with the public. Using the results, Reeves produced a series of now-famous television spots in which Eisenhower criticized the Democratic record on taxes, inflation, and the war in Korea.[48] In addition, the Nielson Marketing Service furnished the campaign with an extensive report in October 1952 that included detailed analysis of key television markets in order to assess when and where campaign spots should be aired. As Nielson explained in its report, "The planning and execution of a comprehensive

Radio-TV campaign is a task of great complexity, requiring the combined experience, facilities and services of an advertising agency, a program producer ... and an audience research organization."[49] In other words, the political use of television required professionals who could determine the efficient use of campaign resources.

For their part, Democrats also made use of television in 1952, with the Baltimore-based advertising firm Joseph Katz and Company handling most of the duties. Although overall television spending by the two major candidates was similar, there were some notable differences between how Stevenson and the Democrats approached the task compared with his Republican competitors. Rather than focus on spots, the Stevenson campaign invested heavily in half-hour television programs. To save money, the Democrats bought airtime months in advance (to avoid expensive fees networks charged to preempt already filmed programs) and purchased cheaper, late-evening slots, hoping viewers would continue to watch political programming after their shows ended at ten o'clock. As Edwin Diamond and Stephen Bates put it sarcastically, the Democratic television strategy was "ideally suited to the radio age."[50] Audience numbers did not materialize as hoped, nor did the intellectual Stevenson make for engaging television.[51]

Democratic miscues signaled differences in how each party approached the political use of television.[52] The Republican emphasis on spots permitted a much more strategic use of the new medium and the ability to target specific audiences in areas of the country thought to be receptive to the Republican message. When Rosser Reeves presented his plan for spot advertisements to the Eisenhower campaign, it included a market analysis that identified forty-nine counties in twelve states Reeves believed could tip the balance of the election.[53] Spot ads saturated cities like New York in the hope that Eisenhower could cut into urban Democratic support and magnify the Republican advantage in rural and suburban areas.[54] By contrast, the Democrats relied on nationally televised broadcasts that did not make use of campaign resources in a targeted or strategic way. This difference may reflect the different roles advertising firms played in the respective campaigns. Whereas firms like BBD&O or Ted Bates enjoyed a degree of control over various elements of Republican television strategy, from ad production to placement, Democratic advertising firms like Katz and Company were mostly "limited to purely technical functions," prompting Stanley Kelley to conclude, "There is little evidence that the Democratic publicity professionals exercised important influence on these strategy decisions made by Stevenson and his principal advisors."[55]

As election postmortems highlighted Eisenhower's use of television, critics lamented the creeping political influence of advertising and public relations. One trade publication placed the number of admen working on both presidential campaigns at well over a hundred.[56] The *Wall Street Journal* reported that "a private group of public relations men, former businessmen, and statistical experts" who helped guide Republican campaign strategy in November was hoping to move its operation into the White House. Working under the name Research Associates, the team offered the new president "scientific analysis of public opinion," so that the administration could "influence the public mind." The *Journal* dubbed Eisenhower's team, with its frequent televised press conferences and planned communication strategies, "the most-public-relations-conscious-administration in history."[57] Others studied the new president and wondered, "Can government be merchandised?"[58] As the salesmanship of the campaign carried over to the White House, it appeared "as though, having created . . . the TV character Likeable Ike, his sponsors found it expedient to continue the installments of his adventures."[59] Popular culture took notice of these political developments as well. The comedic novel *The Golden Kazoo* (1956) portrayed the presidential contest of the future as a battle between Madison Avenue advertising firms. Media manipulation took a darker, more dramatic turn in Elia Kazan's film *A Face in the Crowd* (1957), in which Andy Griffith plays an accidental celebrity who parlays his success as a television personality and pitchman to muster public support on behalf of a presidential candidate.[60]

The fear that advertising debased the democratic process is a familiar trope in American politics. Theodore Roosevelt observed how Mark Hanna "advertised McKinley as if he were a patent medicine."[61] Half a century later, Adlai Stevenson complained that the attempt to "merchandise candidates for high office like breakfast cereal is the ultimate indignity."[62] What changed in the interim, apart from the medium, was the increasing number and prominence of paid experts "who trade in the coin of politics."[63] To scholars such as Kelley and Heard, this reflected the increasing reliance on mass communications to turn out the vote. Even if "the public relations man has replaced the political boss as an object of opprobrium," Heard noted soberly, "whether rated good or bad, [he] . . . fills a functional need in political operations."[64] In fact, Heard observed, these "specialists in persuasion" increasingly occupied "a place among the elite corps of American society."[65] Kelley concurred: "As those who aim at control of government come to regard mass persuasion as their central problem, then the specialist in mass persuasion will rise correspondingly in influence. . . . The public relations man is both a beneficiary of this change and a kind of signal that it is taking place."[66]

Yet a purely functional analysis that sees the rise of professional advice as following directly from the requirements of mass media obscures the salesmanship that accompanied these changes in political technique. As Heard explained, "Public relations has become a label of convenience covering any kind of freewheeling political activity" as those "with a bent for politics" used the professional moniker as "a vocational base from which to sell their political services."[67] In fact, the political use of television spread widely without much hard evidence that it was effective. In 1955, future Nobel laureate Herbert Simon published one of the first studies on the electoral effects of television. Along with a coauthor, Simon compared voting behavior in 1952 in several Iowa counties, some with access to television and some without. After analyzing data on turnout and the share of the Republican vote, Simon found virtually no difference between the counties with television and those where the new medium had yet to penetrate.[68]

The Rise and Fall of Madison Avenue

According to author Joe McGinnis, Richard Nixon's 1968 campaign elevated the Madison Avenue advertising executive to new heights in presidential politics. As McGinnis describes in his well-known account of the campaign, *The Selling of the President, 1968*, Nixon relied on "a group of young men attuned to the political uses of television" who transformed a "grumpy, cold, and aloof" candidate into an image that appealed to a broad swath of voters.[69] Leading the effort was Harry Treleaven, a former vice president at the J. Walter Thompson agency who, in a memo to the campaign, pushed for "imaginative approaches" and "contemporary techniques" to communicate Nixon's strengths while at the same time avoiding "any obvious gimmicks that say 'Madison Ave. at work here.'"[70] According to McGinnis, Treleaven and Nixon were made for each other. Politics and advertising were both a kind of con game, so it came as no surprise that "politicians and advertising men should have discovered one another."[71] With the increasing sophistication of television campaigns since Eisenhower, those responsible for media strategy became a central part of the candidate's inner circle. As McGinnis put it, "The ad men . . . were given a suite upstairs."[72]

If Treleaven represented the political rise of the adman, his desire to avoid the appearance of Madison Avenue "gimmicks" is revealing. In fact, the 1968 election marks the beginning of a decline in the political influence of big advertising firms. During the 1950s and 1960s, commercial agencies jockeyed with one another to land a presidential campaign just as they competed over lucrative corporate accounts. By the 1970s, however, Madison Avenue had mostly turned away from politics. This transition sheds important light on the growth of the political consulting industry, especially the comparative advantage consultants enjoyed over their competitors for control of political work. In particular, advertising firms were less suited to the partisan nature of campaigns than were the political consultants who eventually replaced them.

Initially, political campaigns attracted advertising firms in search of new sources of revenue and a degree of prestige that came from working on a presidential contest. Surveys conducted by the Federal Communications Commission (FCC) showed that station charges for political programs grew at an annual rate of almost 10 percent each year between 1956 and 1968. To put this in perspective, commercial TV ad revenue grew by a modest 2 percent annually, and overall campaign costs remained essentially unchanged during this same period. Much of this growth in political spending on television came from ads, which registered a fivefold increase in real terms between 1956 and 1968.[73]

As television spending rose, so did the money flowing to advertising agencies responsible for the production and placement of campaign commercials. In 1952, two firms, Joseph Katz and Company and the Kudner Agency, each billed more than $1 million in ads to the national Democratic and Republican committees, respectively.[74]

In fact, advertising agencies earned comparable sums earlier in the twentieth century for handling newspaper publicity and radio broadcasts on behalf of the national parties. What changed with the advent of television, however, was that advertising agencies exercised greater control over the content and character of the campaign as presidential candidates and national party committees turned to large commercial advertising firms to handle the creation, production, and placement of political media on a contract basis.

Advertising firms appeared to be a natural place to locate such expertise. Advertisers had ample experience with national campaigns for consumer products and services, and they possessed the creative insight and technical know-how to produce the kind of punchy, memorable ads suitable for television. Most large agencies also knew how to integrate market research and media production, translating survey data into crafted messages that grabbed the attention of the consumer (and voter). As one experienced adman put it, the purpose of an opinion poll is not to find out which candidate voters prefer; rather, surveys could reveal "what [the voters] are troubled about and what are the issues."[75] Political campaigns also offered advertising agencies an additional source of revenue. When Democrats announced the selection of Guild, Bascom & Bonfigli, Inc. to handle advertising for the 1960 presidential campaign, the deal was expected to produce about $3 million in extra billings for the firm, or around one-quarter of its annual revenue.[76] In 1968, the executive in charge of the Nixon account speculated that "total billing could run anywhere from $4 million to $15 million."[77] Signing on to a presidential campaign also raised the profile of an agency as newspaper coverage of the advertising industry routinely included information about which firms were retained by political clients, especially in presidential years.[78]

However, the growing political prominence of advertising firms also led to concerns about inappropriate influence over the issue positions taken by candidates and elected officials. Although the advertising industry worked hard to avoid such perceptions, close association between a politician and an advertising agency could present a political liability nevertheless.[79] During the Eisenhower years, for example, White House critics charged that advertisers dictated how the administration interacted with the public. In 1957, former president Harry

Truman criticized a televised address by President Eisenhower and Secretary of State John Foster Dulles by quipping that the initials of the advertising firm BBD&O (which handled Ike's television needs in 1952 and 1956) stood for "Bunko, Bull, Deceit, and Obfuscation."[80] In fact, both parties relied on advertising firms for election advice, and both parties sought to avoid the appearance that admen played an outsize role in crafting political strategy. Thus, the Republican Party worked hard "to dissociate itself from any stigma that may be attached to Madison Avenue."[81] Similarly, Democratic operatives actively denied "that Madison Avenue is about to take over the policy making function."[82] Nevertheless, charges of "hucksterism" worried the industry, and in 1968 its main trade group, the American Association of Advertising Agencies (AAAA), saw fit to issue the thirty-one-page "Manual of Political Campaign Advertising" that included a code of ethics.[83]

These challenges point toward an inherent tension between the organization of advertising as a commercial enterprise and the inherently partisan nature of political work. Put simply, the appearance that a firm had a partisan leaning could be bad for business. Corporate clients, for example, might rethink their relationship with an agency that was perceived to be on the "wrong side" of the political divide. This proved to be a greater challenge for Democrats, who sometimes found it difficult to secure professional advertising services. Because most corporate executives leaned Republican, it could be risky if the firm took on a Democratic client.[84] Another problem was that an agency might align with one party or another, but its employees could hold a variety of political opinions and affiliations. This raised the possibility that staff working on a campaign might hold partisan views that diverged from those of the candidate their firm was hired to help elect. Fears that this might lead to a halfhearted effort (or worse) prompted the Republican National Committee to establish its own advertising firm for the 1960 presidential campaign. The organization, called Campaign Associates, hired admen from a number of top firms to work for the duration of the campaign.[85] Although some criticized the plan as unwise from a practical standpoint, leading Republicans argued that the idea made political sense.[86] As Daniel Riesner, chairman of the executive committee of the National Republican Club, explained, "The loyalty of people working on a particular political account in an agency is always in question." With the creation of Campaign Associates, Riesner explained, "the Republican party is assured that the workers in its ad vineyards are of [a] friendly political persuasion."[87] The experiment of a party-sponsored firm proved short-lived, however, and in 1963 the Republicans hired the Leo Burnett Company of Chicago to handle their advertising account for the upcoming presidential campaign.[88] In 1968, Republicans adopted an "anchor and loan" system in which staff from a variety of firms worked on a temporary basis for the lead agency that was responsible for the overall campaign.[89]

In other words, advertising firms proved to be ill-suited for political work. Despite the financial resources presidential campaigns devoted to television advertising, for most firms the monetary rewards paled in comparison to what they earned from their corporate accounts. In the five presidential elections between 1952 and 1968, the total money spent on campaign commercials accounted for less than 1 percent of television advertising revenue.[90] David McCall, who ran John Lindsay's campaign in 1965 for New York City mayor, warned that "no good advertising agency is terribly well served financially" by working for a candidate, especially when senior staff time was siphoned off from major accounts that ultimately paid much better than a political campaign.[91] Whereas commercial clients produced a revenue stream that could last for years, political campaigns were fleeting and unpredictable. As McCall colorfully put it, "Instead of a marriage of year-in, year-out budgets and relationships, the agency finds itself in a torrid affair with a demanding mistress who wants it day and night and then in the second week of November has gone off with another man for four years."[92] Of course, this assumed the agency actually got paid. Win or lose, candidates were often unable or unwilling to pay their bills after Election Day.[93] Even the AAAA handbook advised that ad agencies "get cash in advance" to avoid being stiffed by political clients.[94] As *Congressional Quarterly* observed in 1968, many advertising firms simply decided to forgo working on political campaigns given "the uncertainty of payment and the prospect of losing commercial customers."[95]

These organizational and financial challenges opened the door to specialist consultants better suited to the expectations and risks of political work.[96] Unlike ad agencies, for example, consultants readily identified themselves as partisans and, with very few excep-tions, restricted themselves to working for candidates from one party or the other. In fact, partisanship paid. Developing a reputation within party circles connected consultants to a broad network of potential customers throughout the country and at different levels of political office. As one consultant explained, working on behalf of a candidate also entailed working with "the national committee, the finance com-mittee, the boosters club, [and] the whole range of party profession-als." Consequently, a lack of partisan loyalty (or its appearance) could undermine trust between a consultant and the client, causing "some degree, not of hostility, but of hesitancy about someone who was . . . playing both sides of the island in a given year."[97] This willingness to devote oneself to a party and its candidates year in and year out clearly distinguished consultants from the advertising executive who took on the occasional political campaign.

By specializing in political work, consultants claimed that they better understood the dynamics of a race, differentiating their expertise from what an advertising firm could provide. Some consultants, for example, likened elections to a "one-day sale" that required "a whole different kind of strategic mind" than an advertising campaign an agency might roll out over several months.[98] Not only was the speed quicker in poli-tics, but the stakes were higher. "My candidates couldn't afford the long deliberations and goofy people [in advertising]," veteran consultant Ray Strother observed. "Their lives are on the line." Moreover, unlike a commercial product, a candidate is not "looking for a 12-percent mar-ket share, they're looking for a 50-percent market share, and they have to get it in about 6 weeks."[99] Stu Spencer put it more starkly: "I don't think that the big [advertising] agencies . . . have the stomach for what you have to go through in the political process."[100] This was especially the case when dealing with candidates and their inner circle of family and friends who had their own ideas about how to run a campaign.

In addition, consultants saw their work on behalf of a candidate as fundamentally different from advertising a product. More than simply producing an artful commercial, consultants claimed that they could crystallize voters' concerns into a convincing message the candidate would ride to an Election Day victory. According to Walter DeVries, advertisers just "didn't understand politics."[101] In part, DeVries argued, this was because ad agencies operated on a model of broadcasting intended to secure mass appeal. Even if a commercial was aimed at a specific demographic, advertisers generally hoped to reach as wide an audience as possible. Consultants approached things differently, targeting candidate appeals to specific audiences and using specialized tools to identify where critical blocs of voters lived and what issues would likely get them to the polls (or decide to stay at home).[102] In sum, political consultants offered candidates a level of campaign strategy and advice that advertising firms were either unwilling or unable to provide. Specialization reinforced these claims of comparative advantage. As Joe Napolitan put it: "It's like if you want to have a repair job done on your heart, it's better to go to a hospital that does 1,000 of them a year than go to a hospital that does 10."[103]

Business and Politics

The rise and decline of public relations and advertising firms in the conduct of political campaigns illustrates the gradual evolution of political work. Over the course of the twentieth century, a variety of techniques initially developed in the commercial realm made their way into politics as experts drawn from advertising and allied fields adapted their tools to the needs of parties and candidates. A combination of technological change and political circumstance created various opportunities for these early professionals to sell their wares.

Far from being a uniform process, professional opportunities for political work varied considerably during the 1950s and 1960s. With the rise of television, for example, advertising firms took on a prominent role in presidential campaigns. However, congressional candidates utilized professional services far less frequently or intensively. In some states, public relations and advertising firms worked closely with party committees; in other places, close ties between parties and political professionals were mostly lacking.

One other pattern deserves note. Through the end of the 1960s, Republicans appeared to utilize the services of political professionals more often than Democrats. In California, as described in the previous chapter, professional campaign services from the likes of Whitaker and Baxter and others initially flourished on the political right. Similarly, the work of Jon Jonkel in Maryland or Rosser Reeves on behalf of Eisenhower points to a Republican propensity to use public relations and advertising techniques more frequently (and more effectively) than Democrats in the conduct of campaigns. As historian David Greenberg observes, "For more than a generation ... Republicans and conservatives showed a greater comfort with using the sales methods of consumer capitalism in the service of electoral politics."[104]

One reason for this, perhaps, is that Republican ties with corporate interests eased the adoption of business methods in political campaigns. This had a practical dimension, as when a public relations firm or ad agency on corporate retainer could work for a candidate as a way to circumvent state campaign finance laws that barred direct corporate support. Business interests used their existing commercial relationships with public relations or advertising firms to assist Republican candidates or the state party. More generally, it is possible that business leaders accustomed to using market research and advertising as an effective selling tool viewed polling and political media as a more effective and efficient use of campaign resources than the free-flowing money that fueled political machines. In other words, Republicans embraced a "businesslike" approach to politics more quickly than Democrats, who lacked the same kinds of corporate connections in the 1950s and 1960s. Instead of relying on professional services, Democrats developed close ties with labor unions, emphasizing voter registration drives and grassroots mobilization efforts.[105]

These partisan differences disappeared in the 1970s as the modern political consulting industry finally took shape. One reason for this consolidation of the field was the partisan nature of political work. Advertising agencies in particular struggled to incorporate the occasional political campaign with their ongoing commercial responsibilities. Landing the quadrennial account of a presidential candidate may have brought a degree of prestige, but politics also imposed strains on the day-to-day workings of the firm. Specializing in political campaigns avoided this problem, and it enabled a new breed of political consultant to create two distinct markets for political work: one serving Republicans and the other Democrats. By the 1980s, the industry was so firmly established in American politics that most candidates, regardless of party, acquired the services of a political consultant.

7

The Consolidation of Control

THE APRIL 5, 1968, ISSUE of *Congressional Quarterly Weekly Report* featured a ten-page article that described the growing prominence of professional consultants in American politics. Under a headline that read, "Campaign Management Grows into a National Industry," the writers observed, "The future has never looked brighter for a relatively small—but growing—number of professional managers who specialize in running political campaigns."[1] The article described how a collection of "former public relations men, journalists, lobbyists, advertising specialists, radio and television men, data processing technicians, public opinion pollsters, lawyers, college teachers and ministers" conducted paid political work on behalf of candidates running for office.[2]

Two years later, the *National Journal* proclaimed 1970 to be "the year of the free-lance professional campaign director" as a growing number of candidates relied on consultants to provide a range of "sophisticated techniques," including "computers, polling, media and pre-tested issues."[3] According to a *National Journal* survey of all thirty-four Senate races that year, "at least 45 separate consulting firms [were] active in management or in providing other services to the candidates."[4] A similar study by political scientist David Rosenbloom found approximately forty firms that specialized almost entirely in consulting services for political candidates, with as many as two hundred firms engaged at least partly in the "professional campaign management industry."[5]

Rosenbloom published his findings in *The Election Men* (1973), which joined a number of other book-length treatments such as James Perry's

The New Politics (1968) and Dan Nimmo's *The Political Persuaders* (1970) in detailing the rise of a new professional class selling polls, television advertising, and other modern campaign tools to the highest bidder.[6] This view of the consultant as a kind of political mercenary found its fullest expression in the work of journalist Sidney Blumenthal, who in 1982 described what he saw as a fundamental shift in American politics toward "the permanent campaign," a world in which presidents relied on continuous polling and carefully crafted messages in the pursuit of their personal political agenda. "The permanent campaign," Blumenthal wrote, "is the political ideology of our age."[7] Fueling this relentless search for popular support, Blumenthal argued, were legions of political consultants who had replaced the ward heelers and political bosses of the past to become "the new power within the political system."[8] Political scientist Larry Sabato offered a similar assessment, arguing, "There is no more significant change in the conduct of campaigns than the consultant's recent rise to prominence if not preeminence."[9] Like Blumenthal, Sabato saw consultants as responsible for the "triumph of personality cults over party politics" as they exercised "unchecked and unrivaled power" in the conduct of political work.[10]

Although some of these early claims were overdrawn, scholars and journalists did correctly perceive that political consulting was growing into the business we recognize today. In part, this reflected efforts by the industry itself to cement its status as a profession. In 1967, three prominent consultants—Cliff White, Joe Napolitan, and Walter DeVries—met at the Plaza Hotel in New York City to form the American Association of Political Consultants (AAPC) as a forum for the exchange of ideas and the discussion of techniques used in political campaigns. From an initial membership of fewer than forty, the organization boasted more than 800 members just twenty years later.[11] Meanwhile, Neil Fabricant, a former lawyer for the American Civil Liberties Union, joined with Princeton political scientist Stanley Kelley to establish the Graduate School of Political Management at the City University of New York in 1987.[12] The purpose of the new program was to provide specialized training and credentials for the growing ranks of consultants.

These professional trappings added stature to an industry that was already much larger than either the membership of the AAPC or those with a degree in political management might suggest. DeVries estimated in 1989 that 12,000 people earned part or most of their living from campaign consulting.[13] Marking its ten-year anniversary in 1990 as "the magazine for the political professional," the trade publication *Campaigns & Elections* listed thousands of firms in its "Political Pages," a directory of services that ran over 128 pages of print and included 22 pages of general consultants alone.[14] Meanwhile, the profession was penetrating further into the political system. Rosenbloom's survey of consulting firms suggests that around 20 percent of contested House races in 1970 hired a consultant or professional management firm.[15] A 1978 survey of political campaigns found that approximately half of the candidates for the House of Representatives hired a consultant or pollster.[16] By 1992, according to political scientist Stephen Medvic, almost two-thirds of House candidates employed at least one consultant in their campaign. The figure was even higher among incumbents: 85 percent of candidates seeking re-election in 1992 hired a political consultant.[17]

What explains this growth? How did the conduct of political work become the successful business of politics we recognize today? To many observers writing in the 1970s, the growth of consulting was a product of two principal factors, the decline of traditional party organizations and advances in technology. For instance, the writers at *Congressional Quarterly* speculated that campaign consultants flourished where party organizations appeared weakest: "The most important single condition which forces candidates to look to the professionals for help is the absence of a strong and continuing party organization."[18] This pattern seemed to be borne out by the early development of campaign professionals like Whitaker and Baxter in states like California. Similarly, the spread of new technology sparked demand for "highly trained specialists [who] are needed to prepare and analyze public opinion polls, to run sophisticated advertising campaigns and to translate the results of data processing into useful political knowledge."[19]

Although partly correct, these assessments suggest a degree of inevitability that does not square with the evolution of political work over the course of the twentieth century. As described in earlier chapters, publicity experts, public relations men, and pollsters similarly confronted a mix of technological developments and changing political conditions as they plied their wares in the political realm. Whether it was the arrival of radio, the invention of polling, or the rise of television, new technologies created opportunities for experts (real or imagined) to sell their services. Similarly, earlier generations of would-be consultants exploited political developments like the rise of the presidential preference primary, the growing power and prominence of the executive branch, or the unique features of politics in states like California to claim that they alone possessed the requisite skills to secure the support of a large and diverse electorate. Observers writing in the 1970s may have accurately described consultants as the new power behind the throne, but their rise was neither automatic nor predestined. Instead, innovations in technique and assertions of professional status made possible the full-blown business of politics we recognize today.

In other words, the growth of political consulting during the 1970s and 1980s represents the culmination of a decades-long process rather than the emergence of a new phenomenon. The marriage of polling and media first imagined in the 1930s and 1940s influenced the conduct of campaigns in a powerful way. With a few important exceptions, however, many early practitioners found it difficult to earn a living from political work. Television provided important new opportunities in this regard, but it also invited competing sources of expertise and advice such as advertising agencies and public relations firms. Unable to square the partisan nature of political work with their larger commercial interests, many ad agencies turned away from campaigns, opening the door for consultants to consolidate control over a growing business of politics.

However, some things did change in the 1970s. Building on earlier innovations, consultants developed a pricing structure and specialized in a range of services that provided more reliable and more lucrative sources of income. Consultants also exploited low-cost computing, video production, and cheap long-distance telephone service to lower their costs. These developments made it easier to earn a living from political work even as it quickened the pace of campaigns and ushered in a more personalized style of political communication. Most important of all, the passage of campaign finance reform in the wake of the Watergate scandal forced political campaigns to account for every dollar spent, prohibiting certain kinds of expenditures and loose accounting practices. Under the new rules, political consulting became a legitimate campaign expense and a legal way to spend money, helping the industry grow into a critical intermediary linking candidates, political parties, and the various donors who financed capital-intensive campaigns.

Building a Viable Business

For many years, the biggest obstacle to creating a viable business of politics in the United States was financial. Political work was variable and uncertain. Clients did not always pay on time; sometimes they failed to pay at all. Consultant Bob Goodman, who estimated that in any given election season 10 percent of his billings would fail to come through, commented, "I'd never see it. I'd have to write it off."[20] Cash flow problems often plagued consultants, especially in odd-numbered years when few elections were held. Charlie Black recalled that "it would've been very hard to live on what you could make as a political consultant" during the off year of a cycle.[21] Even the writers at *Congressional Quarterly* acknowledged that "most of the several hundred individuals who are paid to plan campaigns will shift to nonpolitical employment after the votes are counted in November."[22] The cyclical nature of political work could make it difficult to stay in business, much less keep qualified staff from one election to the next.[23] For Joe Cerrell, looking back on his early years as a consultant, the operative question was, "How do I stay alive? How do I keep the doors open so that I'm available come the next election season?"[24]

The answer was to devise several coping strategies that placed the consulting business on a sounder financial footing. For instance, many consultants kept the core of their operation flexible and small, adding personnel as needed when the campaign season picked up. This was fairly straightforward in cases where the experience and reputation of one or two consultants were at the heart of the firm's success. During an election year, the number of staff might expand beyond the principals in the firm to twenty or more, and then just as abruptly shrink back down to "a couple of secretaries and an accountant."[25] Consultants might also subcontract aspects of a campaign in order to take on more clients while keeping the core of the firm relatively small. A consultant who specialized in general strategy, for example, might subcontract with a polling firm or a media production company.[26] However, flexible staffing and subcontracting had their limits. For many consultants, the success of their business relied on the formation of a personal relationship with a client, a sense of trust that was not easily replaced by a colleague. As Joe Napolitan explained the dilemma: "I'd say, 'look, I'm not going out there this week, but I can send George,' and they said, 'That's fine. George is a good guy. When are you coming?'" Napolitan's success depended on the formation of "a personal kind of relationship" between himself and the candidate.[27] This kind of handholding made for satisfied clients and positive referrals, but it also limited the number of races a consultant could work during a single campaign cycle. Peter Hart put it simply: "One of the things that we learned is that it's not how many candidates you could get. It was a question of how many races you could effectively serve" in an election year.[28] Hart placed that number at around 14 statewide races for his firm, although numbers likely varied by specialty.[29]

Given these limitations, consultants had to think carefully about what constituted the right mix of clients. A candidate's chance of winning was particularly important in deciding who to take on, as well as expectations about the likelihood of success. "You [have] to be careful ... you don't get caught in the situation where you have somebody in there who is expected to win and loses," Doug Bailey explained, "and you always ... want somebody in there who's expected to lose but really can win."[30] Consultants perceived that their ability to generate business from one cycle to the next depended in large part on a past record of success. As Bailey put it, "We've got to be careful of our reputation, and reputation in this business more than anything else means perceived batting average."[31] Consultants had to balance the need for revenue against the political potential of their clients, protecting themselves from liabilities of the candidate that might prove fatal to the campaign.

Another consideration when choosing clients was whether they could afford the cost of a consultant, or at least had the potential to secure enough campaign contributions to pay for one. According to Bailey, clients needed the "individual capacity to raise the funds to help us meet [our] economic goals."[32] Because even the best-financed candidates possessed a finite set of resources, consultants also developed a pricing structure and a mix of products and services that could maximize their revenues. Typically, consultants worked on a combination of fees and commissions, much like an advertising agency. For instance, a political consultant might charge candidates a markup of 17 or 18 percent on the production cost of a campaign commercial and then charge another 15 percent commission if he or she purchased radio or television airtime on behalf of the candidate. Some consultants also charged a daily rate plus expenses for ongoing consulting services. Other consultants preferred a system of flat fees, in part because it provided a predictable source of revenue. For example, Doug Bailey sometimes waived his commissions "in exchange for payment of a flat fee over a . . . regularly scheduled time frame." Although he might earn more from commissions, Bailey preferred "the certainty of the funds" because it helped his firm "meet some rather radical cash flow problems" by charging for their services up front.[33] As Bob O'Dell, a direct mail consultant explained, "We estimate how much time it's going to take to be involved in a campaign, divide that up into a monthly basis, and that's what the fee will be plus expenses."[34] Consultants like Bailey and O'Dell valued the ability to generate an accurate forecast of future revenue.

Consultants who did work on a commission basis, of course, faced a rather different incentive: the more polls, pieces of mail, or television advertisements a consultant provided, the more money he or she made from the campaign. Although some consultants disliked this aspect of the business, most acknowledged that they were not engaged in charitable work. "It dawned on me pretty early I needed to make money," Ray Strother recalled. "That's my chief, primary reason for being in the business or I would just go be a volunteer occasionally for some good woman or good guy that needs help."[35] Bob Goodman admitted that even if consultants "didn't like to be hired on the idea that the more he spends, the more I make," the profit motive still influenced the structure of the business in important ways.[36] In particular, certain products and services were more attractive than others. Jill Buckley, one of the first women (after Leone Baxter) to make a successful career in the consulting business, specialized in political media because it carried a higher premium than advising clients on general strategy. As she explained, "One of the problems about selling general advice is that you're just one amongst many people who have an opinion on how a candidate ought to be, what he ought to say, and how a campaign ought to run."[37] By contrast, political ads were something campaigns could not provide themselves. For Buckley, "It became abundantly clear ... that if you were selling a real product like the media, you could charge significantly more for it ... [and] you could also get the respect of campaigns because they thought you were selling something that they truly didn't know how to do."[38] Consultant Matt Reese made a similar observation: "I couldn't make it on time. I had to get paid for a product."[39] Providing clients a menu of services created multiple opportunities to make money. In Reese's case, "We made a profit on the letter. We made a profit on the phone calls. We made a profit on the computer work. We made a profit on the polling."[40]

Television clearly illustrates how the financial incentives consultants faced shaped the character of the industry as it developed in the 1970s and 1980s. Because consultants possessed the skills and expertise required to produce political advertising, they were highly valued by causes and candidates seeking access to the airwaves. In fact, buying television time on behalf of a client became an extremely profitable niche as consultants could make money by earning commissions on what stations charged for airtime. Moreover, the price of TV airtime increased just as the consulting industry took off. Between 1975 and 1985, the real per capita cost of television spot advertising rose by 30 percent.[41] For consultants who charged commissions on the ads they placed, this meant a healthy increase to their bottom line. Buying television airtime not only was lucrative but also offered consultants a reliable source of income. Although consultants often waited to get paid for producing commercials, campaigns had to purchase television time up front if they wanted their spot on the air. This allowed consultants to collect the commissions on time buys during the campaign, easing some of their cash flow problems.[42] Some consultants even used a portion of the commissions they collected to offset the fees they charged the campaign. In doing so, consultants created an incentive for campaigns to spend more money on television.[43] For every dollar spent on advertising, campaigns spent less on consulting fees (even as consultants earned more from commissions).

Even with these new ways to make money in politics, consultants still faced significant financial risk working for candidates and campaigns. Therefore, many consultants sought ways to expand their client base as a way to stay in business. For instance, some consultants sought out the relatively small number of races taking place in odd-numbered years, such as governors in some states and down-ballot campaigns for mayor or city council.[44] Other consultants worked for political parties, especially state party organizations, providing ongoing or year-round work such as polling services or soliciting contributions through direct mail.[45] Consultants also found work with advocacy organizations of various kinds, helping them develop grassroots lobbying strategies that relied on campaign-style techniques in the pursuit of legislative goals.[46] Some of the more prominent consultants turned to international work, especially in Latin America and the Caribbean, where there were few restrictions on political spending and American campaign strategies were well suited to the plebiscitary style of politics in the region.[47] Most lucrative of all, consultants often worked for corporate clients seeking to change policy or simply improve their standing with the public. As Joe Cerrell explained, "The knowledge that you have acquired from politics" could be parlayed into year-round work on behalf of a range of clients, including "companies, [trade] associations, labor unions, environmental groups, religious groups, [and] academic organizations."[48] Because of the financial rewards of corporate work, diversifying one's client base promised a degree of financial security that politics alone could not provide.

The career of consultant Matt Reese illustrates how political consulting extended well beyond the realm of campaigns. A native of West Virginia, Reese helped John Kennedy secure a victory in that state's crucial primary during the 1960 presidential campaign. Recognized for his talents, Reese became a deputy chair of the Democratic National Committee and then headed the voter registration drive for Lyndon Johnson in 1964. In August 1966, Reese struck out on his own, forming Matt Reese & Associates as a specialist in voter turnout. Reese quickly established a reputation for success by targeting precincts most likely to turn the election in his client's favor, paying particular attention to undecided voters and those favorably disposed to the candidate but who seldom went to the polls. In the 1970s, Reese teamed up with pollster Bill Hamilton, and together they developed a powerful tool that combined surveys and market research to provide even greater precision in targeting campaign communication and outreach efforts. Using an early form of computer-assisted data analytics called the Claritas Cluster System, Reese and Hamilton could identify zip codes where concentrations of like-minded voters lived. Armed with such knowledge, Reese explained, "you could put the resources where they should be."[49]

In 1978, Reese used this system of data-driven targeting on behalf of organized labor to defeat a statewide ballot initiative that would have turned Missouri into a "right-to-work" state. Although opinion polls suggested that a majority of Missouri voters would approve the measure, the right-to-work initiative lost by a surprisingly wide margin.[50] Reese credited his victory to the effective targeting of almost 600,000 households he believed would vote against right-to-work if persuaded to turn out on Election Day. Spending less than 15 percent of his budget on television, Reese concentrated his resources on these persuadable voters using a combination of door-to-door visits, phone calls, and specially tailored mailings to get them to the polls.[51] The victory demonstrated the power and precision of sophisticated targeting methods to identify voters open to the message of the campaign. Or, as Reese liked to say in his homespun West Virginia manner, "You pick cherries where the cherries is."[52]

Although a self-described "left-leaning Democrat," Reese supplemented his political work with high-paying corporate clients from the oil, gas, and tobacco industries.[53] Like other consultants who took on corporate work, Reese applied the same methods he devised for political campaigns to help companies better understand how the public viewed their products and, especially, the regulations that impacted their bottom line. In 1976, for example, Reese managed a campaign in New York State on behalf of the tobacco industry that sought to build public support for a cut in the cigarette tax.[54] In 1980, Reese and his colleague Bill Hamilton used the same targeting system first deployed in Missouri to analyze which segments of California voters supported the creation of nonsmoking sections in public places.[55] Working for the Natural Gas Supply Association, Reese coordinated a massive grassroots lobbying campaign on behalf of the industry that targeted potential supporters for a letter-writing campaign (complete with computer-generated stationery recipients could sign and mail to Congress). As Reese told an interviewer in 1996, "The corporate [work] was so intriguing and so profitable." Nevertheless, Reese admitted that "you're not doing anything you're particularly proud of. . . . I do good now, to try to make up for that."[56] Moral qualms aside, Reese found corporate work to be an essential part of his business strategy. Many others in the industry followed suit.

In sum, consultants structured their fees, tailored their services, and diversified their client base in order to alleviate the uncertain and uneven character of political work. Combining political and corporate clients while extending the reach of their professional services, either farther down the ballot or across the globe, helped consultants to address the financial risks of the business, whether a nonpaying client or a late surprise that sunk a candidate in the closing days of the race.

Technological Developments and Economic Opportunities

Alongside business adaptations that provided a degree of financial stability in an uncertain political world, consultants benefited from a confluence of factors that improved their bottom line. Through the 1970s and 1980s, in fact, advances in technology coupled with changes in public policy made it possible to provide products and services such as polling, media, and direct mail at a lower cost and higher volume than in the past. As consultants responded to these opportunities, they transformed the character of the profession as well as the conduct of political work.

Notably, the 1970s mark a period of increasing specialization in the consulting business. Although many practitioners still functioned as general strategists and overall campaign managers along the model pioneered by Whitaker and Baxter, consultants increasingly focused on more lucrative parts of the business that combined technical proficiency with political acumen. Polling, for example, blended an academic understanding of statistical sampling techniques with a creative ability to translate survey data into campaign strategy. Media consulting was more than just slick advertisements; it also required molding campaign messages to the changing circumstances of the race.

Similarly, voter targeting or direct mail combined the data-driven precision of direct marketing with the precinct-level political intelligence of a party boss. Consultants were drawn to these specialties in part because it gave them control over a product campaigns could not provide on their own. As much as a seasoned strategist like Joe Napolitan was in demand, his advice was one among many voices in the ear of the candidate. By contrast, the purchase of a survey, advertisement, or mailing was increasingly something only a consultant could provide. However, unlike a general strategist who could work out of a suitcase, polling or media entailed rather high fixed costs that could create cash flow problems given the up-and-down nature of political work. Once these fixed costs declined, the economics of political consulting notably improved.

Polling offers a good example. The commercial survey business that emerged in the 1930s was both labor- and capital-intensive. Pioneer pollsters like Gallup and Roper employed an army of survey takers scattered around the country who conducted door-to-door interviews.[57] Results were then tabulated by hand or using punch card machines. Advances in computing enhanced pollsters' analytical capacity, but the capital expenditures required were far from trivial. In 1976, *Computerworld* magazine reported that the Gallup Corporation's data-processing capabilities included an IBM 1130 computer along with additional disk drives, keypunch machines, punch card readers, and printers.[58] Although marketed as a low-cost business computing system, the IBM 1130 cost more than $40,000 when it was introduced in 1965, and peripherals like punch card readers and printers could add another $15,000 in hardware.[59] Even then, sophisticated statistical analysis required a level of computing power beyond the reach of all but the largest companies (the IBM 370 mainframe computer with 1MB of memory carried a $4.7 million price tag in 1970).[60] Consequently, survey research firms often rented time on an off-site computer in order to conduct more complicated work. This typically took days to complete.[61] Given the high costs of polling, it is not surprising that the field was dominated through the 1960s by a handful of commercial firms like Gallup and Roper plus a few academic institutions like the University of Michigan Survey Research Center and the National Opinion Research Center at the University of Chicago.[62]

In the 1970s, however, several factors combined to make it much cheaper to conduct surveys and analyze the results. First, the telephone replaced face-to-face interviews as the preferred method of collecting data. With home telephone penetration near 100 percent and advances in sampling techniques using random digit dialing, pollsters could employ a single call center staffed by thirty or forty workers rather than a legion of survey takers scattered across the country.[63] Second, changes in the telecommunications industry, precipitated by the breakup of AT&T, dramatically lowered the cost of telephone surveys compared with in-person interviews. Putting aside the complicated story of deregulation, the practical effect of government action was lower prices, especially in the long-distance market.[64] The cost of a flat-rate long distance line for business use (a WATS line) declined in real terms by 30 percent between 1974, when the Justice Department filed its antitrust suit against AT&T, and 1982, when the telephone giant agreed to break up the Bell System. Long-distance costs continued to fall thereafter, declining by almost 50 percent in real terms over the next ten years.[65] Third, with the dawn of the desktop workstation, the cost of computing went down significantly. The nominal price of a small computer dropped from around $15,000 in 1975 to less than $2,000 ten years later. In real terms, this was equivalent to an 80-percent drop in price, or almost 25 percent on an annual basis. Computer memory also became significantly cheaper. Between 1975 and 1984, the cost of random access memory (RAM) fell by 96 percent.[66] In the 1980s, the combination of low-cost long distance and desktop computing led to the development of computer-assisted telephone interviewing (CATI). Using individual workstations equipped with a computer that dialed numbers automatically, interviewers could input survey responses as they went along, eliminating the need for punch card tabulations and giving pollsters almost immediate access to the data they collected.[67]

Other specialties underwent similar changes as low-cost technology made it cheaper for consultants to provide campaigns a steady diet of products and services. With the growing availability of portable video recorders in the 1970s and 1980s, for instance, media consultants could produce campaign advertisements at a fraction of the cost of traditional film recording. Whereas campaign advertisements recorded on film cost $50,000 or more to produce in the 1970s, video made it possible to create a campaign advertisement for just a few thousand dollars.[68] This made political media much more widely available. As Ray Strother observed, "My candidates couldn't afford ... film," but they could afford a campaign commercial "I could produce for $2,000."[69]

Similarly, advances in computing transformed the direct mail business by making it possible to collect, store, and manipulate large databases of voter files that included histories of past contributions, registration information, and various social and demographic characteristics. Using this information, direct mail consultants produced bulk mailings of computer-generated letters tailored to the specific interests or concerns of the recipient. Although the computing power required for direct mail was not cheap, the rate of return made up for the cost. In 1978, direct mail consultant Richard Viguerie teamed up with Republican Party chair William Brock to raise funds for GOP candidates in the congressional midterms. Using a series of targeted appeals aimed at conservatives angered by liberal court decisions on abortion and prayer in schools, Viguerie and Brock raised enormous sums for the party, turning an $8 million investment in direct mail into $25 million in contributions.[70] Direct mail was also lucrative: the *Washington Post* reported in 1978 that Viguerie pocketed $3.2 million out of a total of $5.8 million he raised on behalf of the National Rifle Association.[71] Of course, not all of this was profit. According to Viguerie, he spent $100,000 in monthly fees leasing the powerful mainframe computers he needed to generate up to 500,000 letters for a single campaign.[72] In time, however, lower-cost computing made direct mail techniques more widely available. By the early 1980s, a handful of inexpensive desktop computer software packages (some costing less than $1,000) tailored direct mail to the needs and budgets of individual candidates.[73]

Another important factor in the growth of direct mail was campaign finance reform. Legislation passed in 1974 prohibited large, unregulated contributions from "fat cat" donors; in response, parties and candidates increasingly targeted small, individual contributors using direct mail solicitations to fund their campaigns. In 1978, Congress recognized the political value of direct mail by extending reduced-rate bulk mailing privileges to "qualified political committees" such as national and state parties.[74] Previously limited to nonprofit organizations, reducing the bulk mail rate meant that political causes and campaigns could solicit funds for as little as four cents per letter.[75] Together, the growing reliance on individual contributions and lower postal rates increased the importance of direct mail consultants in the conduct of campaigns.

In sum, a combination of technological and policy developments fueled a process of specialization in products and services that generated a high rate of return. As a result, the economics of consulting improved markedly in the 1970s. As pollster Bob Teeter explained, "The barriers to entry were much lower," especially once low-cost telephone service and data-processing capabilities replaced the need for a "big, mainframe computer" and a "national field force" of in-person interviewers. Lower costs attracted more people to the business. What began in the 1960s with "only a few" pollsters, Tweeter recalled, eventually became a crowded field.[76] Similarly, video lowered the barriers to entry associated with media consulting, making it easier to specialize in one of the most lucrative parts of the business. For an earlier generation of consultants like Tony Schwartz (the creator of the famous "Daisy Ad" for Lyndon B. Johnson's 1964 presidential campaign), a reputation for artistic and technical sophistication came from years of working in TV advertising before turning to politics. In contrast, video made it possible for someone like Jill Buckley, who had extensive campaign experience but no formal background in television, to become a media specialist and reap the financial benefits.

In the case of direct mail, the demand for specialized products and services also had a great deal to do with campaign finance rules. Money in politics was nothing new; Mark Hanna raised unprecedented sums for the Republicans in 1896 to defeat William Jennings Bryan. What distinguished the last quarter of the twentieth century from this earlier period in American politics was the legal requirement that campaigns publicly report how every dollar was spent. For all the weaknesses of campaign finance reform, rules set out in the 1970s for how candidates and parties could spend their money would yield tremendous benefits to the consulting industry in the decades that followed.

Campaign Finance and the Business of Politics

As the Watergate scandal unfolded in 1972, a series of explosive revelations detailed how the Nixon White House, through its Committee to Re-Elect the President (CREEP), raked in vast sums of campaign cash from friends, allies, and industries seeking favor; in some cases, these funds were used for illicit or illegal purposes. In the aftermath of Watergate and the resignation of President Richard Nixon in 1974, Congress passed sweeping legislation intended to overhaul the nation's campaign finance laws. Ambitious in scope, the Federal Election Campaign Act (FECA) Amendments of 1974 set limits on individual contributions, restricted the use of party funds on behalf of candidates running for office, and capped the amount political action committees (PACs) could give to candidates. The 1974 act also set limits on spending by congressional candidates and created a system of public funding for presidential elections. Finally, the act required that each individual candidate submit detailed reports on contributions and campaign expenditures to a newly created independent regulatory agency, the Federal Election Commission (FEC).[77]

Almost immediately, the practical effects of campaign finance reform began to erode through a combination of legal action and clever adaptation. In 1976, the Supreme Court declared spending limits to be an unconstitutional infringement on free speech. Meanwhile, the number of PACs exploded into the thousands, and the national and state parties exploited loopholes in the law that allowed them to raise and spend money almost without limit so long as they were independent of a candidate's campaign. Periodic attempts by Congress to address these gaps in the law did little more than inaugurate another cycle of innovation that further subverted the system.[78] Today, presidential candidates' ability to raise huge sums from millions of individual donors has rendered the system of public funding an antiquated relic, while recent Supreme Court cases have eliminated almost all remaining restrictions on spending and contributions.[79]

Throughout this twisted path of reform, one constant element remained: a high degree of transparency in the conduct of campaigns. Indeed, one feature of reform that did survive the unraveling of the campaign finance system created in the 1970s is the requirement that candidates submit detailed reports on precisely when and how they spend their money. These reporting requirements were a boon to the consulting industry, and not only the relatively small group of professionals (mostly lawyers) who helped candidates comply with the growing list of rules and regulations that governed the conduct of elections. Rather, consultants benefited more generally from the fact that campaigns had to enumerate expenditures. Loose accounting practices that had greased the party system for so long gave way to a new regime in which professional services like polling or media became a clean and legal way to spend money.

The reporting requirements of FECA and its amendments were an uncontroversial element of reform; efforts to bring about greater transparency in political expenditures date back to the Progressive Era.[80] The 1974 legislation differed from these previous efforts by placing a greater onus on individual candidates to report receipts and expenditures. The law also granted the FEC the authority to audit campaigns and levy fines on those who failed to comply with the rules. However, the paper authority of the FEC greatly exceeded the practical capacity of the agency. Particularly in the early years after reform, the FEC struggled to handle the volume and complexity of information it received from candidates or create a workable set of rules and regulations that could keep up with rapidly changing campaign practices that tested legal limits. The manner in which the FEC addressed these administrative challenges redounded to the benefit of the consulting profession.

In 1976, the FEC marked its first full year of operation. A number of factors made it a difficult one for the new agency. First, 1976 was an election year and the first presidential campaign in which candidates were eligible for public matching funds in state primary races and the general election. In addition, the 1976 campaign was the first to take place after the two major parties enacted reforms that assigned convention delegates on the basis of state primary results, the effect of which was to require candidates to run expensive, primary campaigns in multiple states in order to win the nomination.[81] Third, the commission began the year in a partial state of limbo after a January 1976 decision by the Supreme Court in *Buckley v. Valeo* invalidated portions of the 1974 FECA Amendments. The decision forced the FEC to suspend some of its operations until Congress passed new legislation in May 1976.[82]

These factors combined to create a daunting task for the new agency. A total of fifteen candidates running for president submitted almost 1 million individual contribution records to the commission for verification under the matching fund program. At the same time, more than 3,000 candidates for federal office and almost 6,000 campaign committees submitted another half million documents for FEC review, representing $300 million in campaign expenditures. All of this required a set of sophisticated data collection and auditing procedures, most of them constructed on the fly in the midst of a hotly contested presidential election. As the commission noted in its 1976 annual report, "The candidates and Commission were breaking entirely new ground. . . . This situation demanded patience and flexibility on the part of the Commission and campaign treasurers alike."[83]

These challenges were especially daunting in the area of auditing and enforcement, which was plagued by uncertainty and delay from the start. The FEC was still issuing judgments against presidential candidates almost three years after the 1976 election. For instance, the Carter campaign was ordered to pay back some of its public matching funds after a commission audit completed in 1979 deemed certain expenses to be improper or lacking sufficient documentation. Similar judgments were made against the Wallace and Udall campaigns.[84] Meanwhile, the FEC failed to complete even a single audit from the 1978 congressional midterm election, contributing further to a backlog of decisions and mounting criticism of the agency.[85] An outside study by Arthur Anderson & Company in 1979 found "bottlenecks [and] delays . . . at almost every point in the audit process" and further concluded that in many instances the commission was simply unable to determine whether candidates or their committees were "materially complying with the act."[86]

One reason for this difficulty was the lack of clear criteria for what counted as legal campaign expenditures under the law. One of the goals of the FECA Amendments, following on the heels of the Watergate scandal, was to eliminate unregulated slush funds used for unsavory or illegal purposes. Like many complex pieces of legislation, however, the FECA Amendments did not state precisely how this was to be achieved. For instance, the law restricted the use of public funds by presidential candidates to "qualified campaign expanses," but the statute did not specify what, exactly, counted as a qualified expense. Similarly, the statute required that candidates include the "particulars of expenditures" in reports to the commission; however, many campaigns simply provided an itemized list of disbursements that failed to indicate exactly how funds were spent.[87] This left a great deal of room for campaigns to engage in questionable tactics that violated the spirit if not the letter of the law. For instance, many campaigns simply listed cash disbursements such as "advance to fieldman" or "Election Day expenses."[88] Although campaigns often did engage in legitimate efforts to get out the vote, FEC auditors worried that such vague and imprecise categories could conceal more questionable practices like the use of "walking around money" by precinct workers in large cities to round up votes. Auditors also feared that without precise documentation candidates might use campaign funds for personal expenses.[89] The FEC acknowledged the difficulty in bringing these various practices under control by noting in its 1976 annual report that "the variety and ingenuity of political campaigners in spending funds for a campaign [does] not lend itself to easy categorizing."[90]

Despite this "variety and ingenuity," commission staff tried to resolve the legal ambiguity by creating a set of categories campaigns should use for the purpose of reporting their expenses. This would serve two aims: to make it easier for candidates to comply with the law and, second, to help FEC auditors identify violations by standardizing the kind of information they received from each campaign. Accordingly, the commission issued guidelines in 1978 that deemed certain categories "adequate" when considering the legality of campaign expenses. These included "transportation, consultant/professional fees, surveys/polls, advertising, printing/photography, fundraising, administration/operating, postage and meetings, [and] direct mail."[91] The commission further specified that expenditures listed as "advances" or "get-out-the-vote" or "election day expenses" were not acceptable categories by themselves and would require additional information regarding "actual use" of funds, namely, one or more of the acceptable categories listed here.[92] Approved in August 1978, these rules subsequently governed how the commission reviewed reports as well as conducted audits of campaigns.[93]

The creation of FEC rules for reporting expenses had important consequences for the consulting industry. In effect, the commission signaled that the best way for a campaign to avoid an audit was to employ the services of a professional who could carefully document the nature of work they performed. In fact, the commission specifically distinguished "between a commercial firm . . . providing goods and/or services to a committee" using the approved categories for expenditures "and those same terms when used in association with an individual or unregistered political organization/entity as payee." Whereas an expenditure to "ABC Printing" was deemed acceptable, payment to "John Jones" for a "printing expense" was likely to trigger an audit.[94] Commission rules and audit practices had an immediate effect on the conduct of campaigns. As the controller of the 1980 Carter re-election effort acknowledged, "We must now be very specific about . . . spending. . . . We must leave a very careful audit trail" for the FEC.[95] Gone were the days of loose accounting practices when parties and campaigns could distribute cash to precinct workers on Election Day. "It's enough to make a Baltimore boss weep," quipped the *Washington Post*.[96]

Consultants benefited from campaign finance rules in other ways as well. One consequence of the system created in the 1970s was the fragmentation of the political environment into thousands of individual candidate committees, national party committees, congressional campaign committees, state party organizations, and PACs—each one a potential buyer of polling, media, direct mail, and other professional services. The explosive growth in the number of PACs was especially significant in this regard. In the first five years after passage of the 1974 FECA Amendments, the number of PACs increased from just over 600 to 2,000. Five years later, in 1980, the number of PACs had doubled again, exceeding 4,000 in total.[97] Whereas FECA rules limited how much money PACs could contribute to candidates or spend directly on their behalf, the Supreme Court struck down provisions of the 1974 law that restricted so-called independent expenditures. Under the ruling, PACs (and party committees) could advocate for the election or defeat of an individual candidate so long as these expenditures were not made "with the cooperation or with the prior consent of, or in consultation with," the candidate or her committee.[98] Like the definition of particulars, however, the precise meaning of "cooperation" or "consultation" was far from clear, and efforts to resolve this ambiguity were generally beneficial to the consulting industry.

For example, in March 1980 the FEC issued an advisory opinion in response to a series of questions from the National Conservative

Political Action Committee (NCPAC) concerning the use of consultants. At issue was whether the same consultant could simultaneously
work for a candidate seeking office and for NCPAC in its efforts to
defeat the same candidate's opponent. The answer, according to the
FEC, varied considerably depending on the specific circumstances of
the expenditure.[99] In fact, the FEC provided a detailed response that
explained precisely when and how NCPAC could use consultants
without violating the law. According to the advisory opinion, the same
consultant could work for a candidate and for NCPAC during the primary because the candidate seeking the Republican nomination and
the Democratic candidate who was the target of NCPAC expenditures
were not yet opponents. The FEC also explained that the same consultant could work for a candidate and NCPAC so long as activities on
behalf of the latter did not include specific media advocating the election of the former or the defeat of her opponent. This included polls or
fundraising conducted by NCPAC as an "operating expense," as well
as general communication that omitted the name of a candidate, what
became known as "issue ads" in the "soft money" era of the 1980s and
1990s.[100] With the FEC ruling in hand, NCPAC and its leader, Terry
Dolan, went on to spend $3 million on behalf of conservative candi-
dates running in the 1980 election, including more than $1 million on
efforts to defeat six liberal Democratic senators (four of whom lost their
bid for re-election in 1980).[101] As campaign finance expert Frank Sorauf
described NCPAC's innovation, "a potent new political tactic, independent spending, had arrived."[102]

Yet it was the consultants who perhaps benefited the most from
the growth of PACs and the rise of independent expenditures. The
Supreme Court decision in *Buckley v. Valeo* invalidating spending limits combined with the FEC advisory opinion on independent expenditures expanded the number of potential clients in need of consulting
services. Rather than transfer funds to a candidate who may spend the
money unwisely, PAC directors could target spending on specific races
through the services of a consultant working on their behalf. This benefited consultants, who could now work for multiple clients through
a single contract with a PAC rather than having to sell their wares to
individual campaigns.[103] And because consultants were commercial
vendors employed on a contractual basis, they could work for multiple

candidates, parties, and PACs without violating FEC rules that prohibited coordination or collusion in campaign spending—tasks a party
employee or head of a PAC could not legally perform. Even where the
FEC explicitly prohibited a single consultant from working simultaneously for a candidate and a party committee or PAC, it simply created
more opportunities for the profession as a whole. The proliferation of
PACs and the growth in independent spending gave the industry "a
new lease on life," one political consultant observed.[104]

The requirement that committees and candidates submit detailed
reports on spending, the designation of preferred categories of professional services (or risk an audit), and the rules governing independent
expenditures by PACs and party committees created myriad opportunities for consultants to tap into a rich vein of capital flowing through
the political system as campaign contributions. Put simply, it became
difficult to spend money in politics without hiring a consultant. Things
could have been different. Had the Supreme Court upheld spending
limits in political campaigns, considerably less money would have been
available to hire consultants, and the profession likely would not have
grown to the extent it did. Instead, consultants became an important
link in a new political economy of influence, transforming lightly regulated contributions into legal campaign expenditures. As central figures
in these circuits of exchange, consultants were arguably the principal
beneficiaries of reform.

The Transformation of Political Work

By the 1980s, consultants had become key actors in the political process thanks to a series of innovations and adaptations that addressed
the uncertain nature of political work. Consultants diversified their
client base to include advocacy groups, labor unions, and corporations. Consultants also exploited low-cost technology and specialized
in products and services that contributed most to their bottom line.
Finally, campaign finance reform, for all its limitations, allowed consultants to occupy a profitable niche in the political system by serving
as the principal legal way to spend money in campaigns. With these
developments, consultants consolidated their control over the conduct
of political work. By the 1980s, in fact, hiring a consultant itself became

a mark of a professional campaign. In a kind of circular logic, candidates hired consultants to signal their viability to potential donors, thereby attracting the financial contributions needed to pay for the very services that only consultants could provide (and candidates believed were necessary to win).[105]

As they became part of the landscape of American politics, consultants changed the very terrain upon which they worked. One mark of this transformation is the speed and intensity of political campaigns. Starting in the 1970s, a combination of technological developments, economic incentives, and political opportunities created a fast-paced political style. Whereas Whitaker and Baxter took weeks and even months to plan and execute a campaign, consultants working in the 1970s and 1980s could field a survey, analyze the results, and then produce a new television advertisement in a matter of days. "The intensity of campaigns . . . [has] increased just enormously, and it's at every level," Wally Clinton observed. "The media people . . . buy more time on television. The pollsters spend more time in the field. The mail people send more letters. We make more phone calls. . . . The speed of the response has to be immediate. You have to be prepared to respond within minutes."[106] Speed was good for business, of course, because it increased the flow of products and services consultants could sell to their clients.

In the early years of polling a campaign might purchase a benchmark study conducted during the primary followed by one or two additional surveys over the course of the campaign. With low-cost telephone interviews, however, it became possible to conduct tracking polls that examined movements in voter opinion over time using a rolling sample of 200 to 300 respondents contacted each night.[107] With quicker turnaround times, pollsters could measure sudden changes in the campaign, testing, for example, how voters responded to a new advertisement or whether a candidate's performance in a debate had any measurable effect on opinion. Rather than simply provide a snapshot of the race at a single moment in time, pollsters could create a kind of "moving picture" that tracked the daily ups and downs of the campaign. Lance Tarrance likened his job to that of a doctor reading an EKG, watchful for any sign of "erosion in your voter base."[108] The advent of CATI systems sped up the process even further. As Peter Hart recalled, CATI allowed his team to "finish [a survey] at 10:00 at night, and . . . then sit down and talk to the candidate by phone" an hour later.[109] The capacity to conduct more polls more frequently meant the pollster's job interpreting results became an ongoing service rather than a periodic one. As Vince Breglio put it, "The survey researcher becomes a more intimate part of the decision-making apparatus of the campaign structure."[110]

Similarly, it was much faster to produce a commercial on video than on film, enabling consultants to increase their output considerably. Media consultant Bob Goodman described how when he started his career in the 1960s, it took weeks to film, process, and print a political advertisement before it aired on television. Because of the long lead time associated with film, Goodman could create only a handful of ads for a campaign. In fact, his work often ended right after Labor Day: "We'd sit back and say, I wonder what's going to happen in November." Videotape "changed the whole business overnight," Goodman recalled.[111] With the capacity to shoot, edit, and air a new commercial in a matter of days or even hours, a skilled consultant could produce a continuous stream of ads throughout the campaign. Low-cost videotape even allowed media consultants to create multiple ads and then test public responses to different campaign messages using polls and focus groups.[112] Much like polling, the job of the media consultant became one of responding to the unexpected events and changing conditions of the race. Expenditures on political advertising increased accordingly. Between 1972 and 1992, television spending on behalf of political candidates increased in real terms by 150 percent, more than double the rate of growth in both total campaign spending and commercial TV ad revenues over the same period.[113] In addition to more media-intensive campaigns, video altered the very style of political communication, as consultants moved away from the slick production values of commercial advertising in favor of quick "sound bites" and "man-on-the-street" interviews. Videotape was the ideal medium in this regard not only because it was fast and cheap but also because handheld camera work emulated the immediacy voters had grown accustomed to from watching their local news.[114]

The rapid-fire character of political campaigns also reflected a search, frenzied at times, for a more personalized, even intimate, connection with voters. Polling, media, and direct mail offered high returns in part because they were in high demand by parties, interest groups, and candidates in need of money and votes. However, this demand reflected a promise, only partly fulfilled, that a political consultant could provide a more fine-grained portrait of the electorate and a more personal connection with the voter than was previously the case. Polling, for example, became less about the discovery of general trends in opinion and more about detecting small shifts in the allegiance of discrete groups.[115] One of the virtues of low-cost telephone interviews, in fact, was that it enabled pollsters to hone in on a specific demographic or group of voters as needed.[116] Similarly, media strategy focused less on the presentation of the candidate to a broad audience and more on the identification of specific issues or concerns that could bring strategic segments of voters to the polls (or keep them at home). Through the control of political work, consultants became the candidate's principal connection to the people.

The search for what motivated the individual to participate in politics was perhaps most advanced in the area of direct mail. The value of constructing an extensive voter database was that it could be used to craft a personal appeal aimed at a very specific segment of the electorate. As Matt Reese described the advantages of data-driven targeting, "I'd know what kind of folks they are, and consequently I know how to approach them when I send them mail, or call them on the phone. . . . I could tell what they were thinking, and I could tell how they voted."[117] Even more than polling or media, direct mail could drill down to specific constituencies. Wally Clinton explained, "We can be more precise with our messages, we can identify demographically or geographically what messages work with certain segments of the electorate, and deliver complementary messages to those small segments of the electorate."[118] In addition to identifying which voters to target, direct mail consultants working in the 1970s used computers to generate personalized letters that created an appearance of individual attention. As consultant Bill Lacy told political scientist Larry Sabato in 1979, computerized mail services made it possible to create the impression of a personal connection using specific information about the recipient. "All of that's computerized," Lacy explained. "The computer . . . spews out letters that basically . . . [make] a person think that he's actually getting a personal letter from someone."[119] Although such techniques seem dated or even quaint by contemporary standards, advances in direct mail during the 1970s laid the groundwork for more sophisticated targeting weapons in the twenty-first century.[120]

More fundamentally, consultants altered the organizational ecology of American politics. Contemporary observers writing in the 1970s saw consultants as a cause of, or at least an accomplice in, the apparent decline of American political parties. In fact, the story is a more complicated one than that. Consultants did profit from the growing complexity and fragmentation of the American political system by giving voice to multiple actors and interests engaged in the political process. Joe Napolitan, for example, gained national notoriety for helping the multimillionaire Milton Shapp win the 1966 Democratic gubernatorial primary in Pennsylvania. With the help of Shapp's considerable fortune, Napolitan positioned his candidate as an outsider man of the people running against the party machine. Although Shapp lost the general election, his candidacy seemed to herald the rise of a modern, media-savvy politician who, by employing the services of a professional consultant, could operate independently of party in the quest for office.[121] And as we have seen, consultants profited from the expanding array of PACs, advocacy groups, and trade associations that became increasingly active in politics in the 1970s thanks in part to the rules governing independent political expenditures. Consultants contributed to these centrifugal tendencies in American politics by creating a market for products and services that served a myriad of causes and candidates.

However, consultants benefited from and depended on the continued relevance of parties in the American political system. Shapp's famed victory in Pennsylvania illustrated, among other things, how consultants profited from a system in which candidates had to win a primary election to secure their party's nomination. In fact, primaries were good for business. This was certainly the case at the presidential level after party reforms enacted in the 1970s changed the nominating process so that White House aspirants had to compete in statewide primaries in order to become their party's standard-bearer. Similarly, the development of a two-party system in the post–Voting Rights Act South created new opportunities for consultants, especially those working on behalf of Republican candidates in newly contested primary and general election races.[122] Moreover, as careful students of the American party system have pointed out, consultants frequently worked closely with state and particularly national party committees, helping to develop critical resources and capacities in areas such as fundraising, communication, and survey research.[123] During the 1980 electoral cycle, for example, the National Republican Senatorial Committee spent more than $7 million on fundraising, plus another $600,000 on consultants, surveys, and additional research.[124] Consultants and political parties worked together as friends rather than foes, allies in the pursuit of partisan goals rather than adversaries in the political process.[125]

More than simply engaged in a search for profits, consultants sought out causes and candidates they believed in and were willing to devote their considerable energies to help win. This is what attracted consultants to politics in the first place: the excitement of the campaign and the opportunity to work on behalf of a broader set of goals, aspirations, and beliefs. As consultant Charlie Black put it, "Your philosophy kept you going."[126] Often, this lent a strong partisan motivation to consultants' work.[127] For instance, Bob O'Dell noted, "I was a strong Republican long before I was in the business."[128] Matt Reese put it more bluntly: "I don't like Republicans, except for my mother [and] Abraham Lincoln."[129] In fact, many consultants had considerable experience working directly for political parties early in their career. Democratic consultant Joe Cerrell served as the executive director of the California Democratic Party in the years before he began his own firm in 1966.[130] Matt Reese completed a stint with the Democratic National Committee after helping JFK win the White House in 1960.[131] Direct mail consultant Bob O'Dell worked as a summer intern for the Republican Congressional Campaign Committee in 1963 and six years later became the executive director of the Republican National Finance Committee (the fundraising arm of the national party).[132] Republican pollster Lance Tarrance started his career working for the Republican Party of Texas before moving to the Republican National Committee, where he became the director of research in 1968. When Tarrance started his own polling firm in 1977, one of his first clients was the Republican Congressional Campaign Committee, which purchased ten surveys as part of its southern strategy for the 1978 midterms.[133]

Partisanship had economic benefits as well, serving as the bedrock upon which consultants could build the kind of "personal handholding operation" that was critical to their business.[134] Because candidates were unlikely to trust a consultant who did not share the same political beliefs, much less vote for the same party, the vast majority of consultants identified as partisans and restricted themselves to working only for one party or the other. This had important consequences, both for the business of politics and for the character of political competition. Party affiliation granted consultants access to a pool of potential clients, including candidates for office, party committees, and allied advocacy groups. As a result, consultants became a crucial part of the connective tissue linking causes, candidates, and party committees in an extended partisan network.[135] More broadly, consultants helped to define the character and content of partisan campaigns.[136] Through their provision of products and services like polling, media, and direct mail, consultants selected issues, crafted messages, and targeted voters in ways that reinforced and reproduced partisan identities and allegiances. In doing so, consultants helped to create the very partisan context in which they worked.

Nevertheless, some consultants had a complicated and sometimes ambivalent relationship with political parties. Describing his relationship with party operatives in a 1979 interview, Doug Bailey described how "it's not a conflict of interest as much as a conflict in roles."[137] According to Bailey, "The party apparatus is filled with people ... who believe that they already know how to run this guy's campaign." Consequently, party operatives "don't want to admit that [a political consultant] can offer them anything or can really be of any help."[138] The result, Bailey observed, was a "begrudging respect" or even a "kind of jealousy" expressed on the part of party workers toward the consultant. "You sense it in every meeting," Bailey added.[139]

These rivalries may have diminished with time, but the fact remained that most consultants worked for candidates first: partisan goals were secondary to helping your client win. This was because individual officeholders remained largely responsible for their own political fates, a condition magnified by the breakdown of the New Deal coalition and the breakthrough in African American voting rights that transformed the American party system in the late twentieth century. Political consulting rose amid the initial uncertainty of these political shifts, and the industry gained strength as a new era of partisan polarization and closely contested elections took shape. Indeed, the success of the consulting enterprise partly hinged on the heightened sense of insecurity felt by every incumbent or challenger for office, regardless of party. As Matt Reese put it, there is "nothing better than a scared, rich candidate."[140] His comment reflects the complex mix of motives and the complicated relationship, partly symbiotic and partly parasitic, between consultants and their clients. Consultants exploited opportunities for economic gain generated by the high stakes of elections for the winners and the losers, be they candidates for office, party leaders, or the various interests seeking influence through the financial contributions they made to political campaigns.

This mixture of political and pecuniary motives is what makes consulting so unique and also, perhaps, difficult for some observers to grasp completely. Political consulting is a hybrid activity that combines commercial imperatives with ideological and partisan motivations. It is precisely this ability to square political goals with economic realities that made consulting a successful enterprise after the 1970s. Consultants entered the business to make money, but they were not exactly the mercenary operatives early assessments made them out to be. Ray Strother put it best: "I'm a capitalist, [but] I'm a Democratic capitalist."[141] The remark points to the essentially partisan nature of political work, and it illustrates the old saw about those who are drawn to politics to do good, but stay in politics to do well.

8

The Business of Digital Politics

ALTHOUGH THIS BOOK IS PRINCIPALLY focused on the history of political consulting, the origins of the industry shed light on our own time as well. This is because the evolution of political work is ongoing and the occupational struggle that characterized the rise of the consulting industry will continue to shape the nature of elections as well as broader features of the American political system. As in the past, efforts to better understand the dispositions and intentions of the voting public can produce innovations in technique that challenge existing sources of political intelligence and advice. Like radio, polling, or television, digital campaign tools such as Internet advertising or data analytics have altered the character of political work. However, the ability of these newer technologies to target supporters with greater precision and efficiency than traditional media is unlikely to disrupt the occupational control consultants currently enjoy over the conduct of campaigns.

Compared with previous breakthroughs in technique, advances in digital campaigns are taking place amid a fully developed market for political services. The commercialization of political work over the past century makes it less likely that digital politics will produce a radical opening of the campaign field. Instead, recent innovations have become the basis for new products and services that enhance consultants' control over political work. Moreover, the business of politics is increasingly concentrated in a few large firms, and a handful of consulting companies already dominate the digital niche within the industry.

At the same time, advances in digital campaigning are taking place amid a broader trend toward the corporate consolidation of political work. In recent years, a number of prominent consulting firms have become part of global conglomerates, integrating campaign tools with advertising, public relations, crisis communications, and brand management. Consequently, the business of politics is but one facet in a much larger and more lucrative field of corporate communications and public affairs that manages the public sphere on behalf of multinational corporations. In some respects, this corporate consolidation brings the business of politics full circle. The consulting industry emerged in part by adapting the tools of market research and product advertising to political work; now these same skills honed in the course of hard-fought political campaigns are in great demand by corporations that see the cultivation of public support as an essential part of their business strategy.

Innovation, Political Work, and Professional Control

Unlike in most commercial endeavors, there are few patents in politics. Instead, new techniques diffuse through the political system as consultants incorporate lessons from the last campaign. This ongoing innovation partly reflects the uncertainty of political competition. Even with advances in forecasting methods and reliable polls, the intentions of the voting public cannot be fully known until Election Day. Politics remains a speculative enterprise, especially in the midst of a close race, when it is difficult to know whether a particular tactic or strategy will prove to be the decisive factor that separates a candidate from victory or defeat. Even if many elections are decided by the broader political environment rather than the strategies and gambits of a single campaign, the uncertainty of not knowing who will win fuels the search for a more complete picture of the public and a more effective way to communicate the candidate's message.[1] This uncertainty extends to the realm of political work. In fact, because it is so difficult to isolate exactly which techniques were most effective in winning a race, there are rewards to be gained through speculation and innovation, regardless of the result. Winning may validate the wisdom of a new technique, but even in defeat a consultant can point to many factors beyond her control that explain why the client lost. In fact, losing may offer key lessons that spark subsequent invention.

Meanwhile, the number and frequency of elections, coupled with the free flow of political contributions, provide a market rich in opportunities for experiments in the use of novel campaign methods. According to the National Institute on Money in State Politics, in 2012 there were more than 3,800 candidates in 2,500 races for state and federal office who received at least $100,000 in campaign contributions (an additional 200 committees met the $100,000 threshold in state ballot initiatives).[2] The sheer scope of electoral competition in the United States, especially the number of candidates with money to spend, provides fertile ground for consultants offering the newest or most effective tools that can win a competitive race. Indeed, the large number of well-funded potential clients explains why the business of politics is so much larger in the United States than in other democratic nations.[3]

The recent development of digital campaign tools illustrates how this mixture of uncertainty and opportunity fuels innovation and the continuing evolution of political work. Over the past fifteen years, the use of fundraising appeals through email, Internet advertisements, and sophisticated data analytics has become widespread in American campaigns. The story is now a familiar one. In 2004, Howard Dean's unsuccessful run for the Democratic presidential nomination produced a major breakthrough in the use of the Internet to raise money, recruit volunteers, and mobilize supporters. Following his party's bruising defeat in the 2004 election, Dean became the chair of the Democratic National Committee, bringing along key staff from his campaign who then built a sophisticated technology platform so the party could raise more money and target resources more effectively on behalf of Democratic candidates.[4] Meanwhile, several other veterans of the Dean campaign established consulting firms that further developed the tools and techniques of digital campaigning. These pockets of expertise in and outside the party came together during the 2008 presidential race, helping a relatively unknown Barack Obama secure the nomination and then win the general election over John McCain. The development of digital tools continued during Obama's first term through the creation of Organizing for America (OFA), which utilized an enormous database of email addresses collected during the campaign to mobilize support on behalf of the administration's agenda.[5] In 2012, OFA morphed back into a campaign entity (renamed Obama for America) and built an extensive digital operation that utilized sophisticated data analytics in order to "fuse the multiple identities of the engaged citizen—the online activist, the offline voter, the donor, the volunteer—into a single, unified profile."[6] The result was widely hailed as an enormously successful fundraising, targeting, and get-out-the-vote effort that leveraged "big data" in a new and highly effective manner. Election postmortems gave a good part of the credit for Obama's re-election to the "nerds" who created the technology for a ground game that far surpassed what the Romney campaign achieved on Election Day.[7]

From a historical perspective, the arrival of data-driven campaigns resembles the early days of radio and television, when practitioners experimented with new technologies whose practical effects ran just ahead of their commercial value. Although Internet use is widespread in American politics, broadcast media still dwarf the amount of money allocated to online advertising and other digital tools. In the 2012 election, for instance, consulting firms specializing in digital services received only $318 million in campaign spending, compared with $2.6 billion collected by media consultants.[8] Spending in the 2014 midterm elections paint a similar picture. The cost of web ads, software, and other technology totaled only $164 million, compared with the $1.2 billion spent on broadcast media.[9] These figures suggest that consultants have yet to fully reap the commercial opportunities of digital tools. In 2012, the top media consulting firm, GMMB Inc., handled $435 million in campaign expenditures. By contrast, the top digital firm, Targeted Victory, was responsible for $112 million in spending.[10] One reason for this gap may be that digital tools can provide campaigns with a cheaper and more efficient way to allocate resources, for instance, by delivering messages to specific segments of the electorate or assigning volunteers to canvass neighborhoods where pockets of supporters reside. In contrast, television is a rather inefficient way to advertise, especially where media markets cross state lines and there is significant competition for audience attention.[11] The question is whether the advantages of digital tools will ever weaken the hold that media consultants currently enjoy over how campaigns spend their money.

Even without enormous sums spent on Internet advertising or data analytics, however, the new digital tools have transformed campaigns in several important respects. As Daniel Kreiss observes in *Taking Our Country Back: The Crafting of Networked Politics*, "From Howard Dean to Barack Obama, new media have provided campaigns with new ways to find and engage supporters, to run their internal operations, and to translate the energy and enthusiasm generated by candidates and political opportunities into the staple resources of American electioneering."[12] Far from a simple or straightforward story of technological change, Kreiss and others have shown how the developers of digital campaign tools confronted numerous technical challenges, unforeseen setbacks, and occasional clashes with broadcast media consultants over the allocation of campaign resources.[13] In other words, innovation and speculation are an ongoing feature of political work, as is the struggle over the control of that work. For instance, an important consequence of digital campaigning is the renewed emphasis on "ground wars" that marry sophisticated targeting methods with field operations that can mobilize volunteers and canvass would-be supporters.[14] The increasing value placed on face-to-face contacts and other forms of "personalized communication" reminds us that many involved in the day-to-day work of political campaigns are volunteers and low-paid staffers who lack the technical expertise or professional status of political consultants.[15] Media consultants may be the dominant voice in most campaigns, but they must work to remain so in light of digital techniques that challenge their control over political work.

Looking back, previous innovations have also fueled competition in the conduct of campaigns. During the first half of the twentieth century, publicity experts, public relations men, and pollsters challenged party workers and journalists as sources of political intelligence and advice. With the spread of radio and television, advertising agencies provided the personnel and expertise needed to run a modern campaign. In the 1970s, specialized consulting firms largely displaced ad agencies by embracing the partisan nature of political work, as well as tailoring their products and services to the needs and budgets of the candidate.

In a similar fashion, some believe that the new wave of digital technology will undermine the control media consultants currently enjoy in the conduct of campaigns by placing powerful tools of outreach and communication directly in the hands of the candidate. "With a relatively small staff and some creative thinking," one observer suggests, "you could bootstrap an entire campaign with no consultants that would miss out on nothing but paying the commissions."[16] However, there are reasons to be cautious of breathless accounts that foresee radical changes in politics wrought by the Internet.

Cashing In

The "myth of digital democracy," as Matthew Hindman points out, is the misplaced optimism that technology will be the great leveler, generating new avenues for political voice through the creation of online communities.[17] Rather than "democratize democracy" as hopeful advocates sometimes claim, Hindman shows that the online public sphere reproduces many of the same inequalities we see elsewhere in political life.[18] One reason, perhaps, is because the new tools of digital campaigns have become just another service to sell. Unlike the early days of radio or television, campaign innovations today occur in a highly developed marketplace for political work. As a result, new technologies of vote-getting quickly become commercial products and services that consultants sell to candidates in search of an advantage over their adversaries.

The development of digital campaigning illustrates how early advances in new media became part of the larger business of politics in the United States. As noted, the 2004 Dean campaign marked an important breakthrough in online fundraising and voter mobilization as a talented group of young staffers built a technological platform that turned the Internet into a viable and valuable political tool.[19] When Dean's campaign faltered, this previously unknown group of tech-savvy twenty- and thirty-somethings found themselves in high demand in the political world. As one Dean veteran recalled, "We were all pretty well marketable at the time, probably more so than we knew."[20] In fact, experiences gained during the 2004 Dean campaign launched several successful consulting firms that became dominant players in the emerging field of digital politics.

This trajectory is clearly illustrated in the case of Blue State Digital (BSD). Daniel Kreiss describes how four Dean staffers came together in the waning days of the campaign, motivated by "the need for better election tools and the opportunities within Democratic political consulting."[21] As one of the firm's founders put it, "There was a lot of opportunity in this space. . . . All of us recognized that there was a business need."[22] It did not take long for a start-up conceived in a Burlington, Vermont, bar to turn the innovations of the Dean campaign into a successful commercial enterprise. In 2005, BSD worked on behalf of Dean's successful bid to become chair of the Democratic National Committee, and, afterward, members of the firm played a central part in rebuilding the technological capacity of the party. As Kreiss documents so well, BSD developed a modular structure for email fundraising and volunteer recruitment that could be sold to other clients and candidates.[23] During the 2006 midterms, for example, BSD provided digital services to almost two dozen House and Senate candidates (twenty of whom won their election). By 2008, Blue State Digital had fifty employees and was poised for even greater success as one of the firm's founders, Joe Rospars, became new media director for Barack Obama's first presidential campaign.[24]

Two factors were critical to the success of Blue State Digital, one representing an important departure in consulting, the other a decidedly traditional approach to political work. First, an important innovation by BSD was that it secured a client agreement with Democracy for America, Howard Dean's political action committee, giving the firm proprietary control over the technical platform created during the 2004 Dean campaign.[25] By transforming the work of many into the intellectual property of a single company, BSD enjoyed a distinct advantage over its competitors trying to enter the promising field of digital politics. Second, like other successful consulting firms, BSD clearly positioned itself as a partisan player in the market for political work. Rather than develop a digital platform that could be sold to anyone, BSD worked exclusively for Democratic causes and candidates. This enabled the firm to build its client base through a partisan network that included the Democratic Party, allied organizations like America Coming Together (whose director of Internet strategy become managing director of BSD in early 2006), and Democratic candidates (including then junior senator from Illinois, Barack Obama).[26]

Other successful firms in the digital field followed a similar path. Voter Activation Network (VAN), for example, got its start in the 2002 election when its founders developed software that could integrate voter information files, market research, and other data in a single, user-friendly interface. This was particularly useful for get-out-the-vote efforts because it placed valuable data right in the hands of campaign field operations. Unlike commercial vendors who sold voter information to campaigns but retained ownership of the lists, VAN's business model was to sell its software but let clients keep the data. This served partisan ends, as it enabled various state parties, individual campaigns, and allied groups to share information. During the 2004 campaign, VAN software was used by the Kerry campaign's field operations; after Kerry's loss, VAN helped numerous state party committees build up their own valuable voter lists. By 2006, the firm had contracts in twenty-five states.[27]

Like Blue State Digital, VAN emerged from the 2006 election cycle with a strong reputation in Democratic circles as a key provider of digital tools. In 2007, the Democratic National Committee hired VAN to build the interface for its national voter file, and in 2008 VAN and BSD worked together within the Obama campaign to integrate each other's products in a single platform that combined data collected from donors on the public campaign website with the voter files and other valuable sources of information used by field operations on the ground. Although the practical effects of this effort were somewhat limited due to technical challenges in managing large and diverse sources of data, 2008 nevertheless marked an important step in the development and integration of digital technology in presidential campaigns. In particular, data analytics emerged as a powerful tool that could combine online and offline sources of information about voters to identify and mobilize supporters, raise money, and target appeals with greater precision.[28] The various experiments, enhancements, and advances that contributed to the Obama campaign's success in 2008 also had important implications for the rapidly developing business of digital politics.

If 2004 revealed the political potential of the Internet, 2008 demonstrated the commercial viability of sophisticated and increasingly sought-after campaign technologies. Firms like BSD and VAN turned digital tools into proprietary software that could be licensed to parties, candidates, and advocacy groups. As usage of this software spread, these firms captured a significant share of a growing market. Since 2008, several start-ups led by former campaign staffers have translated other digital advances into commercial products and services. For instance, the head of Obama's digital advertising efforts in 2008 established Bully Pulpit Interactive, currently the leading commercial provider of online ads to Democratic clients. A similar pattern is evident on the Republican side. In 2009, the former director of the Republican National Committee's voter turnout program started the consulting firm Targeted Victory along with another veteran from the 2008 campaign. Since then, Targeted Victory has become the leading provider of digital services to the GOP.[29]

In 2012, the Obama re-election effort and the Romney campaign for president invested heavily in digital tools, drawing key personnel from the handful of consulting firms that dominate the field. For instance, the Obama team included a dozen members with ties to Blue State Digital, including its chief digital strategist, Joe Rospars, and digital director, Teddy Goff. The founder of Bully Pulpit Interactive, Andrew Bleeker, directed Internet advertising and tapped four associates from his firm to help with digital marketing on the campaign. Meanwhile, the Romney team hired Targeted Victory cofounder Zac Moffatt as digital director along with ten other employees of the firm.[30] These partisan ties also paid financial dividends: Bully Pulpit Interactive billed the Obama campaign more than $104 million for online ads, while Targeted Victory billed the Romney campaign around $98 million for digital services.[31]

As these examples suggest, the new digital politics reinforces rather than challenges the partisan nature of political work. Although a few nonpartisan consulting firms do exist, these exceptions prove the partisan rule. Aristotle Industries is a longtime vendor of voter lists and campaign software to both Democratic and Republican clients but has recently faced stiff competition from newer, avowedly partisan rivals in the digital marketplace. In fact, Aristotle sued Democratic technology firm NGP for false advertising, arguing that a licensee of NGP software aided Republican candidates (rendering NGP's claims to be a "Democratic firm" misleading). According to NGP founder

Nathaniel Pearlman, Aristotle's lawsuit was an attempt to hobble his company with a costly court battle. A federal judge dismissed the case in 2011 (in 2010, NGP merged with VAN to become the leading provider of campaign software on the Democratic side).[32] A more recent effort to establish a nonpartisan firm is NationBuilder, which offers its clients a low-cost suite of web-based tools that can be tailored to the needs of almost any organization, large or small. Although the firm has attracted venture capital, some question the viability of a nonpartisan firm operating in what is largely a partisan marketplace. As Harper Reed, chief technology officer for the 2012 Obama campaign, put it, "How could we trust [NationBuilder]? What are they sharing? What combined intelligence are they giving . . . to our enemies?"[33] Zac Moffatt of the Republican firm Targeted Victory agreed that "partisanship has a role because of the trust factor," which is compounded by the fact that firms providing digital services are "touching so much of their [clients'] data."[34]

In sum, the growth of Internet advertising and data analytics in American campaigns marks both an important shift and a significant continuity in the history of political work. As noted previously, there are few patents in politics. This is clearly beginning to change as consultants increasingly are able to secure intellectual property rights for their political innovations. At the same time, however, the continued partisan character of political consulting means that the business of digital politics is not much different from the analog model that preceded it.

Corporate Consolidation

In 2010, the world's largest advertising and public relations company, WPP, acquired Blue State Digital for an undisclosed sum. With the move, BSD became part of a large, multinational holding company that generates $17 billion in annual revenues and includes more than 350 firms operating in forty-nine countries around the world. The company's chief executive, Martin Sorrell, built WPP through an aggressive acquisition strategy, turning an obscure UK manufacturer of wire baskets into a global provider of advertising and communications services with marquee holdings that include J. Walter Thompson, Young &

Rubicam, Burson-Marsteller, and Ogilvy & Mather. If it seems strange that Blue State Digital, a firm specializing in campaign services for Democratic candidates, would become part of a global advertising powerhouse, consider that WPP's holdings include twenty-six firms in the United States alone that specialize in political consulting, polling, and lobbying. These companies, in turn, form part of a worldwide group of fifty-six firms based in seventeen countries that specialize in public affairs, a somewhat vague category of activity that combines corporate public relations with grassroots lobbying techniques designed to mobilize or energize public support on behalf of a client, particularly in regulatory matters or other policy areas that potentially impact the bottom line.[35] Because of the skills of its practitioners and the demand for their services, public affairs is an important and growing branch of political work.

In the United States, WPP's holdings in this field include Benenson Strategy Group (whose founder worked as the lead pollster for President Obama in 2012) and the Dewey Square Group (whose principals include former senior strategists for Kerry in 2004 and Hillary Clinton in 2008). Both firms are expected to provide key personnel for Clinton in her 2016 presidential run.[36] Another WPP-owned firm with an impressive Democratic pedigree is the Glover Park Group (founded by the chief strategist for Al Gore's campaign in 2000 along with two veterans of the Clinton administration).[37] On the Republican side, WPP owns the Prime Policy Group, whose chairman, Charlie Black, worked for Presidents Reagan and Bush (I and II) and is an inductee of the American Association of Political Consultants Hall of Fame.[38] Another prominent Republican in the WPP fold is Mark McKinnon, who is currently a senior adviser at Hill+Knowlton Strategies (and was formerly the company's global vice chairman). McKinnon, who served as chief media adviser to George W. Bush in 2000 and 2004, sold the consulting firm he co-owned to WPP in 2006.[39] Another valuable asset is Burson-Marsteller, the third-largest public relations firm in the world (in billings), acquired by WPP in 2000 along with its parent firm, advertising giant Young & Rubicam. The current head of Burson-Marsteller is Donald Baer, a former senior adviser and speechwriter in the Clinton Administration. Baer's predecessor at

Burson-Marsteller was Mark Penn, a fomer pollster for both Clintons who sold his consulting firm to WPP in 2001.[40]

More recently, the company has sought to position itself in the digital marketplace through various mergers, acquisitions, and strategic partnerships. As noted previously, WPP bought Blue State Digital in 2010. In 2013, Burson-Marsteller tapped BSD cofounder and CEO, Thomas Gensemer, to be its chief strategy officer.[41] Meanwhile, in 2011, Burson-Marsteller announced it had entered into a strategic partnership with the Republican firm Targeted Victory, perhaps laying the groundwork for a future acquisition of the leading provider of digital services to the GOP.[42]

The acquisitions by WPP and its subsidiaries point to a corporate consolidation of political work in the United States.[43] Unlike an earlier age when public relations firms and advertising agencies struggled to square their commercial interests with the partisan nature of campaigns, today industry consolidation makes it possible to acquire multiple firms whose principals are connected to Democratic or Republican clients. Although WPP is the most aggressive on this front, it is not the only large player in the political consulting marketplace. Omnicom, Publicis, and InterPublic, rivals of WPP for control of the global advertising market, have also been acquiring assets in political consulting, polling, and public affairs.[44] For instance, the public relations giant Weber Shandwick, a subsidiary of InterPublic, is itself the product of a merger with the firm started by political consulting pioneer David Sawyer. As James Harding detailed in his book *Alpha Dogs*, Sawyer built a profitable consulting firm by bringing American-style campaigns to the Philippines, Colombia, and other countries.[45] Jack Leslie, who went to work for Sawyer after a stint in Ted Kennedy's office, eventually became president of the firm and then managed several successful mergers of the company before it was acquired by InterPublic. Today, Leslie is the chairman of Weber Shandwick, currently ranked as the second-largest public relations firm in the world.[46] Similarly, the French conglomerate Publicis owns political consulting firm Winner & Associates, whose CEO, Chuck Winner, is a leader in the management of ballot initiatives.[47] Finally, Omnicom, through its public relations subsidiary FleishmanHillard, owns the largest Democratic media firm,

GMMB.[48] In 2012, GMMB partner and cofounder Jim Margolis served as senior adviser to the Obama re-election effort (a position he also held in 2008), while his firm billed almost $390 million in media services to the campaign.[49]

What explains the acquisition of these firms and their integration in a broader field of corporate communication and public affairs? In financial terms, political consulting generates paltry revenues compared with advertising agencies and public relations firms. The public may be aghast at the $6 billion spent on the 2012 election, but it is worth remembering that the top 100 advertisers spend more than $100 billion on marketing each year, and Procter & Gamble alone spent $5 billion on advertising in 2012.[50] More than the dollar value of consulting services, however, the value of firms that specialize in political work is their ability to provide corporate clients a menu of services that extend beyond the traditional offerings of an advertising agency or public relations firm. The value of campaign techniques is in the capacity to cultivate public support, whether on behalf of a candidate or a corporation. In the case of the latter, consultants can provide a focused, carefully orchestrated campaign designed to improve a company's public image. In some cases, the same metrics used in politics, such as a candidate's favorable ratings, can be used to measure the success of a corporate campaign. As Mark Penn put it, writing in the *Harvard Business Review*, "While politics has always been an avid spectator sport, lately it's become a field that offers valuable lessons for business." In particular, Penn advised, "Campaigns and consumer choices share one important thing in common: they are about alternatives, not ideals."[51] Whether working for a candidate or a corporation, the job of the consultant is to make the public prefer the client over a lesser alternative.

Looking back on the history of political work, the application of consulting skills to corporate needs is nothing new. Consultants working in the 1970s and 1980s found that corporate clients paid well and helped firms secure a reliable source of revenue immune from the periodic ups and downs of political campaigns. Looking back even further, political consulting itself grew out of the field of public relations, and we can trace polling directly to scientific advances in market research made during the 1930s and 1940s. The effort to understand, measure, and manipulate political behavior grew out of similar efforts and technologies designed and applied first in the commercial realm.

However, the corporate consolidation of political work also represents a new phase in the way campaign tools are integrated into a broader corporate strategy. As Jack Martin, global chairman and CEO of Hill+Knowlton Strategies, put it, "Our approach ... is called the 5th Seat. The 5th Seat puts us in the [corporate] c-suite of our clients, next to the lawyers, accountants, management consultants, and bankers." In Martin's view, his firm offers a valuable skill set that belongs in every boardroom, "not only for interacting with the public but to measure it" as well.[52] Enhancing the public image of the corporation or mobilizing public support on its behalf, especially in matters that touch on government policy, is just as important to business growth as law, finance, advertising, or market research. The innovation of WPP and other communications conglomerates is to provide a one-stop shop for all kinds of corporate communication needs. According to WPP chair Martin Sorrell, a single provider is particularly valuable to large, multinational corporations with "a vast geographical spread and a need for a wide range of marketing services." For these clients, Sorell explains, "WPP can act as a portal to provide a single point of contact and accountability."[53]

The Future of Political Work

The invention of digital campaign tools and the corporate consolidation of the consulting industry help us to understand the present and possible future of political work in the United States. As in the past, competition, uncertainty, and the ability to emulate the successes of the last campaign will produce innovations that diffuse quickly through the political system. Speculative experimentation is a constant feature of political work. While this speculation continues in the business of digital politics, enterprising staffers now look to develop a proprietary technology that can serve as the basis for a successful start-up or be sold to an existing firm. Following the 2012 election, for example, three members of Obama's digital team created NationalField, described as "an online organizing network and dashboard tool for campaigns to integrate and aid their field operations."[54] In 2013, the founders of NationalField sold the business to NGP VAN, adding new features and functionality to what is already the largest provider of campaign software to Democratic clients.[55]

Although it is possible that firms specializing in digital campaign tools could one day displace the traditional media consultants who currently command a dominant position in the industry, this seems unlikely. Instead, media consultants will try to integrate digital tools into their existing products and services, for example, by finding ways to target political ads through media streaming services and smartphone applications. Even so, the partisan character of political work means that consulting services, digital or otherwise, will remain segmented into distinct markets for Democratic and Republican clients. Digital politics can create significant riches for its practitioners without altering the basic structure of the industry.

Another notable trend is that the contemporary business of politics is highly concentrated in a few firms on each side of the partisan divide. Although anyone with a bit of campaign experience can set up a website and call themselves a consultant, most of the money spent on media, fundraising, and other products and services passes through the hands of a select group of firms. Consider the figures from the 2012 election. Just three firms accounted for two-thirds of all spending by the Obama campaign: GMMB (media), Bully Pulpit Interactive (digital), and AB Data (direct mail). Similarly, for the Romney campaign, three firms handled around 64 percent of spending: American Rambler Productions (media), Targeted Victory (digital), and SCM Associates (direct mail).[56] Overall, the top five Democratic media firms handled almost three-quarters of spending, while the top five media firms on the Republican side took in more than half of GOP spending in 2012. This includes congressional races, the presidential campaign, party spending, and independent expenditures. Digital services are even more concentrated. The top five Democratic and Republican firms accounted for 93 percent and 84 percent of digital services, respectively.[57] The two top firms on each side of the partisan divide, Bully Pulpit Interactive and Targeted Victory, accounted for a combined 70 percent of all digital spending in 2012.[58]

This concentration makes it unlikely that new technologies will produce a radical opening of the political process in which candidates have
the capacity to connect directly with a circle of supporters without the
services of a professional consultant. Although recent elections illustrate the enduring importance of grassroots activism and energy, the
ability to locate, engage, and deploy volunteers still relies on technologies supplied by the same industry that provides the traditional tools of
media and direct mail. With the rise of digital campaigns, consultants
have developed another service to sell.

This points to the third and perhaps the most profound development in the evolving business of politics: the consolidation and integration of political work into large, multinational conglomerates that
measure and manage the public on behalf of powerful clients. Together,
WPP, Omnicom, Publicis, and InterPublic control a majority share of
the global advertising and public relations market. In recent years, these
large holding companies have added political consulting firms to their
assets, not because of the revenues generated from campaigns but rather
because of the value of campaign techniques to their corporate clients.
As the leading Democratic digital firm Bully Pulpit Interactive adver-
tises on its website,

> Every organization seeks a bully pulpit. We are just the modern
> version. We use the tools of modern media and the tactics of
> the greatest recent political victories to help you communicate.
> Whether you run for office, steer a company, or chair a founda-
> tion, the public now has an undeniable seat at the table. Many
> leaders are afraid of this. Don't be. Make people part of your team.
> Make them your advocates. Make them your champions. Let us
> show you how. We sit at the intersection of political and corpo-
> rate. While our political mentality keeps us fast and lean, our cor-
> porate experience keeps us on the cutting edge and allows us to
> constantly innovate, not just once every four years. We sit at the
> nexus of persuasion and direct response. From top to bottom, we
> are analysts—constantly testing and optimizing. But tactics with-
> out a message are never enough. We pride ourselves at also being
> master storytellers and we use data to help us shape the most com-
> pelling and credible narratives.[59]

This testimonial captures the continuity of political work, from its Progressive Era origins to the present. By invoking the idea of the "bully pulpit," this cutting-edge, twenty-first-century firm echoes Theodore Roosevelt and others who used publicity to forge a more direct connection with the public. In the words of its founders, the company is "just the modern version." Like an earlier generation of practitioners, Bully Pulpit Interactive celebrates technology as a way to acquire deeper, more reliable information about the public, using "data to help us shape the most compelling and credible narratives." Finally, the company promotes its ability to "sit at the intersection of political and corporate," staying "fast and lean" as well as "cutting edge." This, too, continues a long line of publicity experts, pollsters, and consultants who served both candidates and corporations.

Echoes from the past notwithstanding, the business of digital politics and the corporate consolidation of the industry also represent a departure. Initially, business methods drawn from advertising and public relations influenced the conduct of campaigns; today it is those who practice at the cutting edge of political work who influence the decisions made in corporate boardrooms. For example, the cofounder of Bully Pulpit Interactive (BPI), Andrew Bleeker, now works for WPP subsidiary Hill+Knowlton Strategies as its director of global digital practice (Bleeker continues to serve as BPI president).[60] For a global advertising power like WPP, acquiring expertise in the digital realm is an important part of its strategy to provide a single source for corporate communications, from advertising and market research to crisis management and public affairs. The possibility that digital tools can identify and energize discrete pockets of voters or target ads more efficiently is potentially of great value to WPP and its clients.

This coevolution of business and politics in the United States points to a broader significance in the rise of a modern consulting industry. Over the past century, the blending of advertising, public relations, political consulting, and public affairs has blurred the lines between commerce and politics. Our behavior as consumers and voters is an expression of individual choice that has been constantly measured and continually managed through campaigns of persuasion. And yet, despite the many billions of dollars spent, the ability to convince us to buy a product or vote for a candidate is limited. The available methods and techniques have vastly improved, yet consultants and their clients remain engaged in the continued search for an elusive public whose intentions in the marketplace and the voting booth cannot be fully known.

9

The Evolution of Political Work

OVER THE COURSE OF THE twentieth century, a new industry secured a pivotal role in the American political system. Today, few candidates for office lack the services of a professional consultant; even fewer can succeed without one. Across the political spectrum and at various levels of government, consultants provide products and services considered essential to political competition and electoral success. Pollsters measure the depth of candidate support and help to select the issues of the campaign. Media consultants present the candidate to the public and craft the narrative of the race. Digital tools leverage data analytics to identify and target key groups of voters. Direct mail specialists raise the vast sums of money needed to keep the machine running. Culminating a process that began almost a hundred years earlier, the conduct of political work is now largely a matter of professional control. A full-fledged business of politics has taken shape.

The process by which this occurred was neither inevitable nor automatic. The business of politics arose through a series of innovations that changed how candidates campaigned for office and, more broadly, how elected officials, political parties, and private interests sought to understand and influence public sentiments. Technological advances certainly mattered, as did broader changes in the character of American politics. However, the rise of a political consulting profession was the work of many individual practitioners. Television, for example, created opportunities for those skilled in the use of the new medium, but consultants figured out how to render spot advertisements politically effective and economically viable. Advances in computing, long-distance telephones, and video production lowered the entry barriers to political work, but it was the consultants who turned these low-cost technologies into a profitable niche in media, polling, or direct mail. More recently, specialists in digital campaigning have taken innovations in the political use of the Internet and big data and turned them into proprietary software that is widely used in political campaigns.

These innovations are part of a much longer transformation in the character of political work. Beginning in the early twentieth century, advocates of publicity began to promote the idea that planned campaigns of persuasion and direct appeals to the public were the most effective means to secure popular support. In the 1920s and 1930s, advances in the political use of radio and scientific polling afforded new ways to reach mass publics, creating a new kind of expert in the collection of political intelligence and the interpretation of public sentiment. In California, a recognizable consulting industry began to take shape as early as the 1940s as business interests embraced professional campaign services in the pursuit of political ends. With the advent of television, commercial ad agencies handled much of the advertising for presidential campaigns until the 1960s, when many firms withdrew from political work. In the 1970s, aided by campaign finance rules that privileged professional services, the political consulting industry took off, occupying a critical position in the circuits of capital that connect donors and candidates in the American political system. If the nineteenth-century alchemists of American politics turned whiskey into votes, modern-day consultants transform political contributions into the ubiquitous advertisements and polls of contemporary campaigns.

The consulting profession is firmly established in the political system, but the evolution of political work continues. This ongoing process offers several insights into the character of American politics, past and present. First, consultants continue the search for more effective instruments of persuasion and more reliable sources of information about the attachments and affiliations of individual voters. Running through the entire twentieth-century history of political work, in fact, is an effort to combine a social scientific rendering of the electorate with a personalized style of communication. Just as the invention of radio spurred the twin developments of commercial polling and political broadcasts, advances in data analytics and the development of the Internet as a platform for targeted communication continue the creative blending of science and art in the conduct of political work.[1]

Second, the growth of consulting is both a cause and a consequence of broader changes in the character of American political institutions. As the unimpeded and virtually unlimited flow of campaign contributions makes the economic rewards of political work even greater, the industry continues to benefit from a regulatory structure that privileges consultants as a legal way to spend money. Recent Supreme Court decisions have not altered the basic requirement that campaigns and political committees submit detailed lists of expenditures. However, campaign finance rules are just one example of how government contributed to the development of the consulting industry. From the early days of publicity, the federal executive has fostered experiments in eliciting popular support.[2] During the New Deal, especially, innovations in polling and media contributed simultaneously to the evolution of the modern presidency and the development of professional political work.

Third, alongside the helping hand of government, the consulting industry has long benefited from a close alliance with business, both as a client for professional services and as an incubator of tools and techniques. In the early twentieth century, corporate publicity illustrated the value of public opinion in the pursuit of private interest. In the 1920s and 1930s, public relations experts touted the advantages of modern business methods, including early forms of polling, in the conduct of campaigns. Beginning with Whitaker and Baxter in California and continuing through the consolidation of a national industry in the 1970s, corporate clients helped consultants establish a solid financial footing, compensating for the uneven and uncertain nature of political campaigns. These trends continue as the consulting industry consolidates into larger firms and global conglomerates that provide a menu of services to a wide array of political and corporate clients.

In sum, the origins and evolution of the consulting industry are to be found at the nexus of advances in communication and information technology, the system of campaign finance, and the political awakening of American business. This is not to suggest that the business of politics followed some inevitable logic dictated by technological change or features of the broader political system. Rather, practitioners exploited political opportunities to develop new techniques of persuasion and crafted communication, touting their inventions as essential tools of political competition. Through a process of discovery, trial, and error, the consulting profession changed the conduct of political work and the character of American democracy. This process continues.

Information and Persuasion

As described in chapter 2, presidential campaigns at the turn of the twentieth century combined a progressive belief in rational deliberation with an orchestrated attempt at mass persuasion. This seemingly contradictory impulse marks an important turn in the history of political work. Operating under the general heading of publicity, experts skilled in the techniques of journalism and advertising celebrated the power of the reasoning voter even as they crafted campaign messages designed to create an emotional connection with the public. The resulting tension between reason and emotion, between information and persuasion, and between a world of objective facts and a subjective rendering of the world so that it appeared fact-like shaped the evolution of political work in the United States and altered the character of American politics in ways that are still evident today.

The growth of mass-circulation newspapers and magazines offered unprecedented access to a national electorate. For progressive politicians like Theodore Roosevelt and Woodrow Wilson, the national press made it possible to appeal directly to the voter on the basis of issue positions rather than partisan loyalties. Publicity captured a progressive faith in the power of reason, and it fit well with the criticism of boss rule offered by Roosevelt, Wilson, and others who believed that the character of the individual candidate could stand above the corrupting influence of the party machine.

This emphasis on the individual attributes of the candidate continues to be a staple of American political style long after the party bosses have gone. Contemporary forms of political advertising follow a predictable formula: publicize an opponent's shortcomings in order to elevate one's own position in the public eye. Publicity not only reveals who is honest and who is corrupt but also separates the qualified from the inept. The focus on personal political virtue contributes to the highly personalistic nature of American campaigns and the individualistic self-reliance with which candidates approach their political careers.

As a technique, however, publicity is an instrument of persuasion that frequently draws a mixture of skepticism, derision, and alarm, especially from potential rivals in the provision of political advice. As discussed in chapter 3, revelations of wartime propaganda during the 1920s fueled an occupational struggle over the space between the public and those who endeavored to represent them. Journalists, in particular, defended their role as arbiters of public opinion by portraying those engaged in publicity and public relations as hucksters, con artists, or even master manipulators degrading the democratic process. In response, practitioners adopted the trappings of a profession in an effort to secure occupational control over political work.

Almost a century later, the public image of the political consultant remains mixed at best. Critics sometimes blame the industry for a cynical political style that pollutes the airwaves with negative advertising and turns our leaders into slavish followers of a fickle public.[3] As in the past, entities like the American Association of Political Consultants, graduate programs in political management, and trade publications like *Campaigns & Elections* help the industry foster a professional identity and raise its status in the eyes of a skeptical public.

Throughout this struggle for occupational control, campaign professionals have found common cause with social scientists in search of better ways to measure and manage public opinion. Edward Bernays, for example, corresponded with prominent political scientists who thought the practice of public relations could contribute to a social scientific understanding of mass psychology. For these scholars, propaganda was an essential tool of modern politics; campaigns of persuasion were a feature of a well-functioning democracy. As Harold Lasswell famously put it, propaganda itself was "no more moral or immoral than a pump handle."[4] A version of Lasswell's argument survives in contemporary political science research that finds negative advertising does not repel voters but instead informs and energizes the electorate.[5]

As the consulting profession developed over the next several decades, academia provided both a source of talent and a testing ground for new techniques. As described in chapter 4, commercial pollsters like George Gallup worked closely with academics like Hadley Cantril to perfect their methods, further their professional aims, and raise the status of survey research in the academy. In the 1940s, academic social scientists came to the rescue of commercial pollsters, explaining that the debacle of the 1948 campaign illustrated the need for more polling, not less. Even today, a number of prominent pollsters began their careers in the academy or hold advanced degrees.[6]

More important than the status consultants derive from an affiliation with an academic discipline is the way social scientific techniques helped make the attachments and affiliations of voters legible to consultants crafting the strategy of a campaign. During the 1941 New York mayoral race, for example, Edward Bernays used census data to classify voters and tailor campaign messages that resonated with what he believed to be the interests, aspirations, and fears of discrete racial and ethnic groups. Thirty years later, Matt Reese devised a much more sophisticated targeting method that combined precinct-level demographic, consumer, and electoral data to generate profiles of like-minded voters he believed would be receptive to specific messages and appeals. Today, advances in computer-assisted mapping (geographic information systems) and abundant sources of fine-grained personal data allow for even greater precision in targeting. At the same time, campaigns are using the results of experimental research in political science to gauge the relative efficacy of phone calls, direct mail, and door-to-door contact as inducements to vote.[7]

The Search for an Elusive Public

Close ties between social scientists and campaign professionals reflected a common desire: to understand the motivations and beliefs of an elusive public. The business of politics took shape during a profound growth in the scale and scope of political communication. Mass-circulation newspapers and magazines created new opportunities to craft messages on behalf of a candidate or a corporation. The advent of radio and then television made it possible to engage the electorate more directly, without the intervening influence of an editor. But with new technologies came new challenges as well.

In particular, it was not immediately clear how to integrate the tools of mass communication into the conduct of campaigns. What kind of messages were voters likely to receive? Who was likely to tune in to political programming, and how big was the audience? Which format was best suited to the character of a new medium like radio or television? In the early days of radio, for example, it was difficult to know how the public responded to, or even how many people received, political broadcasts. Whereas circulation data provided a rough measure of a newspaper's reach, radio and television required a new set of techniques that could measure the size and preferences of a largely invisible public. As explored in chapter 4, the development of audience measurement tools was a key step in the origins of the commercial polling industry, as well as a keen interest of academic social scientists like Paul Lazarsfeld, Hadley Cantril, and others interested in the effects of mass communication. By applying the same techniques designed to measure the consumption habits and likes of the radio listener, Cantril along with former business executive Gerald Lambert used survey research to inform White House strategy. Franklin Roosevelt's famed fireside chats represent an early example of crafted talk that combined the science of polling with the art of communication, a union that would transform political work in the decades to come.[8]

Even so, innovation in political work was a halting and uneven process. In the case of radio, political campaigns experimented with a variety of approaches that proved to be of limited use—in some cases they were outright failures. In the 1920s, paid radio programming consisted largely of gavel-to-gavel coverage of nominating conventions that included endless speeches, arcane procedural moves, and long ovations. This was far from scintillating entertainment, and it took at least a decade before political communication adapted to the expectations of a listening audience. With the advent of television, parties and campaigns continued to search for the best way to present a candidate to the public. Initial forays into televised campaigns included issue-focused ads as well as animated spots and jingles that mimicked commercial advertising methods.[9] Throughout the 1950s and 1960s, candidates continued to rely on longer campaign films and paid political programming that lasted fifteen minutes, a half hour, or even longer. It was not until the 1970s that the thirty-second spot became the modal form of political advertising. Even then, the penetration of television in political campaigns was a gradual process. As late as 1978, a survey of general election candidates for the House of Representatives found that only 44 percent of campaigns employed television.[10] The history of political work challenges the notion that technology transforms politics in a linear or straightforward fashion. Rather, communication technology like radio and television first had to be translated into a form that could be used effectively for political ends.

The Internet is the latest in a line of technological advances to influence the character of American politics. As discussed in chapter 8, online fundraising, advertising, and outreach efforts can now target supporters with greater precision and efficiency than was previously the case. As with past innovations, the development of digital campaign tools has implications for the control of political work. Although some foresee a time when the Internet and data analytics will supplant the traditional reliance on television, including the well-paid media consultants and time buyers who currently control the lion's share of campaign resources, the new wave of digital tools is simply another service to sell. In this regard, the business of digital politics is not much different from the analog version that preceded it. In fact, by integrating digital campaigns into a broader menu of corporate communication services, these latest inventions appear to be the most recent phase in the ongoing commercialization of political work rather than some radical departure from the past.

From the spread of mass-circulation newspapers to the development of digital campaigns, practitioners have engaged in an ongoing search for a more immediate and more personal connection to the voter. Newspaper publicity appealed to the reasoning public, using effective copy to reach a national electorate. Radio brought the candidate into the living rooms of Americans and created a far more intimate connection with the voter than ever before. Television added the visceral image. The Internet, mobile technology, and data analytics provide greater immediacy and reach for political communication, and the trove of individual-level information, from consumer habits to voting behavior, can target messages more precisely than in the past. For more than a century, the effort to classify voters, target messages, and track their effects has been central to the development of a consulting industry and will continue to spark innovations that define the character of political work in the United States.

Political Work and American Political Institutions

The twentieth-century transformation of political work also had important implications for American political institutions. The growth of publicity and other tools of mass persuasion placed greater emphasis on the personal characteristics and issue positions of the candidate as opposed to (or at least in addition to) their loyalty to the party standard. The dual character of publicity—a device intended to inform and persuade—liberated politicians like Theodore Roosevelt and Woodrow Wilson whose political views and aspirations cut against the grain of their party. Compared with the nineteenth century, publicity techniques also shifted greater responsibility for the conduct of campaigns onto the candidate and his immediate circle of supporters. This was a gradual process, and one that was far from uniform across the United States. Nevertheless, the upshot was to transform the career politician from one who had faithfully served the interests of the party to one who successfully managed his or her own electoral enterprise.[11]

The effects of this transition are most visible at the level of the president. Cantril and Lambert's work on behalf of the FDR administration illustrates how the rise of a modern executive and a personalistic style of presidential leadership relied on the expertise of those skilled in the modern techniques of polling and media. Although the origins of this development can be seen in the government publicity of the Progressive Era, including the vast propaganda efforts of the Committee on Public Information during World War I, it was during the 1930s and 1940s that contemporary forms of presidential communication took shape amid an ambitious and much-enlarged executive branch that sought to mobilize public support through depression and war.[12] One paradox of the modern presidency is that the growth of executive power focused public attention on the individual character of the president even as it fueled the growth of an institutional apparatus dedicated to the measurement and management of public opinion.[13] The history of political work suggests that politics did not intrude on the modern presidency, bringing with it the unrelenting search for public approval we often associate with the institution today. Instead, polling and media found a receptive home in the executive branch before diffusing to the rest of the political system. The growth of the presidency illustrates how changes in the character of political work interacted with broader changes in the political system, jointly influencing one another in the process. In this manner, the coevolution of political institutions and political work together shaped the trajectory of twentieth-century American politics.

The institutional implications of this transformation extend well beyond the presidency. As examined in chapter 5, Whitaker and Baxter forged a new kind of professional advocacy work in California, helping well-heeled but often inchoate business interests wage successful grassroots lobbying campaigns. Whitaker and Baxter's firm, Campaigns, Inc., enjoyed an impressive run of success during the 1940s and 1950s, helping business groups and professional associations find common cause to defeat popular referendums and legislative initiatives that threatened their political and financial interests. In their work on behalf of the California Medical Association, for example, Whitaker and Baxter defeated Republican governor Earl Warren's proposal for universal sickness protection by touting the benefits of private health insurance while stoking fears of "socialized" medicine. Whitaker and Baxter went on to pursue a similar strategy on behalf of the American Medical Association, and their work continues to echo in national debates over health policy. More broadly, the professional management of grassroots lobbying campaigns, often waged on behalf of corporations seeking to influence policy or simply improve their public image, is widespread in American politics today. This profitable business of public affairs consulting relies on more sophisticated versions of the same tools and techniques Campaigns, Inc. first deployed more than seventy years ago.

The phenomenon of "grassroots for hire" is indicative of the heavy reliance on professional services throughout the contemporary American political system.[14] Consultants work at all levels of government on behalf of candidates for federal, state, and local office, and on behalf of a myriad of interest groups, super PACs, and party committees. The professional control of political work is so nearly complete, in fact, that it can be easy to overlook how the gradual rise of the consulting industry contributed to broader trends in the character of American politics. For instance, early accounts of political consulting keyed its rise to a decline in the strength of party organizations, arguing that the growth of the profession hastened the transition to a more fully candidate-centered political system.[15] In contrast, many contemporary scholars contend that political consultants serve a key function within an extended partisan network of elected officials, activists, allied groups, and national party committees. In this view, political consultants are not antithetical to partisan goals but in fact work closely with the parties in helping candidates win office.[16]

One way to reconcile these two views is to recognize that consultants helped to bring about both the centralizing and centrifugal tendencies in the American political system. The business of politics flourished in part because of the proliferation of individuals and groups in search of public support, including candidates for office, various interests, and often government itself. Consultants benefited from and contributed to the diffuse character of American politics by creating a market for political services that enabled various actors and interests to engage in politics independently from political parties or from one another. However, the changing character of political work, especially the increasing reliance on relatively costly techniques like media, polling, and direct mail, placed a premium on the capacity to raise large amounts of money. This had a centralizing effect on American politics as the national party committees and, more recently, Super PACs have become important brokers in the collection and distribution of campaign contributions from wealthy donors. [17]

Consultants contributed to the concentration of power in the American political system by transforming political donations into valuable polls, media, and mail. As explained in chapter 7, campaign finance reform created a new political economy of influence that cemented the role of consultants in American politics by privileging professional services over traditional forms of political work. The consulting industry benefits both from the utter weakness of campaign finance regulations and from its one enduring strength: transparency in spending. Even in an age of enormous sums flowing into the political system from unknown sources, it is still possible to track exactly where and toward what purpose this "dark money" goes. To a large degree, unlimited political spending has provided a windfall for political consultants who produce the flood of ads and other forms of media, purchase television airtime, and manage the fundraising apparatus needed to raise vast amounts of campaign cash.

Critics sometimes portray consultants as parasites on the political system, but this may be the incorrect metaphor.[18] Rather than feed off the host, the business of politics is more akin to the colonies of microbes that coevolved with humans over thousands of years. Like the microscopic bugs in our gut, the consulting industry is crucial to the metabolic functioning of a system of influence peddling that turns vast amounts of money into legally sanctioned political services. As a result, consultants occupy a rather successful (and profitable) niche within the broader ecology of campaigns and elections. However, the effects of this relationship are far from benign. Political consulting poses a risk to the long run health of the system by enabling the continued growth of unchecked political spending. The consulting industry makes it possible to transform limitless funds into an endless stream of ads and polls, leaving the body politic engorged yet unsatisfied in its appetite for money. The result is a concentration of power and influence, not only among the wealthy interests that finance political campaigns, but also within the handful of consulting firms and global conglomerates that control an increasingly sizable share of the business of politics itself.

The Politics of Business

The system of campaign finance raises troubling questions about political influence in the United States, especially the role of powerful corporate interests. Through their control of political work, consultants serve as a critical intermediary between wealthy contributors and candidates seeking office. In fact, the relationship between the consulting industry and American business goes beyond political campaigns. As described in chapter 8, consultants are in great demand by large multinational holding companies like WPP and Omnicom that offer a package of integrated corporate communications and public affairs services to its clients. This recent consolidation of the industry is part of a longer history of political work that is closely tied to the rise of public relations in the United States. Ivy Lee, working on behalf of railroads and other industrial interests, articulated a vision of corporate publicity that saw the public image of the corporation as an important line of defense against the encroaching powers of the government. Edward Bernays endeavored to make public relations a profession and insert the public relations counsel in business and politics alike. Whitaker and Baxter employed the tools of public relations to defend corporate interests in California and wage political battles on behalf of physicians wary of public health insurance. Close ties between American business and allied fields such as public relations and advertising made the transition from corporate communication to political campaigns a relatively easy one.

In fact, the transformation of political work points to an important affinity between the conduct of business and the business of politics in the United States. Publicity, advertising, public relations, and political consulting all share a common goal: public persuasion. It is not surprising, therefore, that commercial tools designed to tout the merits of a product would find their way into politics. As Michael McGerr so perceptively described, an advertised style of American politics emerged at the turn of the twentieth century that focused on the image and personality of the candidates.[19] During the 1920s and 1930s, the academic study of marketing and the development of commercial survey research gave rise to a new science of selling that shaped the practical conduct of campaigns and provided new tools to measure public opinion on a range of social and political subjects.[20] With the advent of polling, voting became like other consumer acts made legible through social scientific technique. For Paul Lazarsfeld, in particular, elections provided an opportunity to study the psychology of choice during what was, in effect, a one-day sale. This rough equivalence between voting and buying contributed to a broader transformation in the character of political work by treating individual voters as a bundle of affinities and allegiances that could be measured and managed, as well as bought and sold, in the form of polls and surveys.[21] Likening the act of voting to a matter of consumer choice facilitated the commercialization of political work and the creation of a market for products and services such as polls, media, and direct mail.

Looked at this way, the business *of* politics also served as a key conduit for the influence of business *in* politics. Political consultants are key actors in politics today because they transform campaign contributions into a variety of services valued by candidates. This is only one channel of business influence, however. Consultants are also carriers of business methods in the form of coordinated selling campaigns that use tools derived from marketing and advertising to target individual preferences and attachments. With the twentieth century rise of a business of politics in the United States, American democracy increasingly depends on the art (and science) of the sale.

Political Consequences of the Profit Motive

Fundamentally, to say that politics has become a business in the United States is to underscore how commercial incentives inform political practice and shape political campaigns. Money in politics is nothing new. The conduct of political work has always reflected a mixture of partisan and pecuniary interests to some degree. However, a crucial difference separates the political consultant of today from the party worker of the past. Today, politics is heavily influenced by the political consequences of the profit motive. The reliance on surveys, television advertisements, and direct mail in contemporary campaigns reflects the financial incentives of consultants in search of more revenue and more reliable sources of income. Consultants offer tangible goods such as media or polling that campaigns, candidates, and their inner circle are unable to provide themselves. Accordingly, the most commonly used compensation structure in the industry is payment as a percentage of campaign expenditures: the more candidates spend (and the earlier in the campaign they spend it), the more consultants receive in return.[22]

The financial incentives of consultants may help explain why campaigns spend so much money on media and other professional services even when the evidence for their efficacy is far from clear. Beginning with the early voting studies by Lazarsfeld and others in the 1940s, political scientists have tried to measure campaign effects, including the role that media and other forms of mass communication play in shaping political behavior. The accumulated findings from almost seventy-five years of research indicate that campaign tactics do matter, but in ways that can vary quite considerably and often depend on factors that are beyond the control of a candidate or the campaign.[23] However, even though it is difficult to know precisely how political advertising will influence voting or turnout in a given race, the allocation of campaign resources relies heavily on paid media nevertheless. The history of political work suggests that this feature of contemporary campaigns is due to the influence and incentives of the consultants advising the candidate.

The prominent role of media consultants today is a product of gradual transformation over the course of the twentieth century. For innovations in political technique to spread, practitioners had to overcome skepticism and even resistance from candidates who relied on traditional sources of political advice. Edward Bernays used social scientific data to target political messages in ways that look familiar to contemporary eyes, but it is important to remember that William O'Dwyer did not follow his advice in the 1941 campaign for New York City mayor. Bernays failed to close the sale. Similarly, Gerard Lambert could not convince Thomas Dewey's inner circle of the virtues of poll-tested messages in the 1944 presidential race. Even Whitaker and Baxter, whose firm, Campaigns, Inc., boasted an impressive record of success in California, worked hard to convince their clients about the value of their methods.

Things are very different now. Candidates today seek to hire consultants in order to signal the viability of their campaign and secure the support of donors.[24] The use of consultants is so pervasive, in fact, that the structure of the industry and the incentives of individual firms shape the conduct and character of our politics in various ways. As noted earlier, the heavy emphasis on media and mail reflects the fee structure of the business. The broad diffusion of consulting through state and local races, ballot initiatives, public affairs work, and even international campaigns further reflects the desire among consultants to acquire a steady source of revenue.[25] Consulting shapes campaigns in other ways as well. Recent research suggests that certain consulting firms are more likely to employ negative ads, and House candidates who shared the same consultants were more likely to use similar strategies, particularly the kind of issues emphasized during the campaign.[26] Consultants are an important vector for the diffusion of political technique.

The financial incentives of consultants may also diminish the competitiveness of our political system. Consultants are extremely cognizant of the importance of reputation because the business of politics is predicated on the idea that consultants help candidates win office. Within the market for political services, a reputation for winning is critical for the long-run success of a firm. Knowing this, consultants will compete for candidates who can enhance their reputation, which is to say candidates who are likely to win. Consultants may garner attention by helping a previously unknown challenger win a tough race, but from a business perspective, working for an incumbent is a much safer bet. Consequently, larger and more successful firms may seek incumbents as clients. At the same time, incumbents themselves possess limited information about the quality of consultants other than their previous record of success and, therefore, are likely to hire firms with a record of winning. The combined effect of these incentives is to concentrate the work of the largest, most successful firms in the service of incumbents whether or not they face a tough re-election battle. Once hired, consultants tend to work for the same incumbents even if they face little or no opposition to re-election.[27]

In other words, consultants do not necessarily work where they are needed most, in highly competitive races, but where they have established relationships with clients. This does not make sense from the perspective of a party, which might allocate consulting resources according to need, or really from the perspective of a candidate who would presumably spend less money on consultants when the probability of winning is quite high (as is the case for most incumbents). However, the pattern does make sense from the perspective of a consultant who, rather than take the chance of losing a close race, works for an incumbent who is likely to win (and likely to pay). In this manner, the business of politics contributes to the entrenchment of a political elite who rely on consultants partly as a form of electoral insurance and partly as a way to legally dispose of political contributions.

Implications for American Democracy

The business of politics has transformed our democracy in fundamental ways. In assessing the significance of these changes, two conclusions come into view. One is a bit more hopeful; the other is less so. One view embraces and celebrates the uncertainty of political competition and the attendant opportunities to experiment. The other view acknowledges that the very same drive to innovate contributes to the ephemeral quality of our politics and the almost daily search for political advantage in the United States.

The rise and growth of the consulting business is part of a broader entrepreneurial style that has taken hold of American politics over the past fifty years. Across a range of institutions, political actors have carved out greater space for independent action. A myriad of elected officials, interest groups, super PACs, party committees, individuals, and firms pursue their political goals at the federal, state, and local levels; within legislatures, bureaucracies, and courts; and in the public, private, and nonprofit sectors. The capacity for independent action in the pursuit of a political career, a single issue, a legal ruling, or a specific regulation contributes to the cacophony of voices in politics today. Yet governing remains a collective enterprise, a task that is often ill-suited to the entrepreneurial drive for individual reward.[28]

The modern business of politics is both emblematic of this entrepreneurial style and an important factor contributing to its rise. Of course, consultants themselves are entrepreneurs in the literal sense that they have embarked on a drive for economic success through the innovation of political technique. The consulting industry is engaged in a constant search for new sources of revenue, new products and services, and new clients. As a result of this search, the business of politics produces a steady stream of advertisements, polls, and solicitations of public support that make up the crowded and often noisy public sphere. However, consultants are more than just another voice. In important respects, the consulting industry itself serves as a critical handmaiden for others to engage in an entrepreneurial search for political success. Candidates for office, corporate interests, parties, and super PACs, among others, rely on the services of a professional political class to help them measure the public, craft messages, and target supporters in ways that further their particular goals.

What is the consequence of this for our politics? Although the speed and sophistication of modern techniques may add a certain precision to the conduct of political work, they also render political conditions more fleeting as consultants continually interpret and reinterpret the public. At the same time, the steady probing and the constant bombardment of messages may contribute to a creeping cynicism as people tire of a media-intensive politics born from an unending search for more precise measures of public opinion and more effective means of political persuasion. This is perhaps an ironic result of the Progressive

Era hope for a well-informed public. Progressives valued the free flow of information as an antidote to the influence of special interests, but they failed to anticipate that the supposed revelation of "facts" would appear to most of us as highly contrived messages designed to persuade. The public knows that half of what it sees, reads, and hears about politics is often a half-truth, but we do not know which half. The incessant flow of political talk adds to a sense of ambivalence many voters share about politics; many Americans tune out altogether. It is doubly ironic that the diminishing returns from political communication may actually help consultants sell more of their wares.

The transformation of political work has also contributed to an evolving set of techniques that help define the character of democratic practice. The rise of a multi-billion-dollar business of politics has had profound consequences for the conduct of campaigns, the articulation of various interests, and the functioning of our institutions. The consolidation of the industry into larger firms and multinational holding companies points to the rise of a professionally managed public sphere in which corporations leverage their vast resources in order to improve their image or sway the electorate much the same way they would sell us a product. Over the past century, these developments have contributed to a set of practices we associate with American politics today: a media-intensive style of political campaigns funded by wealthy donors seeking influence through the provision of legally sanctioned products and services. Consultants are central to this exchange and will continue to play a significant role in American politics so long as there is an unlimited flow of money that can be spent in a limited number of ways.

Yet there is a hopeful side to this story. The thrill of political competition will always attract inspired believers willing to work long hours for little or no pay.[29] Even if political work is largely the domain of the professional speculator who turns a handsome profit by controlling critical aspects of democratic practice, a place still remains for the speculative volunteer. Indeed, the relentless drive to innovate, to construct political identities anew, and to create messages and appeals that may produce a victory at the polls reflects the enduring uncertainty of politics and the actions of the public that cannot be entirely known, completely predicted, or easily reduced to the affiliations or attachments of individual voters. We should take hope in the fact that after a century of advances in mass communication, including radio, television, and the Internet, the evolution of political work continues to play out in an ongoing search for a clearer picture of the public that is stubbornly incomplete. Even with each new technological advance, our inner selves remain just out of view. It is this elusiveness that makes spontaneous expressions of collective action a durable feature of democratic politics, even as it drives further efforts to develop new and possibly more effective instruments of persuasion.

Appendix

Estimating the Size of the Political Consulting Industry

IT IS DIFFICULT TO MEASURE the economic size of the political consulting industry with precision. In part, this is because the boundaries of the industry itself are unclear. In addition, most of the reported expenditures for media and to a lesser extent direct mail include sums that pass through individual consulting firms as purchases of television time or mailings. In order to estimate how much the consulting industry received during the 2012 election, I had to make decisions about what to include and what to exclude from the total.

First, the estimate includes only commercial firms that provide specialized political services to candidates, parties, or super PACs. This list of services includes media, polling, fundraising, digital services, and general consulting (I will say more about these categories later). I exclude expenditures to individuals who provide services, and I also exclude firms that provide services but do not specialize in political work. For instance, even though candidates may purchase web ads through Google, Inc., I do not include Google in my estimate of the consulting industry. If I was unsure about a firm, I used information on the company's website to decide whether to include it in the industry count.

Second, my estimate includes all expenditures made to a firm as listed in the Federal Election Commission (FEC) reports. In the case of media consultants, this includes purchases of television time for which a firm typically collects a commission. Frequently, the description of expenditures reported to the FEC will simply state "media" without stipulating what portion went to the purchase of airtime and what part went to the consulting firm. Consequently, my estimates for these firms are like billings, as one would find in the advertising industry, rather than revenue or profits. Put another way, the estimate captures the importance of the industry as the conduit through which a majority of the $6 billion in political expenditures moved during the 2012 campaign. The estimate also reveals which firms were particularly important by virtue of the fact that they handled such a large share of the money spent on the election. The estimate tells us nothing about the profitability of these firms.

Aggregating these expenditures into totals for individual firms is a difficult task. The data files available on the FEC website include more than 1 million individual expenditures to tens of thousands of vendors made during the 2012 election. Rather than construct one data set, I created and analyzed separate data sets for the House, the Senate, presidential candidates, party committees, and independent expenditures. For the party data, I combined monthly expenditure reports for the two national party committees and the four congressional party committees. The presidential data include expenditures for fourteen candidate committees and two presidential PACs, Romney Victory, Inc. and Obama Victory Fund.

After eliminating duplicate expenditures and transfers to other committees, I consolidated the records of each data set into subtotals for each vendor, candidate, and expenditure description. For instance, the media firm GMMB received 175 payments from the Obama campaign in 2012 for services listed in the FEC reports as "media buy." The same firm, GMMB, received 227 payments for "media production services" and four payments for "media consulting." I consolidated these 406 separate payments to GMMB into subtotals for each of the three expenditure categories in my presidential data set. One of the major challenges in analyzing the FEC data is that campaigns do not use consistent naming conventions for vendors or for descriptions of expenditures. For instance, whereas one campaign might report payments to the software vendor NGP VAN, another might list the vendor as NGP-VAN (or NGP VAN, Inc.). In order to avoid counting each version of the name as a separate vendor, I removed spaces and symbols as well as words or designations such as "and," "inc.," or "LLC" from the vendor names. Even then, some vendors such as Mentzer Media Services might be listed simply as Mentzer Media. In order to consolidate these records into a single vendor name, I used the software OpenRefine to locate clusters of similar names and create a uniform naming convention.[1] Even then, I often discovered slightly altered spellings of the same vendor and manually cleaned the data accordingly.

Addressing the variety of descriptions for expenditures posed a different challenge. Rather than create uniform descriptions, I used search terms to create categories of expenditures for media, fundraising, polling, digital services, and general consulting. In the case of media, for example, I wanted to include things like media, advertising, and television, but I wanted to exclude from the media category expenditures for GOTV (get out the vote), newspapers, or billboards. My five categories of expenditures are not mutually exclusive; for instance, Internet advertisements could be counted as expenditures for media and for digital services. However, this overlap was only an issue for determining the specialty of the firm. If a firm performed multiple services, I determined the specialty using the largest category of expenditures (media, polling, etc.). Once my coding was complete, I excluded vendors that did not have expenditures in one of the five categories. Table A1 includes the search terms used for each category.

The next step was to manually clean each of the five data sets in order to eliminate payments to individuals, commercial vendors like

TABLE A1 Search Terms for Consulting Services

Service	Search Terms
Media	("media" OR "advert" OR "ads" OR "television") AND NOT ("gotv" OR "newspaper" OR "signs" OR "billboard")
Fundraising	("direct mail" OR "telemarket" OR "fundrais") AND NOT ("event" OR "postage")
Polling	("poll" OR "research" OR "survey") AND NOT ("monitor" OR "worker" OR "watcher")
Digital	"internet" OR "web" OR "online" OR "digital" OR "data" OR "software"
Consulting	"consult"

printers, television stations, and other firms (like Google or Facebook) that received payments from campaigns but do not specialize in political work. To make this task more tractable, I included only vendors that received at least $25,000 in expenditures during the 2012 cycle.[2] Once this process was complete, I then calculated the total expenditures received by these firms (in addition to the sums they received for media, polling, or other specific services). Combining the firms from each of the five data sets yielded a list of 1,765 firms that met the criteria (political firms receiving over $25,000 in expenditures on consulting services). Each firm in the list includes a party designation based on the party affiliation of its clients (for independent expenditures, I used the party designation of the candidate supported or opposed in the advertisements).

The following tables provide information about total campaign expenditures by service (media, polling, etc.), by source (Congress, president, etc.), and top firms by party and specialty.

TABLE A2 Consulting Expenditures by Specialty and Party

	Republican	Democrat	Both/Other	Total
Media	$1,481,273,939	$1,099,180,930	$7,745,858	$2,588,200,727
Fundraising and direct mail	$294,294,952	$178,683,807	$8,505,846	$481,484,605
Digital services	$159,408,524	$141,784,637	$16,661,076	$317,854,237
General consulting	$77,431,563	$26,672,517	$2,191,656	$106,295,736
Polling	$32,669,715	$48,351,804	$740,378	$81,761,897
Grand total	$2,045,078,693	$1,494,673,695	$35,844,814	$3,575,597,202

TABLE A3 Consulting Expenditures by Source and Party

	Republican	Democrat	Both/Other	Total
Independent expenditures	$822,047,770	$366,440,418	$6,012,487	$1,194,500,675
President	$504,636,538	$607,061,959	$14,176,195	$1,125,874,692
Senate	$313,154,389	$227,699,458	$4,040,126	$544,893,973
House	$297,695,226	$219,303,519	$7,504,523	$524,503,268
Party committees	$107,544,780	$74,168,347	$4,111,483	$185,824,610
Grand total	$2,045,078,693	$1,494,673,695	$35,844,814	$3,575,597,202

TABLE A4 Top Ten Democratic Firms

Firm	Specialty	Expenditures
GMMB	Media	$411,505,600
Media Strategies & Research	Media	$115,583,096
Great American Media	Media	$109,662,728
Bully Pulpit Interactive	Digital services	$108,626,291
Waterfront Strategies	Media	$92,993,968
Mundy Katowitz Media	Media	$62,080,292
Shorr Johnson Magnus	Media	$41,498,381
AB Data	Fundraising/direct mail	$37,209,316
Buying Time LLC	Media	$29,177,360
Adelstein Liston	Media	$21,883,604
Share of Democratic Total		69%

TABLE A5 Top Ten Republican Firms

Firm	Specialty	Expenditures
Mentzer Media Services	Media	$245,945,842
American Rambler Productions	Media	$240,597,648
Crossroads Media, LLC	Media	$185,956,608
Targeted Victory	Digital services	$112,570,704
National Media Research	Media	$105,457,994
Strategic Media Services	Media	$66,807,584
OnMessage Inc.	Media	$61,018,616
FLS Connect	Fundraising/direct mail	$57,216,688
SCM Associates	Fundraising/direct mail	$56,632,788
Strategic Media Placement	Media	$48,206,204
Share of Republican Total		58%

TABLE A6 Five-Firm Concentration
(Share of Expenditures) by Specialty and Party

Specialty	Democrat	Republican
Media	72%	57%
Digital services	93%	84%
Fundraising and direct mail	40%	54%
Polling	39%	64%
General consulting	28%	19%

TABLE A7 Top Five Firms by Specialty

Media

Firm	Party	Expenditures
GMMB	DEM	$411,505,600
Mentzer Media Services	REP	$245,945,842
American Rambler Productions	REP	$240,597,648
Crossroads Media, LLC	REP	$185,956,608
Media Strategies & Research	DEM	$115,583,096

Digital Services

Firm	Party	Expenditures
Targeted Victory	REP	$112,570,704
Bully Pulpit Interactive	DEM	$108,626,291
CMDI	REP	$12,708,331
Piryx Inc	BOTH	$11,158,674
Well & Lighthouse	DEM	$7,795,367

Fundraising and Direct Mail

Firm	Party	Expenditures
FLS Connect	REP	$57,216,688
SCM Assoc	REP	$56,632,788
AB Data	DEM	$37,209,316
Strategic Fundraising	REP	$17,767,062
Arena Communications	REP	$16,582,817

Polling

Firm	Party	Expenditures
Public Opinion Strategies	REP	$11,103,838
David Binder Research	DEM	$4,864,140
Tarrance Group	REP	$4,598,882
Benenson Strategy Group	DEM	$4,105,875
Anzalone Liszt Grove Research	DEM	$3,586,048

General Consulting

Firm	Party	Expenditures
Red Curve Solutions	REP	$3,539,073
Redwave Communications	REP	$3,180,223
WWP Strategies	REP	$2,957,878
Perkins Coie	DEM	$2,693,069
Patton Boggs LLP	REP	$2,601,428

NOTES

Chapter 1

1. http://www.mentzermedia.com/.
2. For a list of Mentzer Media's clients in 2012, see Center for Responsive Politics, http://www.opensecrets.org/expends/vendor.php?year=2012&vendor=Mentzer+Media+Services.
3. For data on GMMB, see http://www.opensecrets.org/expends/vendor.php?year=2012&vendor=GMMB.
4. Author's calculation using Federal Election Commission (FEC) data. See the appendix for an explanation of how I estimated revenues for the consulting industry.
5. Because many consultants place advertisements and purchase television airtime on behalf of their clients (for which these firms typically charge a commission), a large portion of campaign spending passes through, rather than goes directly to, consulting firms.
6. For data on the top fifty vendors, see Center for Responsive Politics, http://www.opensecrets.org/expends/vendors.php. Comparisons over time have to be made with some caution because of data quality. Whereas the 2008 figures do not include independent expenditures, the 2012 figures do include them. To estimate independent expenditures on consulting services for 2008, I multiplied total outside spending in 2008 by the share of independent expenditures received in 2012 by the top fifty firms (around 87 percent). This amounts to an extra $318 million (in GDP 2012 dollars) in my estimate for 2008 (see http://www.opensecrets.org/outsidespending/). I excluded vendors that were not political consulting firms, such as the US Postal Service or Paychex (a commercial payroll service). In calculating

real growth, I used nominal GDP/2012 GDP as a deflator to account for economic growth, or the size of the industry relative to the overall economy.

7. Of the $1.3 billion reported to the Federal Election Commission as independent expenditures, $1.2 billion went to just under 300 firms.

8. According to data from the Center for Responsive Politics (http://www. opensecrets.org/expends/vendors.php), GMMB received $837 million in expenditures between 2008 and 2012, more than any other firm. The vast majority of this money came in the form of media buys; assuming a standard 15 percent commission, this translates into $125 million in revenues for the firm.

9. Erin Quinn, "The Misinformation Industry," Center for Public Integrity, http://tinyurl.com/publicintegritypr, accessed April 16, 2015.

10. The figure of 40 percent comes from Matt Grossmann, "Campaigning as an Industry: Consulting Business Models and Intra-party Competition," *Business and Politics* 11.2 (2009): article 2, p. 9. Grossmann surveyed eighty consulting firms in 2003 and 2007.

11. This distinction was first identified by the German sociologist Max Weber in his *Political Writings*, ed. Peter Lassman and Ronald Spiers (Cambridge: Cambridge University Press, 1994 [1919]), 318.

12. Weber, *Political Writings*, 352.

13. Joe Klein, *Politics Lost: How American Democracy Was Trivialized by People Who Think You're Stupid* (New York: Doubleday, 2006).

14. Sidney Blumenthal, *The Permanent Campaign* (New York: Simon and Schuster, 1982).

15. John Aldrich, *Why Parties? The Origin and Transformation of Political Parties in America* (Chicago: University of Chicago Press, 1995); Robin Kolodny, "Electoral Partnerships: Political Consultants and Political Parties," in *Campaign Warriors: Political Consultants in Elections*, ed. James A. Thurber and Candace J. Nelson (Washington, DC: Brookings Institution Press, 2000); see Robin Kolodny and David Dulio, "Political Party Adaptation in US Congressional Campaigns: Why Political Parties Use Coordinated Expenditures to Hire Political Consultants," *Party Politics* 9 (2003): 729–746; David Dulio, "Party Crashers? The Relationship between Political Consultants and Political Parties," in *Handbook of Party Politics*, ed. Richard Katz and William Crotty (London: Sage, 2006), 348–358; Robin Kolodny and Angela Logan, "Political Consultants and the Extension of Party Goals," *PS: Political Science & Politics* 31 (1998): 155–159.

16. On the limits of functional explanations for political development, see Daniel Galvin, "Political Parties in American Politics," in *Oxford Handbook of Historical Institutionalism*, ed. Orfeo Fioretos, Tulia Falleti, and Adam Sheingate (New York: Oxford University Press, 2016).

17. The literature is vast. For good summaries, see Richard Lau, Lee Sigelman, and Ivy Brown Rovner, "The Effects of Negative Political Campaigns: A Meta-analytic Reassessment," *Journal of Politics* 69

(2007): 1176–1209; Stephen Ansolabehere, "The Paradox of Minimal Effects," in *Capturing Campaign Effects*, ed. Henry E. Brady and Richard Johnston (Ann Arbor: University of Michigan Press, 2006), 29–44.

18. John Sides and Lynn Vavreck, *The Gamble: Choice and Chance in the 2012 Presidential Election* (Princeton, NJ: Princeton University Press, 2013). See also Seth Hill, James Lo, Lynn Vavreck, and John Zaller, "How Quickly We Forget: The Duration of Persuasion Effects from Mass Communication," *Political Communication* 30 (2013): 521–547.

19. Derek Willis, "Political TV Ads Can Be Wasteful. But That's Changing," *New York Times*, October 21, 2014, http://tinyurl.com/nytmespoliticaltvads, accessed April 17, 2015.

20. Donald Green and Alan Gerber, *Get Out the Vote: How to Increase Voter Turnout* (Washington, DC: Brookings Institution, 2008).

21. Erika Franklin Fowler and Travis Ridout, "Negative, Angry, and Ubiquitous: Political Advertising in 2012," *Forum* 10 (2012): 51–61.

22. Anthony King, *Running Scared: Why America's Politicians Campaign Too Much and Govern Too Little* (New York: Free Press, 1997).

23. Michael Franz and Travis Ridout, "Political Advertising and Persuasion in the 2004 and 2008 Presidential Elections," *American Politics Research* 38 (2010): 303–329. For additional evidence that spending advantages matter, see Larry Bartels, *Unequal Democracy: The Political Economy of the New Gilded Age* (Princeton, NJ: Princeton University Press, 2008), 122.

24. My view of political work is heavily influenced by the work of sociologist Andrew Abbott. See especially Andrew Abbott, *The System of Professions: An Essay on the Division of Expert Labor* (Chicago: University of Chicago Press, 1988); Andrew Abbott, "Linked Ecologies: States and Universities as Environments for Professions," *Sociological Theory* 23 (2005): 245–274.

25. Richard Bensel, *The American Ballot Box in the Mid-Nineteenth Century* (New York: Cambridge University Press, 2004), 295.

26. Bensel, *The American Ballot Box in the Mid-Nineteenth Century*, 294.

27. Bensel, *The American Ballot Box in the Mid-Nineteenth Century*, 294.

28. Bensel, *The American Ballot Box in the Mid-Nineteenth Century*, 294.

29. Bensel, *The American Ballot Box in the Mid-Nineteenth Century*, 296n20.

30. Moisei Ostrogorski, *Democracy and the Organization of Political Parties*, vol. 2, *The United States* (New Brunswick, NJ: Transaction Books, 1982 [1902]), 146.

31. Harold Gosnell, "Thomas C. Platt—Political Manager," *Political Science Quarterly* 38 (1923): 443–469.

32. Sarah Igo, *The Averaged American: Surveys, Citizens, and the Making of a Mass Public* (Cambridge, MA: Harvard University Press, 2007), 113; see also Coleman Harwell Wells, "Remapping America: Market Research and American Society, 1900–1940" (PhD diss., University Virginia, 1999); Brian Balogh, "Mirrors of Desires: Interest Groups, Elections, and the Targeted Style in Twentieth-Century America," in *The Democratic Experiment: New*

Directions in American Political History, ed. Meg Jacobs et al. (Princeton, NJ: Princeton University Press, 2003), 222–249.

33. Stanley Kelley, *Professional Public Relations and Political Power* (Baltimore: Johns Hopkins University Press, 1956), 42–43.

34. Between 1968 and 1988, the share of items in Google Books that include the term "political consultant" or "political consulting" increased by 16 percent per year. http://tinyurl.com/p2axobe.

35. My interest in political practice has been influenced by a range of work on American elections, including Bensel, *The American Ballot Box in the Mid-Nineteenth Century*; Michael McGerr, *The Decline of Popular Politics: The American North, 1865–1928* (Oxford: Oxford University Press, 1986); Stanley Kelly, *Professional Public Relations and Political Power* (Baltimore: Johns Hopkins University Press, 1956); Larry Sabato, *The Rise of the Political Consultants: New Ways of Winning Elections* (New York: Basic Books, 1981); Daniel Galvin, "The Transformation of Political Institutions: Investments in Institutional Resources and Gradual Change in National Party Committees," *Studies in American Political Development* 26 (2012): 50–70; Rasmus Kleis Nielsen, *Ground Wars: Personalized Communication in Political Campaigns* (Princeton, NJ: Princeton University Press, 2012); Daniel Kreiss, *Taking Our Country Back: The Crafting of Networked Politics from Howard Dean to Barack Obama* (Oxford: Oxford University Press, 2012); Edward Walker, *Grassroots for Hire: Public Affairs Consultants in American Democracy* (Cambridge: Cambridge University Press, 2014).

36. The first set of interviews was made by Larry Sabato during his research for *The Rise of the Political Consultants*. The second set was made under the auspices of the American Association of Political Consultants in an oral history project initiated by John Franzen.

37. Daniel Kreiss, "People as Media: Campaigns and Actually Existing Democracy," *Mobilizing Ideas* (blog), September 3, 2012, http://tinyurl.com/ kreissmobilizingideas, accessed January 9, 2015.

Chapter 2

1. Francis Rourke, *Secrecy and Publicity: Dilemmas of Democracy* (Baltimore: Johns Hopkins University Press, 1966). See also "Publicity Topsy-Turvy," *Independent*, August 17, 1905, 401.

2. Jeremy Bentham, *The Works of Jeremy Bentham*, quotes available at http:// www.ucl.ac.uk/Bentham-Project/Faqs/fquote.htm.

3. Bentham quoted in Slavko Splichal, "The Right to Communicate," *Critical Review* 15 (2003): 292.

4. Quoted in Slavko Splichal, *Principles of Publicity and Press Freedom* (Lanham, MD: Rowman and Littlefield, 2002), 45.

5. Bentham quoted in Splichal, "The Right to Communicate," 291.

6. Kant quoted in Splichal, "The Right to Communicate," 293.

7. Kant quoted in John Christian Laurson, "The Subversive Kant: The Vocabulary of 'Public' and 'Publicity,'" *Political Theory* 14 (1986): 599.

8. David M. Kennedy, *Over Here: The First World War and American Society* (Oxford: Oxford University Press, 1980), 47; Stuart Ewen, *PR! A Social History of Spin* (New York: Basic Books, 1996), 50.

9. "The Searchlight: Use and Abuse," *Outlook*, April 14, 1906, 830.

10. "Publicity the Remedy," *Zion's Herald*, August 2, 1905, 967.

11. Shaw quoted in Jonathan Kahn, *Budgeting Democracy: State Building and Citizenship in America, 1890–1928* (Ithaca, NY: Cornell University Press, 1997), 23.

12. Henry C. Adams, "What Is Publicity?," *North American Review*, December 1, 1902, 896, 899.

13. Henry Clews, "Publicity and Reform in Business," *Annals of the American Academy of Political and Social Science* 28 (1906): 154.

14. John Dewey, *The Public and Its Problems* (Athens, OH: Swallow Press, 1991 [1927]), 167.

15. Henry Bruère, "Government and Publicity," *Independent*, December 12, 1907, 1422 (emphasis in original). See also Kenneth Finegold, *Experts and Politicians: Reform Challenges to Machine Politics in New York, Cleveland, and Chicago* (Princeton, NJ: Princeton University Press, 1995), 30; Kahn, *Budgeting Democracy*, 42–45.

16. William H. Baldwin Jr., "Publicity as a Means of Social Reform," *North American Review*, December 1901, 845–846.

17. "Publicity the Remedy," 967. The quoted passage is in Matthew 10:26. For the link between social science and the social gospel, see Bradley W. Bateman, "Make a Righteous Number: Social Surveys, the Men and Religious Forward Movement, and Quantification in American Economics," *History of Political Economy* 33 (2001): 57–85.

18. Daniel Rodgers, "In Search of Progressivism," *Reviews in American History* 10 (1982): 123.

19. Arthur T. Vance, "The Value of Publicity in Reform," *Annals of the American Academy of Political and Social Science* 29 (1907): 88–89.

20. Brian Balogh, "Mirrors of Desires: Interest Groups, Elections, and the Targeted Style in Twentieth-Century America," in *The Democratic Experiment: New Directions in American Political History*, ed. Meg Jacobs, William Novak, and Julian Zelizer (Princeton, NJ: Princeton University Press, 2003), 228.

21. "Alcohol versus Publicity," *Outlook*, November 8, 1913; "Getting Temperance Facts before the Public," *Outlook*, February 17, 1915.

22. Peter H. Odegard, *Pressure Politics: The Story of the Anti-Saloon League* (New York: Columbia University Press, 1928), 231–232.

23. Alice Winter, quoted in Elisabeth Clemens, *The People's Lobby: Organizational Innovation and the Rise of Interest Group Politics in the United States, 1890-1925* (Chicago: University of Chicago Press, 1997), 216.

24. "New Suffrage Campaign," *New York Times*, January 17, 1911, 1.
25. H. Wirt Steele, "Publicity," *Survey*, June 11, 1910, 465.
26. Ewen, *PR!*, 132–146.
27. Ivy Lee, "The Technique of Publicity," *Electric Railway Journal*, January 6, 1917, 18.
28. Stephen Ponder, *Managing the Press: Origins of the Media Presidency, 1897–1933* (New York: St. Martin's Press, 1998), xiii.
29. For figures on newspaper circulation, see *Historical Statistics of the United States, Colonial Times to the Present*, series R244–R257. For figures on magazines, see Ponder, *Managing the Press*, 3.
30. Michael Schudson, *Discovering the News: A Social History of American Newspapers* (New York: Basic Books, 1978).
31. William Kittle, "The Making of Public Opinion," *Arena*, July 1909, 440.
32. Interstate Commerce Commission, "Letter from the Chairman of the Interstate Commerce Commission submitting a report of an investigation of the subject of railroad discriminations and monopolies in oil," 59th Cong., 2nd sess. H. Doc 606, pp. 4–5.
33. Kittle, "The Making of Public Opinion," 450.
34. Will Irwin, "The Press Agent, His Rise and Decline," *Collier's*, December 2, 1911, 24.
35. "Public Opinion and the Press Agent," *Youth's Companion*, February 19, 1920, 102.
36. "Press Agents and Public Opinion," *New York Times*, September 5, 1920, 3.
37. Frederick Cleveland, a founding director of the bureau, established the Institute of Governmental Research, the forerunner of the Brookings Institution. Kahn, *Budgeting Democracy*, 103–104, 129.
38. Bureau of Municipal Research, "A National Program to Improve Methods of Government," 10.
39. Allen quoted in Kahn, *Budgeting Democracy*, 104.
40. Theodore Roosevelt, "First Annual Message to Congress," December 3, 1901, http://www.presidency.ucsb.edu/ws/print.php?pid=29542.
41. Theodore Roosevelt, "Third Annual Message to Congress," December 7, 1903, http://www.presidency.ucsb.edu/sou.php.
42. On the Bureau of Corporations and James R. Garfield, see Martin Sklar, *The Corporate Reconstruction of American Capitalism, 1890–1916: The Market, The Law, and Politics* (New York: Cambridge University Press, 1988), 186; Arthur M. Johnson, "Theodore Roosevelt and the Bureau of Corporations," *Mississippi Valley Historical Review* 45 (1959): 571–590. For reference to the "publicity bureau," see "New Cabinet Officer," *New York Times*, February 17, 1903, 7.
43. "Report of the Commissioner of Corporations," in *Reports of the Department of Commerce and Labor, 1906* (Washington, DC: Government Printing Office, 1906), 71.

44. Theodore Roosevelt, *The New Nationalism* (Englewood Cliffs, NJ: Prentice Hall, 1961 [1910]). See also James Ceaser, *Presidential Selection: Theory and Development* (Princeton, NJ: Princeton University Press, 1979), 176. Ceaser makes a similar argument about openness and transparency in Roosevelt's conception of leadership.

45. George Kibbe Turner, "Manufacturing Public Opinion: The New Art of Making Presidents by Press Bureau," *McClure's Magazine*, July 1912, 322.

46. J. J. Dickinson, "Theodore Roosevelt: Press Agent," *Harper's*, September 28, 1907, 1410.

47. Ponder, *Managing the Press*; Jeffrey Tulis, *The Rhetorical Presidency* (Princeton, NJ: Princeton University Press, 1987), chap. 4.

48. Turner, "Manufacturing Public Opinion," 322. Turner described Pinchot as "a master and promoter of political publicity, second—if to anybody—only to Theodore Roosevelt" ("Manufacturing Public Opinion," 320).

49. Turner, "Manufacturing Public Opinion"; Stephen Ponder, "Gifford Pinchot: Press Agent for Forestry," *Journal of Forest History* 31 (1987): 26.

50. Ponder, "Gifford Pinchot," 29.

51. For examples, see Ponder, "Gifford Pinchot"; Mordecai Lee, *Congress vs. the Bureaucracy: Muzzling Agency Public Relations* (Norman: University of Oklahoma Press, 2011); Harold Pinkett, *Gifford Pinchot: Private and Public Forester* (Urbana: University of Illinois Press, 1970); Clifford McGeary, *Gifford Pinchot, Forester-Politician* (Princeton, NJ: Princeton University Press, 1960); Brian Balogh, "Scientific Forestry and the Roots of the Modern Administrative State: Gifford Pinchot's Path to Progressive Reform," *Environmental History* 7 (2002): 198–225; Daniel P. Carpenter, *The Forging Bureaucratic Autonomy: Reputations, Networks, and Policy Innovation in Executive Agencies, 1862–1928* (Princeton, NJ: Princeton University Press, 2001).

52. Forest Service Order 80, August 19, 1905, Records of the Office of the Chief, Record Group 95, National Archives, quoted in Ponder, "Gifford Pinchot," 28.

53. Treadwell Cleveland Jr. to Gifford Pinchot, July 25, 1905, Gifford Pinchot Papers, Library of Congress, Box 578; "Press Bulletins," Forest Service Order 32, May 25, 1904, Records of the Forest Service, Circulars and Orders from the Office of the Chief, 1903–1917, Record Group 95, National Archives.

54. "Circular Letter to Newspaper Unions," n.d. (possibly March 1905), Records of the Division of Information and Education, Box 16, Record Group 95, National Archives; Gifford Pinchot to Hon. Charles F. Scott, Chairman, Committee on Agriculture, House of Representatives, February 14, 1908, Office of the Chief, Selected Records Relating to the Administration of Gifford Pinchot, Box 7, Record Group 95, National Archives.

55. "Press Bulletins Issued by the Bureau of Forestry," Records of the Division of Information and Education, News Articles and Press Releases, Box 15, Record Group 95, National Archives.

56. "Another Press Agency Attacked by Senator," *New York Times*, January 30, 1906, 4; Stephen Ponder, "Executive Publicity and Congressional Resistance, 1905–1913: Congress and the Roosevelt Administration's PR Men," *Congress & the Presidency* 13 (1986): 177–186.

57. Gifford Pinchot to Hon. Charles F. Scott, Chairman, Committee on Agriculture, House of Representatives, February 14, 1908.

58. Gifford Pinchot to Hon. Ernest M. Pollard, House of Representatives, April 1, 1908, Office of the Chief, Selected Records Relating to the Administration of Gifford Pinchot, Box 7, National Archives.

59. Ponder, "Executive Publicity and Congressional Resistance," 181–182.

60. As Price and Shaw put it in their letter to Pinchot explaining their actions, "Feeling that there was no alternative but to appeal to the people by giving further publicity to the material contained in the Glavis report [concerning evidence of Ballinger's corruption], we accordingly communicated with Glavis respecting the publication [in *Collier's*]." Joint Committee to Investigate the Interior Department and Bureau of Forestry, *Investigation into the Interior Department and Bureau of Forestry*, (Washington, DC: Government Printing Office, 1911), 4:1277.

61. *Investigation into the Interior Department*, 9:5378.

62. *Investigation into the Interior Department*, 9:5310–5311. Pinchot employed similar language in his book *The Fight for Conservation* (New York: Doubleday, Page, 1910): "It is just as necessary for the people to know what is being done to help them as to know what is begin done to hurt them. Publicity is the essential and indispensable condition of clean and effective public service" (119).

63. McGeary, *Gifford Pinchot*, 198.

64. Thomas R. Shipp to Gifford Pinchot, November 16, 1910; Gifford Pinchot to Thomas R. Shipp, December 2, 1910; Thomas R. Shipp to Gifford Pinchot, December 5, 1910. all in General Correspondence of National Conservation Commission, Box 470, Gifford Pinchot Papers, Library of Congress.

65. "A Plan for Publicity," n.d., Gifford Pinchot Papers, Box 701, Library of Congress. Although it is unclear if Pinchot is the author, other parts of the document clearly indicate close working knowledge of Forest Service publicity efforts, noting, for example, that "in May, 1907, the combined 'circulation record'—that is papers accepting [Forest Service] material—was 74 papers, with a circulation of 1,144,855; while in September 1908 the record was over one thousand papers, with an average monthly circulation over 40,000,000."

66. Timothy Cook makes a similar point about progressive politics in *Governing with the News: The News Media as a Political Institution* (Chicago: University of Chicago Press, 2005), 82.

67. Henry Litchfield West, "American Politics: The President and the Campaign," *Forum*, November 1908, 421.

68. Michael McGerr, *The Decline of Popular Politics: The American North, 1865–1928* (Oxford: Oxford University Press, 1986), 145.

69. McGerr, *Decline of Popular Politics*, 159.

70. Oscar King Davis, "The Game and Cost of Making a President," *New York Times Magazine*, August 9, 1908, 2.

71. McGerr, *Decline of Popular Politics*, 145.

72. The earliest reference to these "booms" I have found is in the promotion of Secretary of the Treasury John Sherman as a presidential candidate in 1880. See "Hunting for Sherman Men: A Secret Service Agent Vainly Looking for the 'Boom' in Philadelphia," *New York Times*, April 12, 1880, 1.

73. "Tells of His Work to Boom Chanler," *New York Times*, January 8, 1910, 5.

74. Davis, "The Game and Cost of Making a President," 2.

75. Woodrow Wilson, "Government by Debate" (1882), in *The Papers of Woodrow Wilson*, vol. 2, edited by Arthur S. Link (Princeton, NJ: Princeton University Press, 1967), 27, 191.

76. Woodrow Wilson, "Two Interviews" (1910), in *The Papers of Woodrow Wilson*, vol. 22, edited by Arthur S. Link (Princeton, NJ: Princeton University Press, 1976), 5.

77. Woodrow Wilson, "An Address to the Conference of Governors in Frankfort, Kentucky" (1910), in *The Papers of Woodrow Wilson*, vol. 22, edited by Arthur S. Link (Princeton, NJ: Princeton University Press, 1976), 109.

78. Woodrow Wilson, "A Campaign Address" (1910), in *The Papers of Woodrow Wilson*, vol. 21, edited by Arthur S. Link (Princeton, NJ: Princeton University Press, 1976), 228.

79. Woodrow Wilson, *The New Freedom* (Englewood Cliffs, NJ: Prentice Hall, 1961 [1913]), 77. For a similar turn of phrase, see Woodrow Wilson, "A Campaign Address in Trenton, New Jersey" (1910), in *The Papers of Woodrow Wilson*, vol. 21, edited by Arthur S. Link (Princeton, NJ: Princeton University Press, 1976), 232–233.

80. Woodrow Wilson, "Notes for a Campaign Speech in Montclair, New Jersey" (1910), in *The Papers of Woodrow Wilson*, vol. 21, edited by Arthur S. Link (Princeton, NJ: Princeton University Press, 1976), 509.

81. James D. Startt, *Woodrow Wilson and the Press: Prelude to the Presidency* (New York: Palgrave Macmillan, 2004), 90.

82. Startt, *Woodrow Wilson and the Press*.

83. Frank P. Stockbridge, "How Woodrow Wilson Won His Nomination," *Current History* 20 (1924): 561.

84. Stockbridge, "How Woodrow Wilson Won His Nomination," 561.

85. Stockbridge, "How Woodrow Wilson Won His Nomination," 564.

86. Turner, "Manufacturing Public Opinion," 317.

87. L. Ames Brown, "The President on the Independent Voter," *World's Work*, September 1916, 494–495.

88. "H. L. Wilson Gives G.O.P. Mexico Data," *New York Times*, July 23, 1916, 14.
89. "A Lesson in Publicity," *Wall Street Journal*, November 9, 1916, 1.
90. "Bureau of Publicity," n.d., Robert Woolley Papers, Box 34, Library of Congress. For more on Woolley, see McGerr, *Decline of Popular Politics*, 164–165.
91. Dan Balz and John Maxwell Hamilton, "In 2016, We're Going to Campaign Like It's 1916," *Washington Post*, January 2, 2015, http://wapo.st/177AdoI, accessed June 30, 2015.
92. "A Publicity Campaign about the Constructive Work of the Wilson Administration," n.d., Robert Woolley Papers, Box 12. Although Creel's name does not appear, McGerr attributes the memo to Creel due to its similarities in prose and typing styles to another memo signed by Creel in the Woolley Papers. See McGerr, *Decline of Popular Politics*, 271n98.
93. Robert Woolley to Vance C. McCormick, March 1, 1917, Robert Woolley Papers, Box 13, Library of Congress, p. 10.
94. "A Publicity Campaign."
95. Woolley to McCormick, March 1, 1917; "A Publicity Campaign"; McGerr, *Decline of Popular Politics*, 164–168.
96. "A Plan for Publicity," n.d., Gifford Pinchot Papers, Box 701, Library of Congress.
97. John A. Morello, *Selling the President, 1920: Albert D. Lasker, Advertising, and the Election of Warren G. Harding* (Westport, CT: Praeger, 2001).
98. McGerr, *Decline of Popular Politics*, 169.
99. Morello, *Selling the President*, 65–66.
100. Quoted in McGerr, *Decline of Popular Politics*, 170.
101. Richard Boeckel, "The Man with the Best Story Wins: Which Explains Why Pitiless Publicity Looms So Large in the Presidential Campaign," *Independent*, May 22, 1920, 244–245.
102. McGerr, *Decline of Popular Politics*, 170–171.
103. Scott Cutlip, "The Nation's First Publicity Firm," *Journalism Quarterly* 43 (1966): 275–276.
104. Ray Stannard Baker, "Railroads on Trial: How Railroads Make Public Opinion," *McClure's Magazine*, March 1906, 537.
105. Baker, "Railroads on Trial," 537.
106. Margaret Susan Thompson, *The "Spider Web": Congress and Lobbying in the Age of Grant* (Ithaca, NY: Cornell University Press, 1985).
107. "Statement of Mr. William Wolff Smith," in *Hearings on the Estimates of Appropriations for the Department of Agriculture for the Fiscal Year Ending June 30, 1908*, Committee on Agriculture, House of Representatives, 59th Cong., 2nd sess., p. 55.
108. "Tainted News," *Collier's*, February 23, 1907, 25.
109. "Tainted News," 25.
110. "Statement of Mr. William Wolff Smith," 67, 76, 82.

111. Ken Kollman, *Outside Lobbying: Public Opinion and Interest Group Strategies* (Princeton, NJ: Princeton University Press, 1998). See also Edward Walker, *Grassroots for Hire: Public Affairs Consultants in American Democracy* (Cambridge: Cambridge University Press, 2014).

112. E. Pendleton Herring, *Group Representation before Congress* (Baltimore: Johns Hopkins Press, 1929), 59–60. Herring's use of quotation marks around the word "information" captures the ambiguity between objectivity and subjectivity.

113. "Loses His Libel Suit: W. W. Smith Not Damaged by Collier's, Jury Finds," *Washington Post*, June 21, 1912, 14.

114. Ray Eldon Hiebert, *Courtier to the Crowd: The Story of Ivy Lee and the Development of Public Relations* (Ames: Iowa State University Press, 1966), 32–49.

115. Lee, "The Technique of Publicity," 16.

116. Ivy Lee, "Enemies of Publicity," *Electric Railway Journal*, March 31, 1917, 599.

117. Ivy Lee, *Publicity: Some of the Things It Is and Is Not* (New York: Industries Publishing Company, 1925), 21.

118. Schudson, *Discovering the News*, 135.

119. Schudson, *Discovering the News*, 136.

120. Lee, "Enemies of Publicity," 600.

121. Lee, "The Technique of Publicity," 17.

122. Ivy Lee, quoted in Ewen, *PR!*, 84.

123. Lee, "Enemies of Publicity," 600.

124. Tulis, *The Rhetorical Presidency*, 18.

125. Lee, "The Technique of Publicity," 16.

126. Dewey, *The Public and Its Problems*, 167.

127. "The 'Publicity Men' of Corporations," *World's Work*, July 1906, 7703.

Chapter 3

1. Stephen Vaughn, *Holding Fast the Inner Lines: Democracy, Nationalism, and the Committee on Public Information* (Chapel Hill: University of North Carolina Press, 1980), 213.

2. Creel quoted in Vaughn, *Holding Fast the Inner Lines*, 17. See also Stuart Ewen, *PR! A Social History of Spin* (New York: Basic Books, 1996), 102–130.

3. George Creel, "Public Opinion in War Time," *Annals of the American Academy of Political and Social Science* 78 (July 1918): 185.

4. Creel, "Public Opinion in War Time," 189–190.

5. George Creel, *How We Advertised America: The First Telling of the Amazing Story of the Committee on Public Information That Carried the Gospel of Americanism to Every Corner of the Globe* (New York: Harper and Brothers, 1920), 4.

6. Vaughn, *Holding Fast the Inner Lines*.

7. George Creel, "Propaganda and Morale," *American Journal of Sociology* 47 (November 1942): 346.

8. Vaughn, *Holding Fast the Inner Lines*, 149–150.

9. Charles H. Hamlin, *The War Myth in United States History* (New York: Vanguard Press, 1927), 91–92, quoted in Barry Alan Marks, "The Idea of Propaganda in America" (PhD diss., University of Minnesota, 1957), 44–45.

10. Irwin quoted in J. Michael Sproule, *Propaganda and Democracy: The American Experience of Media and Mass Persuasion* (New York: Cambridge University Press, 1997), 19.

11. Sproule, *Propaganda and Democracy*, 52. See also Brett Gary, *The Nervous Liberals: Propaganda Anxieties from World War I to the Cold War* (New York: Columbia University Press, 1999), 23–26.

12. Marks, "The Idea of Propaganda," 53; Frederic William Wile, "Government by Propaganda," *Outlook*, December 1928, quoted in Marks, "The Idea of Propaganda," 52.

13. Sproule, *Propaganda and Democracy*, 53.

14. Gary, *The Nervous Liberals*, 3.

15. Wallas, quoted in Sproule, *Propaganda and Democracy*, 31.

16. Walter Lippmann, *Public Opinion* (New York: Free Press Paperbacks, 1997 [1922]), 217, 220, 223.

17. Lippmann, *Public Opinion*, 218.

18. Lippmann, *Public Opinion*, 158.

19. Lippmann, *Public Opinion*, 158.

20. Lippmann, *Public Opinion*, 158.

21. Gary, *The Nervous Liberals*, 1.

22. Michelson quoted in Ralph D. Casey, "Party Campaign Propaganda," *Annals of the American Academy of Political and Social Science* 179 (May 1935): 103.

23. Michael McGerr, *The Decline of Popular Politics: The American North, 1865–1928* (Oxford: Oxford University Press, 1986).

24. "Text of Ex-Governor's Radio Address," *New York Times*, January 17, 1929, 2. See also Thomas S. Barclay, "The Publicity Division of the Democratic Party," *American Political Science Review* 25 (February 1931): 68–72.

25. "Democrats Cheer Raskob and Shouse as Party Builders," *New York Times*, June 11, 1929, 10.

26. Charles Michelson, *The Ghost Talks* (New York: Putnam's, 1944), 20.

27. Timothy Cook, *Governing with the News: The News Media as a Political Institution* (Chicago: University of Chicago Press, 1998).

28. Michelson, *The Ghost Talks*, 32.

29. Frank Kent, "Charley Michelson," *Scribner's*, September 1930, 291.

30. Oliver McKee, Jr., "Publicity Chiefs," *North American Review* 230 (October 1930), 411, 416.

31. Will Irwin, *Propaganda and the News or What Makes You Think So?* (New York: McGraw-Hill, 1936), 301.

32. Irwin, *Propaganda and the News*.

33. Marshall Andrews, "Michelson Wit Marked Party Speech, Harassed Foes through New Deal Era," *Washington Post*, January 9, 1948, B2.

34. Andrew Abbott, *The System of Professions: An Essay on the Division of Expert Labor* (Chicago: University of Chicago Press, 1988), 225.

35. E. Pendleton Herring, "Official Publicity under the New Deal," *Annals of the American Academy of Political and Social Science* 179 (May 1935): 167.

36. Sidney Blumenthal, *The Permanent Campaign* (New York: Simon and Schuster, 1982); Theodore Lowi, *The Personal President: Power Invested, Promise Unfulfilled* (Ithaca, NY: Cornell University Press, 1986); Hugh Heclo, "Campaigning and Governing: A Conspectus," in *The Permanent Campaign and Its Future*, ed. Norman J. Ornstein and Thomas E. Mann (Washington, DC: American Enterprise Institute, 2000).

37. William E. Berchtold, "Press Agents of the New Deal," *New Outlook*, June 1934, 23.

38. "Response Is Nation-Wide," *New York Times*, July 28, 1933, 1.

39. Michelson, *The Ghost Talks*, 120.

40. "Whole NRA Reorganized," *New York Times*, April 10, 1934, 1.

41. John Kennedy Ohl, *Hugh S. Johnson and the New Deal* (Dekalb, IL: Northern Illinois University Press, 1985), 140–143.

42. "Text of General Johnson's Portland Speech," *New York Times*, July 16, 1934, 2.

43. Elisha Hanson, "Official Propaganda and the New Deal," *Annals of the American Academy of Political and Social Science* 179 (May 1935): 179.

44. Frank R. Kent, "Washington's Ballyhoo Brigade," *American Magazine*, September 1937, 61.

45. Irwin, *Propaganda and the News*, 308.

46. Hanson, "Official Propaganda and the New Deal," 180–181.

47. "Charges Attempt to Control Press," *New York Times*, July 10, 1936, 17.

48. Mordecai Lee, *Congress vs. the Bureaucracy: Muzzling Agency Public Relations* (Norman: University of Oklahoma Press, 2011), 147–165.

49. 38 US Statute 212 (October 22, 1913); James L. McCamy, *Government Publicity* (Chicago: University of Chicago Press, 1939), 6–7; Lee, *Congress vs. the Bureaucracy*, 147.

50. US Senate, Select Committee to Investigate the Executive Agencies of the Government, "Investigation of Executive Agencies of the Government, No. 13: Report on the Government Activities on Library, Information and Statistical Services by the Brookings Institution," 75th Cong., 1st sess., p. 12.

51. Lee, *Congress vs. the Bureaucracy*, 154–155; Ewen, *PR!*, 210.

52. McCamy, *Government Publicity*, 138–139.

53. "Expensive Propaganda," *Washington Post*, January 19, 1937, 8.

54. In 1936, the chairman of the Republican National Committee did complain that "a Democratic publicity campaign of unprecedented magnitude" was being waged by New Deal agencies in the run-up to Roosevelt's re-election

campaign. "Avers Democrats Use Federal Funds," *New York Times*, May 18, 1936, 2.

55. Lee, *Congress vs. the Bureaucracy*, 173–175. Early forays into presidential polling posed a similar threat. Robert M. Eisinger, *The Evolution of Presidential Polling* (New York: Cambridge University Press, 2002).

56. Jay Franklin, "We, the People," *Washington Evening Star*, January 8, 1937, A9. According to McCamy, Franklin was the pen name of John Carter, first director of information for the Resettlement Administration. See McCamy, *Government Publicity*, 10.

57. Harold W. Stoke, "Executive Leadership and the Growth of Propaganda," *American Political Science Review* 35 (June 1941): 493–494, 497–498.

58. Herring, "Official Publicity under the New Deal," 174–175 (emphasis in original).

59. Ewen, *PR!*, 292. See also Roland Marchand, *Creating the Corporate Soul: The Rise of Public Relations and Corporate Imagery in American Big Business* (Berkeley: University of California Press, 1998).

60. Edward L. Bernays, *Biography of an Idea: Memoirs of Public Relations Counsel Edward L. Bernays* (New York: Simon and Schuster, 1965), 56–57; Ewen, *PR!*, 158–161.

61. The "torch" parade was only one of several ways Bernays promoted cigarettes among women. In addition, he championed smoking as a way to lose weight, crafting the slogan "Reach for a Lucky Instead of a Sweet." See Larry Tye, *The Father of Spin: Edward Bernays and the Birth of Public Relations* (New York: Crown, 1998), 28–31.

62. Ewen, *PR!*, 216.

63. Tye, *The Father of Spin*.

64. Henry F. Pringle, "Mass Psychologist," *American Mercury*, February 1930, 155–156.

65. Ernest Boyd, "Portrait of a Press Agent," *Bookman*, July 1924, 563–565.

66. Bernays, *Biography of an Idea*, 187.

67. Edward L. Bernays, *Crystallizing Public Opinion* (New York: Boni and Liveright, 1923), 173; Edward L. Bernays, "Counsel of Public Relations—a Definition," January 1927, Edward L. Bernays Papers, Library of Congress (hereafter ELB Papers), Box 422.

68. Bernays quoted in Wayne W. Parrish, "He Helped Make Press-Agentry a Science," *Literary Digest*, June 1934, 26.

69. Edward L. Bernays, *Propaganda* (New York: Horace Liveright, 1928), 93, 96.

70. Emily Newell Blair, "Another Job for the Supersalesman," *Independent*, March 10, 1928, 222.

71. Blair, "Another Job for the Supersalesman," 223.

72. Bernays, *Propaganda*, 105.

73. Edward L. Bernays, "Crystallizing Public Opinion for Good Government," speech, National Municipal League, Pittsburgh, PA, November 1925, ELB Papers, Box 422.

74. Edward L. Bernays, "The Public Relations of the National Government," speech, annual meeting of the American Political Science Association, December 27, 1934, Chicago, IL, ELB Papers, Box 423.

75. Edward L. Bernays, "Public Relations as a Career," speech, Newark, NJ, June 27, 1934, ELB Papers, Box 422.

76. Edward L. Bernays, "Speech at New York Newspapers Women's Club," October 21, 1930, ELB Papers, Box 422.

77. Bernays quoted in Parrish, "He Helped Make Press-Agentry a Science," 26.

78. Edward L. Bernays, "The Engineering of Consent," *Annals of the American Academy of Political and Social Science* 250 (March 1947): 114.

79. Michael Heaney and John Mark Hansen, "Building the Chicago School," *American Political Science Review* 100 (November 2006): 590.

80. Gary, *The Nervous Liberals*, 59.

81. Lasswell quoted in Gary, *The Nervous Liberals*, 59.

82. Harold D. Lasswell, *Propaganda Technique in the World War* (New York: Knopf, 1927), 5.

83. Lasswell, *Propaganda Technique in the World War*, 2.

84. Lasswell, *Propaganda Technique in the World War*, 34.

85. Harold D. Lasswell. "The Theory of Political Propaganda," *American Political Science Review* 21 (August 1927): 631.

86. Lasswell, "The Theory of Political Propaganda," 627.

87. Lippmann, *Public Opinion*, 150.

88. Harold D. Lasswell. "The Function of the Propagandist," *International Journal of Ethics* 38 (April 1928): 264.

89. E. Pendleton Herring, *Group Representation before Congress* (Baltimore: Johns Hopkins University Press, 1929).

90. Peter Odegard, *Pressure Politics: The Story of the Anti-Saloon League* (New York: Columbia University Press, 1928), 73.

91. Peter Odegard, *The American Public Mind* (New York: Columbia University Press, 1930), vi, 178, 197.

92. Gary, *The Nervous Liberals*, 72.

93. Harold D. Lasswell, Ralph D. Casey, and Bruce Lannes Smith, *Propaganda and Promotional Activities: An Annotated Bibliography* (Minneapolis: University of Minnesota Press, 1935).

94. Harwood L. Childs, "Foreword," *Annals of the American Academy of Political and Social Science* 179 (May 1935): xi.

95. Lasswell, "The Function of the Propagandist," 260–261.

96. Harold D. Lasswell. "The Person: Subject and Object of Propaganda," *Annals of the American Academy of Political and Social Science* 179 (May 1935): 193.

97. In the opening pages of *Propaganda Technique*, Lasswell noted how "members of the new propaganda, or publicity, profession have begun to rationalize their own practices," adding that Bernays and others were "pioneers in this direction." Lasswell, *Propaganda Technique in the World War*, 2.

98. Bernays, "Public Relations as a Career."
99. Bernays, "Public Relations as a Career."
100. Edward L. Bernays, "The Science of Propaganda," text of radio address, April 15, 1937, ELB Papers, Box 426.
101. Childs, "Foreword," xi; Edward L. Bernays, "Molding Public Opinion," *Annals of the American Academy of Political and Social Science* 179 (May 1935): 87.
102. Pendleton Herring to Edward Bernays, November 16, 1934, and Edward Bernays to Pendelton Herring, November 19, 1934, ELB Papers, Box 423; Frederick A. Ogg, "Thirtieth Annual Meeting of the American Political Science Association," *American Political Science Review* 29 (February 1935): 109.
103. Harwood Childs to Edward Bernays, September 29, 1934, ELB Papers, Box 422; Harwood L. Childs, *A Reference Guide to the Study of Public Opinion* (Princeton, NJ: Princeton University Press, 1934), ii–iii.
104. Abbott, *The System of Professions*, 54–55, 102.
105. Harwood Childs to Edward Bernays, October 26, 1936; Ralph Casey to Edward Bernays, October 27, 1936; Harold Lasswell to Edward Bernays, October 26, 1936, ELB Papers, Box 423.
106. *Universities—Pathfinders of Public Opinion: A Survey by Edward L. Bernays In Collaboration with Doris E. Fleischman*, Self-published pamphlet (New York, 1937), 6, ELB Papers, Box 73.
107. A. Percy Block to Edward Bernays, February 21, 1936, ELB Papers, Box 423.
108. A. Percy Block to Edward Bernays, February 21, 1936, ELB Papers, Box 423.
109. Edward Bernays to Henry Epstein, April 9, 1936, ELB Papers, Box 425.
110. "Comparison between the Legal Profession and the Profession of Public Relations," n.d., ELB Papers, Box 423.
111. Bernays, *Crystallizing Public Opinion*, 143.
112. Chris McNickle, *To Be Mayor of New York: Ethnic Politics in the City* (New York: Columbia University Press, 1993), 48–52.
113. Charles Garrett, *The La Guardia Years: Machine and Reform Politics in New York City* (New Brunswick, NJ: Rutgers University Press, 1961), 252–253.
114. Garrett, *The La Guardia Years*, 271.
115. Edward L. Bernays, "Putting Politics on the Market," *Independent*, May 19, 1928, 470, 472.
116. Bernays, "Putting Politics on the Market," 470. See also Bernays, *Propaganda*, 97.
117. Bernays, *Crystallizing Public Opinion*, 143.
118. Bernays, "Putting Politics on the Market," 472.
119. Bernays, *Crystallizing Public Opinion*, 147.

120. Bernays, "Putting Politics on the Market," 472; *Public Relations: Edward L. Bernays and the American Scene; Annotated Bibliography of and Reference Guide to Writings by and About Edward L. Bernays from 1917 to 1951* (Boston: F. W. Faxon, 1951), 40.

121. Bernays, "Crystallizing Public Opinion for Good Government."

122. Edward L. Bernays, Recommendations to the O'Dwyer Campaign Committee, n.d. (likely 1941), ELB Papers, Box 301, 1.

123. Bernays, Recommendations to the O'Dwyer Campaign, 2.

124. Bernays, Recommendations to the O'Dwyer Campaign, 16.

125. Bernays, Recommendations to the O'Dwyer Campaign, 18–19.

126. Bernays, Recommendations to the O'Dwyer Campaign, 9.

127. Bernays, Recommendations to the O'Dwyer Campaign, 10.

128. Bernays, Recommendations to the O'Dwyer Campaign, 14.

129. Bernays, Recommendations to the O'Dwyer Campaign, 18.

130. Bernays, Recommendations to the O'Dwyer Campaign, 14.

131. Bernays, Recommendations to the O'Dwyer Campaign, 28.

132. To express the projected cost of the 1941 campaign in 2013 dollars, I deflated the 1941 amount by nominal GDP in 1941 divided by nominal GDP in 2013 (GDP figures from www.measuringworth.com). De Blasio expenditures for 2013 are available at http://www.nyccfb.info/searchabledb/Start.aspx?from_screen=Expenditure, accessed January 30, 2015.

133. Financial statements 1941, O'Dwyer Campaign Committee, September 23, 1941: "For balance of fee in connection with survey and sampling public attitudes regarding candidates and issues in present city campaign, together with general recommendations . . . $1,750"; ELB Papers, Box 5.

134. Garrett, *The La Guardia Years*, 273.

135. McNickle, *To Be Mayor of New York*, 63.

136. Robert Westbrook, "Politics as Consumption: Managing the Modern Election," in *The Culture of Consumption: Critical Essays in American History, 1880–1980*, ed. Richard W. Fox and T. J. Jackson Lears (New York: Pantheon, 1983), 145–173.

Chapter 4

1. Edward Bernays, "Molding Public Opinion," *Annals of the American Academy of Political and Social Science* 179 (May 1935): 82.

2. Bernays, "Molding Public Opinion," 82.

3. Bureau of the Census, *Historical Statistics of the United States: Colonial Times to 1970* (Washington, DC: Government Printing Office, 1975), 796.

4. David Michael Ryfe, "Franklin Roosevelt and the Fireside Chats," *Journal of Communication* 49 (Autumn 1999): 81.

5. Edward L. Bernays, "The Engineering of Consent," *Annals of the American Academy of Political and Social Science* 250 (March 1947): 113–114.

6. Bernays, "The Engineering of Consent," 113–114.

7. Becky M. Nicolaides, "Radio Electioneering in the American Presidential Campaigns of 1932 and 1936," *Historical Journal of Film, Radio and Television* 8 (Summer 1988): 115.

8. Louise M. Benjamin, "Broadcast Campaign Precedents from the 1924 Presidential Election," *Journal of Broadcasting and Electronic Media*, 31 (Fall 1987): 454.

9. Douglas B. Craig, *Fireside Politics: Radio and Political Culture in the United States, 1920–1940* (Baltimore: Johns Hopkins University Press, 2000), 117–119.

10. Craig, *Fireside Politics*, 149.

11. Craig, *Fireside Politics*, 146–149. As a share of GDP, this is equivalent to $164 million in 2012 dollars. By comparison, the two presidential candidates spent $763 million on media in the 2012 election. For presidential expenditures, see https://www.opensecrets.org/pres12/expenditures.php, accessed February 3, 2015.

12. Nicolaides, "Radio Electioneering," 117, 120–121.

13. Coolidge quoted in Craig, *Fireside Politics*, 142.

14. Gil Troy, *See How They Ran: The Changing Role of the Presidential Candidate* (Cambridge, MA: Harvard University Press, 1996), 155–156.

15. Craig, *Fireside Politics*, 154.

16. Troy, *See How They Ran*, 162–164; Nicolaides, "Radio Electioneering," 120.

17. Ellis, "Accepting the Nomination," 127–129.

18. Alan Brinkley, *Voices of Protest: Huey Long, Father Coughlin and the Great Depression* (New York: Vintage Books, 1983), 193.

19. Brinkley, *Voices of Protest*, 97.

20. Brinkley, *Voices of Protest*, 97.

21. "Priest of a Parish of the Air Waves, *New York Times*, October 29, 1933, SM8.

22. Brinkley, *Voices of Protest*, 100–101, 119.

23. Craig, *Fireside Politics*, 161.

24. Brinkley, *Voices of Protest*, 207–209.

25. Nicolaides, "Radio Electioneering," 121.

26. Craig, *Fireside Politics*, 124; Nicolaides, "Radio Electioneering," 117, 121; Richard W. Steele, *Propaganda in an Open Society: The Roosevelt Administration and the Media, 1933–1941* (Westport, CT: Greenwood Press, 1985), 18; "Campaign Trips of Candidates Today Scientifically Planned," *Washington Post*, October 14, 1928, 13.

27. "Politics Irks Broadcasters," *New York Times*, October 23, 1932, XX6; Nicolaides, "Radio Electioneering," 122.

28. Nicolaides, "Radio Electioneering," 121, 128–130.

29. "Doubt Radio Value in Convention Use," *New York Times*, June 28, 1936, 24.

30. Nicolaides, "Radio Electioneering," 134.

31. "Republicans to Launch New Kind of Campaign," *New York Times*, August 16, 1936, 3.

32. Ralph D. Casey, "Republican Propaganda in the 1936 Campaign," *Public Opinion Quarterly* 1 (April 1937): 33–34.
33. Nicolaides, "Radio Electioneering," 133.
34. Bureau of the Census, *Historical Statistics of the United States*, 796.
35. "Talk Will Not Be Cheap," *New York Times*, May 10, 1936, 10; Nicolaides, "Radio Electioneering," 131.
36. Troy, *See How They Ran*, 158.
37. Troy, *See How They Ran*, 158.
38. On the history of market research, see Coleman Harwell Wells, "Remapping America: Market Research and American Society, 1900–1940" (PhD diss., University Virginia, 1999); Lawrence C. Lockley, "Notes on the History of Marketing Research," *Journal of Marketing* 14 (April 1950): 733–736; Robert Bartels, "Influences on the Development of Marketing Thought," *Journal of Marketing* 16 (July 1951): 1–17.
39. Walter Dill Scott, *The Theory of Advertising: A Simple Exposition of the Principles of Psychology and Their Relation to Successful Advertising* (Boston: Small, Maynard, 1903), 5; Walter Dill Scott, *The Psychology of Advertising* (Boston: Small, Maynard, 1908), v.
40. Selden O. Martin, "The Scientific Study of Marketing," *Annals of the American Academy of Political and Social Science* 59 (May 1915): 77–85. Martin was the first director of the bureau.
41. Jean Converse, *Survey Research in the United States: Roots and Emergence 1890–1960* (Berkeley: University of California Press, 1987), 89–90; Lockley, "Notes on the History of Marketing Research," 733. On Cherington's career, see Archibald M. Crossley, "Paul Terry Cherington," *Journal of Marketing* 21 (October 1956): 135–136; Wells, "Remapping America," 68–76.
42. Resor quoted in Peggy J. Kreshel, "John B. Watson at J. Walter Thompson: The Legitimation of 'Science' in Advertising," *Journal of Advertising* 19 (1990): 51.
43. Kreshel, "John B. Watson at J. Walter Thompson," 53. See also Peggy J. Kreshel, "The 'Culture' of J. Walter Thompson, 1915–1925," *Public Relations Review* 16 (Fall 1990): 80–93; Wells, "Remapping America," 163–171.
44. Paul T. Cherington, "Statistics in Market Studies," *Annals of the American Academy of Political and Social Science* 115 (September 1924): 132.
45. Cherington, "Statistics in Market Studies," 133.
46. Cherington was not the only one to develop quota sampling. Others included Harvard Business School professors Daniel Starch and Theodore Brown, who developed the mathematical formula that related sample size to standard error. Converse, *Survey Research*, 93; Crossley, "Paul Terry Cherington," 135–136; Daniel J. Robinson, *The Measure of Democracy: Polling, Market Research, and Public Life, 1930–1945* (Toronto: University of Toronto Press, 1999), 16–17.

47. On the limitations of quota sampling, see Converse, *Survey Research*, 203–204. On the biases of polling more generally, see Sarah Igo, *The Averaged American: Surveys, Citizens, and the Making of a Mass Public* (Cambridge, MA: Harvard University Press, 2007).

48. On the creation of a segmented mass market, see especially Wells, "Remapping America," 206–219.

49. James Mark Banks, "A History of Broadcast Audience Research in the United States," (PhD diss., University of Tennessee, 1981), 28.

50. "Survey Reveals New Radio Facts," *New York Times*, November 18, 1928, 18.

51. C. W. Steffler, "Classifying the Invisible Audience," *Commerce and Finance*, October 24, 1928, 2271.

52. Converse, *Survey Research*, 112; Archibald Crossley, "Early Days of Public Opinion Research," *Public Opinion Quarterly* 21 (Spring 1957): 160, 162.

53. James G. Webster, Patricia F. Phalen, and Lawrence W. Lichty, *Ratings Analysis: The Theory and Practice of Audience Research*, 3rd ed. (London: Routledge, 2006), 95–96.

54. Walter K. Kingson, "Measuring the Broadcast Audience," *Quarterly Journal of Film and Television* 3 (Spring 1953): 291–303.

55. "Exit Crossley," *Time*, September 30, 1946, 98.

56. Webster, Phalen, and Lichty, *Ratings Analysis*, 96–98; Banks, "A History of Broadcast Audience Research," 34–35, 60–63; Craig, *Fireside Politics*, 193–194.

57. Igo, *The Averaged American*, 113, 173.

58. Robinson, *The Measure of Democracy*, 6. For other work on the link between marketing and polling, see Converse, *Survey Research*, 87–127; Igo, *The Averaged American*, 113–118; Wells, "Remapping America," 360–422.

59. For biographical information on Gallup, see Becky Wilson Hawbaker, "Taking the 'Pulse of Democracy': George Gallup, Iowa, and the Origin of the Gallup Poll," *Palimpsest* 74 (Fall 1993): 98–113; J. J. O'Malley, "Black Beans and White Beans," *New Yorker*, March 2, 1940, 20–24; Igo, *The Averaged American*, 116–118; Converse, *Survey Research*, 114–124.

60. Hawbaker, "Taking the 'Pulse of Democracy,'" 107.

61. Igo, *The Averaged American*, 117; Converse, *Survey Research*, 117.

62. Susan Herbst, *Numbered Voices: How Opinion Polling Has Shaped American Politics* (Chicago: University of Chicago Press, 1993).

63. Converse, *Survey Research*, 117–119; "Results Today Point to Close November Race," *Washington Post*, July 12, 1936, B1.

64. On region, see "Drought States Give President Chief Gains," *Washington Post*, August 9, 1936, B1, and "Poll Indicates Roosevelt Slipping a Bit in South," *Washington Post*, September 10, 1936, X9. On income, see "President Polls 81% of Relief Vote Today," *Washington Post*, September 13, 1936, B1. On support among different occupational groups, see "Survey First to Test Workers' Sentiment," *Washington Post*, August 16, 1936, B1. On age, see "Roosevelt Draws Younger, Landon Older Voters, Poll Shows," *Washington*

Post, September 27, 1936, B1. On religion, see "Roosevelt Is Strongest with Catholics, Jews," *Washington Post*, October 11, 1936, B1. On support among partisans, see "Growing Third Party a Threat to Democrats, Poll Finds," *Washington Post*, July 26, 1936, B1, and "Landon Gains 4 1-2 Million Shift Votes, Roosevelt 2 Million," *Washington Post*, August 30, 1936, B1. Notably absent in Gallup's analysis was any discussion of race, and Gallup routinely undersampled women and minorities in his election polls. On Gallup's sampling biases, see Igo, *The Averaged American*, 134–137; Robinson, *The Measure of Democracy*, 51–57.

65. "Campaign to Center in Five Close States," *Washington Post*, August 23, 1936, B1.

66. For explanations of method, see "Institute Poll a 'Sampling' of Public Opinion," *Washington Post*, August 9, 1936, B1; "Poll Methods Used Daily by Industry and Science," *Washington Post*, August 23, 1936, B1; "Probability of Error," *Washington Post*, September 6, 1936, B1; "Institute Poll and Straw Vote Are Different," *Washington Post*, September 20, 1936, B1.

67. "How Correct Will Poll Be on Nov. 3d?," *Washington Post*, October 4, 1936, B1.

68. "Voting Tuesday to Test Clashing Methods," *Washington Post*, November 1, 1936, B1.

69. "Exclusive Survey Gave Landon 3 'Sure' States," *Washington Post*, November 8, 1936, B1. In 1936, FDR polled 61 percent of the electorate and received 523 electoral votes. On Gallup's errors in 1936, see Converse, *Survey Research*, 119.

70. "Gallup Announces Expansion of Institute Poll Policy," *Washington Post*, November 15, 1936, B1.

71. Wells, "Remapping America," 393–395.

72. On the increasing overlap between commerce and politics, see Roland Marchand, *Creating the Corporate Soul: The Rise of Public Relations and Corporate Imagery in American Big Business* (Berkeley: University of California Press, 1998).

73. Wells, "Remapping America," 397.

74. Wells, "Remapping America," 406–408.

75. "A New Technique in Journalism," *Fortune*, July 1935, 65.

76. "The Fortune Quarterly Survey: III," *Fortune*, January 1936, 46–47, 156–157; Wells, "Remapping America," 413.

77. Converse, *Survey Research*, 113–114; Igo, *The Averaged American*, 115–116.

78. Converse, *Survey Research*, 119; "The November Elections," *Fortune*, October 1936, 130–132.

79. George Gallup to Elmo Roper, November 18, 1940, Elmo Roper Papers, Thomas J. Dodd Research Center, University of Connecticut Libraries (hereafter Elmo Roper Papers), Box 3; Elmo Roper to George Gallup, November 19, 1940, Elmo Roper Papers, Box 3. Roper's letter is marked "not sent" in blue pencil.

80. Elmo Roper to Jay N. Darling, November 6, 1944, Elmo Roper Papers, Box 3.
81. Igo, *The Averaged American.*
82. Chester Bowles to Elmo Roper, September 3, 1946, Elmo Roper Papers, Box 4.
83. Elmo Roper Statement Profit and Loss, September 30, 1946, Elmo Roper Papers, Box 48.
84. Elmo Roper to Charles Farnsley, March 13, 1942, Elmo Roper Papers, Box 3.
85. Elmo Roper to Chester Bowles, March 15, 1949, Elmo Roper Papers, Box 6.
86. Elmo Roper to Frank Altschul, August 21, 1957, Elmo Roper Papers, Box 10; Elmo Roper to Roger S. Stevens, November 4, 1957, Elmo Roper Papers, Box 11; memo from Elmo Roper, September 19, 1957, Elmo Roper Papers, Box 10.
87. Herbst, *Numbered Voices*; Taeku Lee, *Mobilizing Public Opinion: Black Insurgency and Racial Attitudes in the Civil Rights Era* (Chicago: University of Chicago Press, 2002).
88. Igo, *The Averaged Americans*, 173.
89. "Riddles for Social Planners," *New York Times*, October 20, 1935, X13.
90. Hadley Cantril and Gordon W. Allport, *The Psychology of Radio* (New York: Harper and Brothers, 1935), vii.
91. Cantril and Allport, *The Psychology of Radio*, 11, 14.
92. Cantril and Allport, *The Psychology of Radio*, 7.
93. Cantril and Allport, *The Psychology of Radio*, 18 (emphases in original).
94. "Riddles for Social Planners," X13.
95. Hadley Cantril, *The Human Dimension: Experiences in Policy Research* (New Brunswick, NJ: Rutgers University Press, 1967), 22.
96. Cantril, *The Human Dimension*, 23.
97. Cantril quoted in Converse, *Survey Research*, 148.
98. O'Malley, "Black Beans and White Beans," 23; Cantril, *The Human Dimension*, 23.
99. Igo, *The Averaged American*, 118.
100. Converse, *Survey Research*, 144.
101. "Foreword," *Public Opinion Quarterly* 1 (January 1937): 4.
102. Whereas the number of articles by authors with business affiliations averaged more than 20 percent during the first decade of publication, by the 1960s articles by business-affiliated authors accounted for less than 10 percent of the total. Converse, *Survey Research*, 398–399.
103. Rockefeller Foundation, *Annual Report* (1937), 322, 325.
104. Timothy Glander, *Origins of Mass Communications Research during the Cold War* (Mahwah, NJ: Erlbaum, 2000), 85; Converse, *Survey Research*, 149, 151.
105. Rockefeller Foundation, *Annual Report* (1939), 344–345.
106. Lindsay Rogers, *The Pollsters: Public Opinion, Politics, and Democratic Leadership* (New York: Knopf, 1949); Amy Fried, "The Forgotten Lindsay

Rogers and the Development of American Political Science," *American Political Science Review* 100 (November 2006): 555–561.

107. Hadley Cantril and Norman Frederiksen, "How Society Shapes Our Mind," *Science Digest* 7 (February 1940): 45–46.

108. Paul Lazarsfeld, "An Episode in the History of Social Research: A Memoir," in *The Intellectual Migration: Europe and America, 1930–1960*, ed. Donald Fleming and Bernard Bailyn (Cambridge, MA: Harvard University Press, 1969), 279; Todd Gitlin, "Media Sociology: The Dominant Paradigm," *Theory and Society* 6 (September 1978): 205–253.

109. Allen H. Barton, "Paul Lazarsfeld and Applied Social Research: Invention of the University Applied Social Research Institute," *Social Science History* 3 (October 1979): 15.

110. Paul Lazarsfeld, Bernard Berelson, and Hazel Gaudet, *The People's Choice: How the Voter Makes Up His Mind in a Presidential Campaign* (New York: Columbia University Press, 1948 [1944]), 1.

111. Converse, *Survey Research*, 143–144; Peter Rossi, "Four Landmarks in Voting Research," in *American Voting Behavior*, ed. Eugene Burdick and Arthur J. Brodbeck (Glencoe, IL: Free Press, 1959), 15; Paul Lazarsfeld and Marjorie Fiske, "The 'Panel' as a New Tool for Measuring Opinion," *Public Opinion Quarterly* 2 (October 1938): 596–612.

112. Paul F. Lazarsfeld, "The Psychological Basis of Market Research," *Harvard Business Review* 13 (1934): 68; Max Visser, "The Psychology of Voting Action: On the Psychological Origins of Electoral Research, 1939–1964," *Journal of the History of Behavioral Sciences* 30 (January 1994): 43–52.

113. Lazarsfeld, Berelson, and Gaudet, *The People's Choice*, 1.

114. Paul F. Lazarsfeld, "The Election Is Over," *Public Opinion Quarterly* 8 (August 1944): 317.

115. Elmo Roper, "It's Dewey over Truman by a Landslide," *Evening Independent*, September 9, 1941, 1.

116. Robert K. Merton and Paul K. Hatt, "Election Polling Forecasts and Public Images of Social Science: A Case Study in the Shaping of Opinion among a Strategic Public," *Public Opinion Quarterly* 13 (Summer 1949): 185–222.

117. Igo, *The Average American*, pp. 153–154, 346n.1.

118. Mosteller et al., *The Pre-election Polls of 1948*, 291.

119. Igo, *The Averaged American*, 186–187.

120. Seymour M. Lipset, Paul F. Lazarsfeld, Allen H. Barton, and Juan Linz, "The Psychology of Voting: An Analysis of Political Behavior," in *Handbook of Social Psychology*, vol. 2, ed. Gardner Lindsey (Cambridge, MA: Harvard University Press, 1954), 1124. See also Robert Westbrook, "Politics as Consumption: Managing the Modern Election," in *The Culture of Consumption: Critical Essays in American History, 1880–1980*, ed. Richard W. Fox and T. J. Jackson Lears (New York: Pantheon, 1983), 162.

121. Brinkley, *Voices of Protest*, 207–209, 284–286. For Farley's assessment, see James A. Farley, *Jim Farley's Story: The Roosevelt Years* (New York: McGraw-Hill, 1948), pp. 50–51.

122. Melvin G. Holli, *The Wizard of Washington: Emil Hurja, Franklin Roosevelt, and the Birth of Public Opinion Polling* (New York: Palgrave, 2002), 66–67.

123. Emil Hurja quoted in Thomas Sugrue, "Hurja: Farley's Guess Man," *American Magazine* 71 (1936): 87. See also Holli, *The Wizard of Washington*, 41; Robert M. Eisinger, *The Evolution of Presidential Polling* (Cambridge: Cambridge University Press, 2003), 81.

124. Holli, *The Wizard of Washington*, 43.

125. Holli, *The Wizard of Washington*, 43–44.

126. Holli, *The Wizard of Washington*, 52.

127. Holli, *The Wizard of Washington*, 63–64.

128. Holli, *The Wizard of Washington*, 40.

129. Robert M. Eisinger and Jeremy Brown, "Polling as a Means toward Presidential Autonomy: Emil Hurja, Hadley Cantril, and the Roosevelt Administration," *International Journal of Public Opinion Research* 10 (1998): 242.

130. Alva Johnston, "Prof. Hurja, the New Deal's Political Doctor," *Saturday Evening Post*, June 13, 1936), 8.

131. Johnston, "Prof. Hurja, the New Deal's Political Doctor," 72.

132. Eisinger, *The Evolution of Presidential Polling*.

133. Stephen Schoenherr, "Selling the New Deal: Stephen T. Early's Role as Press Secretary to Franklin D. Roosevelt" (PhD diss., University of Delaware, 1976), 62.

134. Schoenherr, "Selling the New Deal," 67; A. S. Draper, "President Employs Air, Press to Educate Nation," *Literary Digest*, January 27, 1934, 9.

135. Early quoted in Betty Houchin Winfield, *FDR and the News Media* (Urbana: University of Illinois Press, 1990), 109.

136. Craig, *Fireside Politics*, 56, 91, 93.

137. Steele, *Propaganda in an Open Society*, 22–23.

138. Schoenherr, "Selling the New Deal," 68–69.

139. Craig, *Fireside Politics*, 158; James L. McCamy, *Government Publicity* (Chicago: University of Chicago Press, 1939), 94–99.

140. Craig, *Fireside Politics*, 127.

141. Ryfe, "Franklin Roosevelt and the Fireside Chats," 90–91; see especially the detailed discussion of the preparation and delivery of the fireside chats in Schoenherr, "Selling the New Deal," 110–122.

142. Brandon Rottinghaus, "Dear Mr. President: The Institutionalization and Politicization of Public Opinion Mail in the White House," *Political Science Quarterly* 121 (Fall 2006): 456–458.

143. Schoenherr, "Selling the New Deal," 123–124; Winfield, *FDR and the News Media*, 108–109, 121.

144. On the importance of crafted communication see Lawrence Jacobs and Robert Shapiro, *Politicians Don't Pander: Political Manipulation and the Loss of Democratic Responsiveness* (Chicago: University of Chicago Press, 2000).

145. Converse, *Survey Research*, 144.

146. Gisela Cramer and Ursula Prutsch, "Nelson A. Rockefeller's Office of Inter-American Affairs (1940–1946) and Record Group 229," *Hispanic American Historical Review* 86 (November 2006): 785–806.

147. Converse, *Survey Research*, 153. See also Cantril, *The Human Dimension*, 28; Glander, *Origins of Mass Communications Research*, 88.

148. Cantril, *The Human Dimension*, 28–29.

149. Cantril, *The Human Dimension*, 35–38, 43. For a discussion of the methodological limitations of this work, see Adam Berinsky, "American Public Opinion in the 1930s and 1940s: The Analysis of Quota-Controlled Sample Survey Data," *Public Opinion Quarterly* 70 (2006): 499–529.

150. Cantril, *The Human Dimension*, 38.

151. "Father of Halitosis," *Time*, January 14, 1957, 106; Gerard B. Lambert, *All Out of Step* (Garden City, NY: Doubleday, 1956), 264.

152. Cantril, *The Human Dimension*, 39–40.

153. Lambert, *All Out of Step*, 251–252.

154. Lambert, *All Out of Step*, 259–260.

155. Richard W. Steele, "The Pulse of the People: Franklin D. Roosevelt and the Gauging of American Public Opinion," *Journal of Contemporary History* 9 (October 1974): 210.

156. Cantril, *The Human Dimension*, 52–54, 65–66, 69–72.

157. Cantril, *The Human Dimension*, 56.

158. Cantril, *The Human Dimension*, 59–60.

159. Cantril, *The Human Dimension*, 61.

160. "Mr. Roosevelt at His Best," *Time*, September 27, 1943, 19. Steele, "The Pulse of the People," 211–214.

161. Cantril, *The Human Dimension*, 41.

162. Cantril, *The Human Dimension*, 41.

163. Lambert, *All Out of Step*, 262.

164. Jeffrey Tulis, *The Rhetorical Presidency* (Princeton, NJ: Princeton University Press, 1987). See also Richard J. Ellis, "Accepting the Nomination: From Martin Van Buren to Franklin Delano Roosevelt," in *Speaking to the People: The Rhetorical Presidency in Historical Perspective*, ed. Richard J. Ellis (Amherst: University of Massachusetts Press, 1998), 112–133.

Chapter 5

1. Max Weber, *Political Writings*, ed. Peter Lassman and Ronald Spiers (Cambridge: Cambridge University Press, 1994 [1919]), 318.

2. Carey McWilliams, "Government by Whitaker and Baxter," *Nation*, April 15, 1951, 346–348; Stanley Kelley, *Professional Public Relations and Political Power* (Baltimore: Johns Hopkins University Press, 1956), 43.

3. McWilliams, "Government by Whitaker and Baxter," 346. For the other installments in the series, see "Government by Whitaker and Baxter, II," *Nation*, April 21, 366–369, and "Government by Whitaker and Baxter, III," *Nation*, May 5, 1951, 418–421.

4. Kelley, *Professional Public Relations*, 39.

5. Robert Pitchell, "The Influence of Professional Campaign Management Firms in Partisan Elections in California," *Western Political Quarterly* 11 (June 1958): 286.

6. Other notable clients in this period include Pacific Telephone and Telegraph, Standard Oil of California, the California Medical Association, and the California Teachers Association. Kelley, *Professional Public Relations*, 42–43.

7. Kelley, *Professional Public Relations*, 43. The efforts of Whitaker and Baxter on behalf of Eisenhower, Nixon, and the AMA are located in "Whitaker and Baxter Campaigns, Inc. Records," California State Archives (hereafter Whitaker and Baxter Papers). For AMA fees, see "Income-Fees from A.M.A.," Whitaker and Baxter Papers, Box 153.

8. Kelley, *Professional Public Relations*, 40, 55–56.

9. "Re: Advertising Schedules," May 6, 1936, Whitaker and Baxter Papers, Box 1, Folder 13 (emphasis in original).

10. "Re: Ad Schedules Northern California Citizens against 30-Thursday," August 10, 1939, Whitaker and Baxter Papers Box 1, Folder 50.

11. Clem Whitaker, "The Public Relations of Election Campaigns," *Public Relations Journal* 2 (July 1946): 8 (emphasis in original).

12. Whitaker, "The Public Relations of Election Campaigns," 8.

13. Whitaker, "The Public Relations of Election Campaigns," 8.

14. "Bond Proposal to Be Fought," *Los Angeles Times*, October 10, 1938, 6; "Strong-Arm Tactics for Budget Told," *Los Angeles Times*, April 23, 1939, 1.

15. Will H. Fischer to P. M. Downing, October 31, 1938; Clem Whitaker to Will H. Fischer, September 27, 1938, Whitaker and Baxter Papers, Box 1, Folder 32.

16. Clem Whitaker to Will H. Fischer, August 15, 1938, Whitaker and Baxter Papers, Box 1, Folder 32.

17. Kelley, *Professional Public Relations*, 45.

18. Clem Whitaker, "The Public Relations of Election Campaigns," *Public Relations Journal* 2 (July 1946): 7.

19. Whitaker, "The Public Relations of Election Campaigns."

20. Leone Baxter, "Public Relations Precocious Baby," *Public Relations Journal* 6 (January 1950): 18.

21. Baxter, "Public Relations Precocious Baby," 23.

22. "Plan of Campaign for Proposition 9—Elementary School Initiative, General Election, November 7, 1944," Whitaker and Baxter Papers, Box 3, Folder 41.

23. Kelley, *Professional Public Relations*, 52–53 (emphasis in original).

24. Baxter, "Public Relations Precocious Baby," 23.

25. Kelley, *Professional Public Relations*, 52–53 (emphasis in original).

26. "Hetch Hetchy Campaign Memorandum," Whitaker and Baxter Papers, Box 2, Folder 17, 1. The Raker Act, passed in 1913, granted San Francisco rights to the Hetch Hetchy Valley but sought to limit the role of private utilities in generating and distributing power and water. The sale of rights to Pacific Gas and Electric violated the spirit, if not the letter, of the law and resulted in a long struggle between Harold Ickes, secretary of the interior under FDR, and the City of San Francisco over the deal. For background, see Robert Righter, *The Battle over Hetch Hetchy: America's Most Controversial Dam and the Birth of Modern Environmentalism* (Oxford: Oxford University Press, 2005), especially chap. 8.

27. "Hetch Hetchy Campaign Memorandum," 1–2.

28. "Hetch Hetchy Campaign Memorandum," 6.

29. "Hetch Hetchy Campaign Memorandum," 6–7.

30. "Hetch Hetchy Campaign Memorandum," 6.

31. "Hetch Hetchy Campaign Memorandum," 7.

32. "Hetch Hetchy Campaign Memorandum," 7.

33. "Hetch Hetchy Campaign Memorandum, 10; "Radio Schedule," Whitaker and Baxter Papers, Box 2, Folder 23.

34. Letter from Joe Robinson to Clement Whitaker, October 25, 1941, Whitaker and Baxter Papers, Box 2, Folder 20. On Robinson & Company and other professional signature firms, see David Magleby, *Direct Legislation: Voting on Ballot Propositions in the United States* (Baltimore: Johns Hopkins University Press, 1984), 73. For results of the bond measure, see San Francisco Ballot Propositions Database, San Francisco Public Library, http://sfpl.org/index. php?pg=2000027201&propid=504, accessed June 25, 2012.

35. Seth Masket, *No Middle Ground: How Informal Party Organizations Control Nominations and Polarize Legislatures* (Ann Arbor: University of Michigan Press, 2011), 59–62; Carey McWilliams, *California: The Great Exception* (New York: A. A. Wyn, 1949), 193.

36. McWilliams, *California*, 194–195.

37. Harold F. Gosnell, quoted in McWilliams, *California*, 196.

38. McWilliams, *California*, 193.

39. Masket, *No Middle Ground*, 59.

40. McWilliams, *California*, 196.

41. McWilliams, *California*, 196.

42. McWilliams, *California*, 196.

43. Greg Mitchell, *The Campaign of the Century: Upton Sinclair's Race for Governor of California and the Birth of Media Politics* (New York: Random House, 1992), 85–86; "Vote Count Complete," *Los Angeles Times*, September 29, 1934, 2.

44. Mitchell, *The Campaign of the Century*, 85–86; Jill Lepore, "The Lie Factory: How Politics Became a Business," *New Yorker*, September 24, 2012, 53.

45. Mitchell, *The Campaign of the Century*, 354.
46. "Sinclair Hit by Hatfield," *Los Angeles Times*, October 21, 1934, 18.
47. Warren quoted in Mitchell, *The Campaign of the Century*, 54; "Warren Assails Sinclair Bait," *Los Angeles Times*, October 6, 1934, 12. Eight years later, in 1942, Campaigns, Inc. managed Warren's successful run for governor of California.
48. Greg Mitchell's blog also contains a video link to anti-Sinclair newsreels (http://gregmitchellwriter.blogspot.com/search?q=sinclair). On the role of MGM studios, see "Hollywood Masses the Full Power of Her Resources to Fight Sinclair," *New York Times*, November 4, 1934, X5.
49. Upton Sinclair, *I, Candidate for Governor, and How I Got Licked* (Berkeley: University of California Press, 1994 [1934]), 99, 144; Lepore, "The Lie Factory," 53.
50. Greg Mitchell, "Beyond Obama: Could a True Socialist Actually Gain Power in America? How One Almost Did," weblog, *Nation*, September 15, 2012, accessed January 23, 2013.
51. Jonathan Bell, *California Crucible: The Forging of Modern American Liberalism* (Philadelphia: University of Pennsylvania Press, 2012), 108.
52. Knight quoted in Bell, *California Crucible*, 107.
53. Bell, *California Crucible*, 126.
54. Daniel J. B. Mitchell, "Impeding Earl Warren: California's Health Insurance Plan That Wasn't and What Might Have Been," *Journal of Health Politics, Policy and Law* 27 (December 2002): 957–960.
55. McWilliams, "Government by Whitaker and Baxter, II," 366.
56. McWilliams, "Government by Whitaker and Baxter, II," 366.
57. "Preliminary Outline of Campaign against Compulsory Health Insurance and for the Extension of Voluntary Pre-paid Medical and Hospital Systems in California," April 8, 1945, Whitaker and Baxter Papers, Box 4, Folder 39, 2.
58. "Preliminary Outline of Campaign against Compulsory Health Insurance," 8.
59. Mitchell, "Impeding Earl Warren," 953.
60. "Preliminary Outline of Campaign against Compulsory Health Insurance," 8.
61. "Preliminary Outline of Campaign against Compulsory Health Insurance," 8.
62. "Preliminary Outline of Campaign against Compulsory Health Insurance," 7.
63. "Report to the Council of the California Medical Association—May 6th, 1946," Whitaker and Baxter Papers, Box 4, Folder 39, 5.
64. "The Fifth Freedom," Campaign Material, Whitaker and Baxter Papers, Box 5, Folder 20.
65. "A Doctor's Diagnosis of Compulsory Health Insurance," Campaign Material, Whitaker and Baxter Papers, Box 5, Folder 20.

66. "Preliminary Outline of Campaign against Compulsory Health Insurance," 9.
67. "Preliminary Outline of Campaign against Compulsory Health Insurance," 11.
68. "Preliminary Outline of Campaign against Compulsory Health Insurance," 13.
69. Knight and Parker California Associates, "Public Opinion Survey Made Expressly for California Medical Association, March 1945," Whitaker and Baxter Papers, Box 5, Folder 5, 2, 4.
70. "Preliminary Outline of Campaign against Compulsory Health Insurance," 14.
71. "Preliminary Outline of Campaign against Compulsory Health Insurance," 16.
72. "Report to the House of Delegates of the California Medical Association," April 11, 1948, Whitaker and Baxter Papers, Box 5, Folder 4, 4.
73. "Report to the Council of the California Medical Association—May 6th, 1946," 6.
74. "Preliminary Outline of Campaign against Compulsory Health Insurance," 22.
75. "Report to the House of Delegates," 6.
76. "Report to the House of Delegates," 4–8.
77. "Report to the House of Delegates," 13.
78. "Report to the House of Delegates," 9.
79. "Report to the House of Delegates," 14.
80. "Report to the House of Delegates," 16.
81. McWilliams, "Government by Whitaker and Baxter, II," 368.
82. William Strang, Strang & Prosser Advertising Agency, to John Hunton, California State Medical Association, July 10, 1947, Whitaker and Baxter Papers, Box 5, Folder 1.
83. Monte Poen, *Harry S. Truman versus the Medical Lobby* (Columbia: University of Missouri Press, 1979); Christy Ford Chapin, *Ensuring America's Health: The Public Creation of the Corporate Health Care System* (New York: Cambridge University Press, 2015).
84. Edward Walker, *Grassroots for Hire: Public Affairs Consultants in American Democracy* (New York: Cambridge University Press, 2014).
85. Poen, *Harry S. Truman versus the Medical Lobby*, 133; Oscar Ewing, *The Nation's Health—A Ten-Year Program: A Report to the President* (Washington, DC: Government Printing Office, September 1948).
86. Tentative Program, National Medical Public Relations Conference, November 27, 1948, Whitaker and Baxter Papers, Box 9, Folder 26.
87. McWilliams, "Government by Whitaker and Baxter, II," 368.
88. "Medical Association Moves against Socialized Medicine," *New York Times*, December 17, 1948, 33.
89. Chapin, *Ensuring America's Health*, 75.

90. "Medical Association Moves against Socialized Medicine"; Lepore, "The Lie Factory," 56; "Leaders Rally Doctors of the Country to All-Out Fight on Socialized Medicine," *New York Times*, December 7, 1949, 33; "AMA Told to Gird for Climax of State Medicine Fight in '50," *Christian Science Monitor*, December 7, 1949, 17. Using the Consumer Price Index, Whitaker and Baxter's annual fee is equivalent to $993,000 in 2014; relative to the total output of the economy (share of GDP), this is equivalent to $6.4 million in 2014 (relative values calculated using www.measuringworth.com).

91. Kelley, *Professional Public Relations*, 74–75.

92. "Address of Mr. Clem Whitaker," *Journal of the American Medical Association* 140 (June 25 1949): 697.

93. Kelley, *Professional Public Relations*, 77.

94. "Address of Miss Leone Baxter," *Journal of the American Medical Association* 140 (June 25 1949): 696.

95. "Address of Miss Leone Baxter," 696.

96. Kelley, *Professional Public Relations*, 76.

97. Kelley, *Professional Public Relations*, 73.

98. "Compulsory Health Plans Fail to Win Women's Clubs," *Christian Science Monitor*, April 20, 1949, 15.

99. "Compulsory Health Plans Fail to Win Women's Clubs," 15.

100. Kelley, *Professional Public Relations*, 80–82.

101. Progress Report of the Coordinating Committee, *Journal of the American Medical Association* 143 (July 15, 1950): 987–988; Kelley, *Professional Public Relations*, 81–85.

102. Kelley, *Professional Public Relations*, 85.

103. "Address of Mr. Clem Whitaker," 698.

104. Kelley, *Professional Public Relations*, 85–86.

105. Adjusted for economic growth (GDP), the AMA spent around $147 million in 2010 dollars. By comparison, the US Chamber of Commerce spent more than $275 million during the struggle over the Affordable Care Act in 2009–2010. However, this only accounted for around 4 percent of all lobbying in 2010. For historic lobbying data, see "CQ Listing of Lobby Financial Reports," in *CQ Almanac 1949* (Washington, DC: Congressional Quarterly, 1950), 866–879; "Lobby Spending Breaking Records," in *CQ Almanac 1950* (Washington, DC: Congressional Quarterly, 1951), 768–70; "Roundup of 1950 Lobby Spending," in *CQ Almanac 1951* (Washington, DC: Congressional Quarterly, 1952), 718–719; "1951 Lobby Spending Roundup," in *CQ Almanac 1952* (Washington, DC: Congressional Quarterly, 1953), 432–434; "Lobby Spending Plunges," in *CQ Almanac 1953* (Washington, DC: Congressional Quarterly), 1954, 578–580. For 2010 figures, see Center for Responsive Politics, OpenSecrets.org, http://www.opensecrets.org/lobby/top.php?showYear=2010&indexType=s, accessed January 15, 2013.

106. "Address of Miss Leone Baxter," 696.

107. "Address of Miss Leone Baxter," 696.
108. Kelley, *Professional Public Relations*, 86.
109. "Address of Mr. Clem Whitaker," 696.
110. "Address of Mr. Clem Whitaker," 697.
111. Kelley, *Professional Public Relations*, 92.
112. Kelley, *Professional Public Relations*, 96.
113. Kelley, *Professional Public Relations*, 96.
114. Drew Pearson, "Ike's Crowd Alienated the AFL," *Washington Post*, September 28, 1952, B5.
115. "Professional Men to Aid Eisenhower," *New York Times*, September 23, 1952, 14.
116. Chapin, *Ensuring America's Health*, 94.
117. Mitchell, *The Campaign of the Century*.
118. Pitchell, "The Influence of Professional Campaign Management Firms"; Kelley, *Public Relations*; Joseph Pratt Harris, *California Politics* (Stanford, CA: Stanford University Press, 1956); McWilliams, *California*.
119. Including corporate public relations and their occasional work for the Republican Party in California, Campaigns, Inc. served fifty-nine different clients during the period when the firm was at its height in California politics. Figures are calculated from the inventory of the Whitaker and Baxter Records in the California State Archives, available online at http://oac.cdlib.org/findaid/ark:/13030/kt7p3036z9/, accessed January 28, 2013. For a list of all California propositions between 1912 and 1998, see John M. Allswang, *The Initiative and Referendum in California, 1898–1998* (Stanford, CA: Stanford University Press, 2000), 251–269.
120. Herbert Baus, Oral History Interview, Conducted 1989 by Enid H. Douglass, Oral History Program, Claremont Graduate School, for the California State Archives Oral History Program, 130.
121. Ned Burman, "Value of Television as Campaign Media," July 27, 1954, Whitaker and Baxter Papers, Box 18; Ned Burman to Leone Baxter and Clem Whitaker, May 10, 1954, Whitaker and Baxter Papers, Box 18.
122. By comparison, Whitaker and Baxter ran 3,400 radio spot announcements on behalf of the Knight campaign in 159 stations. "Campaign Materials Used, Knight for Governor Campaign 1954," Whitaker and Baxter Papers, Box 18; Clem Whitaker to Jerry Campbell, October 22, 1954, Whitaker and Baxter Papers, Box 19.
123. Clem Whitaker to Howard Ahmanson, February 23, 1954, Whitaker and Baxter Papers, Box 19; Harris, *California Politics*, 45, 47.
124. Herbert M. Baus, Oral History Interview, 31, 56–57.
125. The Nixon campaign operated separate organizations in Northern and Southern California under the management of Whitaker and Baxter and Baus and Ross, respectively. Organization of Nixon Campaign, Whitaker and Baxter Papers, Box 60, Folder 1.

126. When Clem Whitaker learned that Goodwin Knight had appointed a rival to manage his re-election campaign for lieutenant governor, Whitaker wrote to his son that he was "madder than hell" and instructed him to inform the Knight camp that they would play no part in a campaign if it meant playing "a subordinate part to fellows of this caliber." Clement Whitaker Sr. to Clement Whitaker, Jr., January 31, 1950, Whitaker and Baxter Papers, Box 68, Folder 1.

127. William Ross, Oral History Interview, Oral History Interview, Conducted 1990 by Enid H. Douglass, Oral History Program, Claremont Graduate School, for the California State Archives Oral History Program, 49.

128. For insights into political polling, see Dorothy D. Carey, Oral History Interview, Conducted 1990 by Enid H. Douglass, Oral History Program, Claremont Graduate School, for the California State Archives Oral History Program. On the dominant signature-gathering firm in California, Robinson and Co., see Allswang, *The Initiative and Referendum in California*, 48.

129. Stuart K. Spencer, "Developing a Campaign Management Organization," Oral History Interview, in *Issues and Innovations in the 1966 Republican Gubernatorial Campaign*, Regional Oral History Office, University of California, Berkeley, p. 4.

130. William E. Roberts, "Professional Campaign Management and the Candidate, 1960–1966," Oral History Interview, in *Issues and Innovations in the 1966 Republican Gubernatorial Campaign*, Regional Oral History Office, University of California, Berkeley, p. 2.

131. When Herbert Baus worked for Democrat Pat Brown in his campaign against Ronald Reagan in 1966, he attracted criticism from Republicans and was effectively blacklisted from future candidate campaigns. Herbert Baus, Oral History Interview, 168–169.

132. On Democratic operatives and consultants, see Donald L. Bradley, "Managing Democratic Campaigns, 1943–1966," an oral history conducted 1977–1979 by Amelia R. Fry, Regional Oral History Office, University of California, Berkeley. On California Democrats more generally, see Bell, *California Crucible*.

133. On Baus's early career, see Herbert Baus, Oral History Interview, 30–32.

134. Baxter, "Public Relations Precocious Baby."

135. Walker, *Grassroots for Hire*.

136. Although no authoritative source exists, the quote is widely attributed to Unruh. See Richard Bergholz, "After Political Honey Comes That Big Money," *Los Angeles Times*, September 6, 1963, A4.

Chapter 6

1. Angus Campbell, Philip Converse, Warren Miller, and Donald Stokes, *The American Voter* (New York: Wiley, 1960). Bernard Berelson, Paul F. Lazarsfeld, and William N. McPhee, *Voting: A Study of Opinion Formation in a Presidential Campaign* (Chicago: University of Chicago Press, 1954).

For work that does examine campaign effects, see Samuel J. Eldersveld, "Experimental Propaganda Techniques and Voting Behavior," *American Political Science Review* 50 (March 1956): 154–165.

2. Stanley Kelley, *Professional Public Relations and Political Power* (Baltimore: Johns Hopkins University Press, 1956).

3. Kelley, *Professional Public Relations*, 110.

4. William White, "Tydings Charges McCarthy Perjured Himself at Inquiry," *New York Times*, July 20, 1950, 1.

5. Kelley, *Professional Public Relations*, 135.

6. Clayton Knowles, "Inquiry Set Today in Tydings Charge," *New York Times*, February 20, 1951, 17.

7. Knowles, "Inquiry Set Today in Tydings Charge."

8. Edward Ryan, "Carpetbagging in the Free State," *Washington Post*, April 22, 1951, B1.

9. US Senate, *Maryland Senatorial Election of 1950*, Subcommittee on Privileges and Elections, 82nd Cong., 1st sess. (Washington, DC: Government Printing Office, 1951), 278.

10. US Senate, *Maryland Senatorial Election of 1950*, 272.

11. Kelley, *Professional Public Relations*, 109, 141.

12. United States Senate, *Maryland Senatorial Election of 1950*, 302.

13. Kelley, *Professional Public Relations*, 141.

14. Kelley, *Professional Public Relations*, 142.

15. Jon Jonkel quoted in Kelley, *Professional Public Relations*, 142.

16. Kelley, *Professional Public Relations*, 141.

17. Kelley, *Professional Public Relations*, 143.

18. Kelley, *Professional Public Relations*, 143.

19. United States Senate, *Maryland Senatorial Election of 1950*, 5–6.

20. "Jonkel Pays $5,000 Fine in Election Case," *The Baltimore Sun* (June 5, 1951), 34.

21. "Jon Jonkel Dies; Former Publicist," *The New York Times* (July 1, 1959), 25.

22. Kelley, *Professional Public Relations*, 35.

23. Kelley, *Professional Public Relations*.

24. Daniel Galvin, *Presidential Party Building: Dwight D. Eisenhower to George W. Bush* (Princeton, NJ: Princeton University Press, 2009).

25. Kelley, *Professional Public Relations*, 35–36. The states were Washington, Minnesota, Michigan, Ohio, Kansas, Arizona, Iowa, Massachusetts, Nevada, New Mexico, New Jersey, New York, California, Maryland, Illinois, Pennsylvania, and Oregon. Unfortunately, Kelley does not discuss states where public relations firms were not active.

26. Kelley, *Professional Public Relations*, 37.

27. Alexander Heard, *The Costs of Democracy* (Chapel Hill: University of North Carolina Press, 1960).

28. Heard, *The Costs of Democracy*, vii–viii; US Senate, *1956 Presidential and Senatorial Campaign Contributions and Practices*, pts. 1 and 2, Subcommittee

on Privileges and Elections (Washington, DC: Government Printing Office, 1956).

29. Heard, *The Costs of Democracy*, 417–419. Two hundred firms in twenty-nine states received questionnaires; 130 firms in twenty-four states responded. Of these firms, seventy-eight (60 percent) reported providing services to political campaigns.

30. These were all large states: California, Illinois, Michigan, New York, Ohio, Pennsylvania, and Texas. Heard, *The Costs of Democracy*, 417.

31. Heard, *The Costs of Democracy*, 415.

32. Heard, *The Costs of Democracy*, 416.

33. Heard, *The Costs of Democracy*, 420.

34. Heard, *The Costs of Democracy*, 419.

35. Heard, *The Costs of Democracy*, 416.

36. Warren E. Miller and Donald E. Stokes, *American Representation Study, 1958: Candidates*, ICPSR Study 7226, conducted by University of Michigan, Survey Research Center (Ann Arbor, MI: Inter-university Consortium for Political and Social Research, 1959). Miller and Stokes conducted a survey of 251 congressional candidates running in 146 districts scattered across thirty-nine states. Although mainly interested in studying the relationship between House members and their districts, they included a number of questions in their survey that shed light on the conduct of campaigns during this period. Warren E. Miller and Donald E. Stokes, "Constituency Influence in Congress," *American Political Science Review* 57 (1963): 45–56.

37. To calculate these percentages, I used the sampling weights from the study. Candidates who did not campaign, for instance if they ran unopposed, are not included in the analysis.

38. Miller and Stokes, *American Representation Study, 1958*.

39. In order to calculate figures for 2014 House candidates, I used data from the Center for Responsive Politics that included subtotals for various categories of expenditures for each House candidate. My calculation of professional services includes the following categories: media (miscellaneous media, unspecified media buys, broadcast ads, print ads, web ads, media production, media consulting), fundraising (fundraising mailings, data, fees, consulting), polls and surveys, campaign data and technology, strategy and communications consulting, administrative data and technology, administrative consulting, and unclassifiable data and consulting. My denominator is the total number of major party candidates who received at least $100,000 in contributions. Overall, 659 out of 857 candidates spent at least $100,000 on professional services. Among incumbents, 357 out of 391 candidates met this criterion. I am extremely grateful to Andrew Mayersohn at the Center for Responsive Politics for providing me with these data.

40. Heard, *The Costs of Democracy*, 404–405; US Senate, *Proposed Amendments to the Federal Corrupt Practices Act*, Subcommittee on Privileges and Elections, 83rd Cong., 1st sess. (Washington, DC: Government Printing Office, 1953), 2;

US Senate, *1956 Presidential and Senatorial Campaign Contributions and Practices*, "Exhibit 24: 1956 General Election Payments for Radio and Television Broadcasts, September 1–November 6."

41. Heard, *The Costs of Democracy*, 22. For overall campaign spending between 1952 and 1956, see Herbert Alexander, *Financing Politics: Money, Elections and Political Reform* (Washington, DC: Congressional Quarterly Press, 1976), 17. I deflated expenditures by 1956 GDP to control for economic growth.

42. Robert Humphreys, "Campaign Plan—Document 'X,'" Robert Humphreys Papers, Box 10, Dwight D. Eisenhower Presidential Library, 13.

43. Humphreys, "Campaign Plan—Document 'X'" 13.

44. Kelley, *Professional Public Relations*, 150.

45. Kelley, *Professional Public Relations*, 151.

46. Robert Humphreys, "Memorandum on Advance Men for Major National TV-Radio or Radio Appearances of General Eisenhower at Public Rallies or in Studio Shows," August 31, 1952, Robert Humphreys Papers, Box 10.

47. Kelley, *Professional Public Relations*, 19.

48. Kelley, *Professional Public Relations*, 19. Clips of the spots are available at http://www.livingroomcandidate.org/commercials/issue/change.

49. Nielson Marketing Service, "Recommendations Re Spot Radio-TV Campaign for Eisenhower-Nixon," October 2, 1952, Robert Humphreys Papers, Box 10, 4.

50. Edwin Diamond and Stephen Bates, *The Spot: The Rise of Political Advertising on Television* (Cambridge, MA: MIT Press, 1988), 47.

51. Diamond and Bates, *The Spot*, 47–48.

52. For an insightful treatment of these differences, see David Greenberg, "A New Way of Campaigning; Eisenhower, Stevenson, and the Anxieties of Television Politics," in *Liberty and Justice for All: Rethinking Politics in Cold War America*, ed. Kathleen Donohue (Amherst: University of Massachusetts Press, 2012), 185–212.

53. Gordon Cotler, "That Plague of Spots from Madison Avenue," *Reporter*, November 25, 1952, 7–8.

54. Charles A. H. Thomson, *Television and Presidential Politics: The Experience in 1952 and the Problems Ahead* (Washington, DC: Brookings Institution, 1956), 59n.

55. Kelley, *Professional Public Relations*, 160.

56. "Admen Analyze the Campaign Strategy," *Tide*, November 7, 1952, 15.

57. Philip Geyelin, "GOP's 'PR': Public Relations Gets Sharp Attention from New Washington Team," *Wall Street Journal*, February 25, 1953, 1.

58. William Lee Miller, "Can Government Be Merchandised?," *Reporter*, October 27, 1953, 11–16.

59. Miller, "Can Government Be Merchandised?," 15.

60. John G. Schneider, *The Golden Kazoo* (New York: Reinhart, 1956); *A Face in the Crowd*, directed by Elia Kazan, Warner Bros., 1957.

61. Quoted in Michael McGeer, *The Decline of Popular Politics: The American North, 1865–1928* (New York: Oxford University Press, 1986), 145.

62. Stevenson quoted in David Halberstam, *The Powers That Be* (New York: Dell, 1979), 323.

63. Heard, *The Costs of Democracy*, 414.

64. Heard, *The Costs of Democracy*, 413.

65. Heard, *The Costs of Democracy*, 413.

66. Kelley, *Professional Public Relations*, 210.

67. Heard, *The Costs of Democracy*, 414.

68. Herbert A. Simon and Frederick Stern, "The Effect of Television upon Voting Behavior in Iowa in the 1952 Presidential Election," *American Political Science Review* 49 (June 1955): 470–477.

69. Joe McGinnis, *The Selling of the President, 1968* (New York: Trident Press, 1969), 31, 35.

70. Harry Treleaven, "Notes re Nixon for President Advertising in the Primary Campaigns," reprinted in McGinnis, *The Selling of the President*, 175.

71. McGinnis, *The Selling of the President*, 26–27.

72. McGinnis, *The Selling of the President*, 28.

73. For data on political television, see United States Federal Election Commission, *Survey of Political Broadcasting: Primary and General Election Campaigns of 1968* (Washington, DC: Government Printing Office, 1969). For overall advertising spending, see *Coen Structured Advertising Expenditure Data Set*, http://purplenotes.net/2008/09/14/us-advertising-expenditure-data/. For overall political spending, see Alexander, *Financing Politics*, 17. All figures deflated by 2013 GDP.

74. Heard, *The Costs of Democracy*, 415.

75. Carl Spielvogel, "Advertising: Madison Ave. Has Its Hat in Both Rings," *New York Times*, July 30, 1958, 41.

76. Carl Spielvogel, "Advertising: Democrats Pick Guild, Bascom," *New York Times*, November 13, 1959, 40.

77. Walter Troy Spencer, "The Agency Knack of Political Packaging," in *The New Style in Election Campaigns*, ed. Robert Agranoff (Boston: Holbrook Press, 1972), 79.

78. See for example, "B.B.D.&O. Joins Kudner in Eisenhower Campaign," *New York Times*, August 29, 1952, 25. On the political role of firms more generally, see Spielvogel, "Advertising: Madison Ave. Has Its Hat in Both Rings."

79. "Ad Men Dispute Role in Politics," *New York Times*, October 27, 1958, 15.

80. Philip Benjamin, "Truman Derides TV NATO Report," *New York Times*, December 27, 1957, 4.

81. Robert Alden, "Advertising: G.O.P. Planning Its Own Unit," *New York Times*, July 19, 1960, 38.

82. "Ad Men Dispute Role in Politics."

83. Spencer, "The Agency Knack of Political Packaging," 80; Robert Alden, "Advertising: Industry Unsullied in Election," *New York Times*, November 9, 1960, 54.

84. Heard, *The Costs of Democracy*, 412.

85. Alden, "Advertising: G.O.P. Planning Its Own Unit."

86. Robert Alden, "Advertising: GOP Plan Called Unwise," *New York Times*, July 21, 1960, 30.

87. Robert Alden, "Advertising: Plan for a G.O.P. Agency Is Supported," *New York Times*, July 26, 1960, 38.

88. Peter Bart, "Advertising: Republicans Sign with Leo Burnett," *New York Times*, January 9, 1963, 15.

89. Spencer, "The Agency Knack of Political Packaging," 90–91.

90. Calculation based on United States Federal Election Commission, *Survey of Political Broadcasting* and *Coen Structured Advertising Expenditure Data Set*.

91. Quoted in Spencer, "The Agency Knack of Political Packaging," 88.

92. Spencer, "The Agency Knack of Political Packaging," 88–89.

93. This was the case as early as 1916, when one New York ad agency struggled to collect $238,000 from the Democratic Party for newspaper ads that ran in several hundred papers around the country during the presidential campaign. "Agency Wants Full Payment from Democratic Committee," *Printer's Ink*, February 8, 1917, 122–123.

94. Quoted in Spencer, "The Agency Knack of Political Packaging," 88.

95. "Campaign Management Grows into National Industry," CQ Fact Sheet on Campaign Consultants," *Congressional Quarterly Weekly Report*, April 5, 1968, 709.

96. "Campaign Management Grows into National Industry," 709.

97. Roy Pfautch, interview with Larry Sabato (July 27, 1979), University of Virginia Center for Politics, p. 9.

98. Peter Hart, interview with John Franzen (December 22, 1997), American Association of Political Consultants Interview Collection, George Washington University Library (hereafter AAPC Interview Collection), p. 16.

99. Ray Strother, interview with John Franzen (October 10, 1997), AAPC Interview Collection, p. 7.

100. Stu Spencer interview with unidentified individual (February 2, 1999), AAPC Interview Collection, p. 8.

101. Walter DeVries, interview with John Franzen (November 7, 1997), AAPC Interview Collection, pp. 29–30

102. DeVries, AAPC Interview Collection, p. 30.

103. Joe Napolitan, interview with John Franzen (December 3, 1996), AAPC Interview Collection, p. 11.

104. Greenberg, "A New Way of Campaigning," 208.

105. For a discussion of political funds by labor unions, see Heard, *The Costs of Democracy*, 169–211.

Chapter 7

1. "Campaign Management Grows into National Industry," *Congressional Quarterly Weekly Report*, April 5, 1968, 706.
2. "Campaign Management Grows into National Industry," 706.
3. "Campaign Report/Professional Managers, Consultants Play Major Roles in 1970 Political Races," *National Journal*, September 26, 1970, 2077.
4. "Campaign Report/Professional Managers, Consultants Play Major Roles in 1970 Political Races," 2077.
5. David L. Rosenbloom, *The Election Men: Professional Campaign Managers and American Democracy* (New York: Quadrangle Books, 1973), 54.
6. Rosenbloom, *The Election Men*; James M. Perry, *The New Politics: The Expanding Technology of Political Manipulation* (New York: Clarkson N. Potter, 1968). Dan Nimmo, *The Political Persuaders: The Techniques of Modern Election Campaigns* (Englewood Cliffs, NJ: Prentice-Hall, 1970). See also Robert Agranoff's edited volume *The New Style in Election Campaigns* (Boston: Holbrook Press, 1972).
7. Sidney Blumenthal, *The Permanent Campaign* (New York: Simon and Schuster, 1982), 23.
8. Blumenthal, *The Permanent Campaign*, 12.
9. Larry Sabato, *The Rise of the Political Consultants: New Ways of Winning Elections* (New York: Basic Books, 1981), 3.
10. Sabato, *The Rise of the Political Consultants*, 3.
11. Walter DeVries, "American Campaign Consulting: Trends and Concerns," *PS: Political Science and Politics* 22 (1989): 21. According to DeVries, almost three-quarters of AAPC members in 1988 had joined in the last five years. Joe Napolitan, one of the cofounders of the AAPC, dates the beginning of the organization to December 1968. Joe Napolitan, interview with John Franzen (December 3, 1996), American Association of Political Consultants Interview Collection, George Washington University Library (hereafter AAPC Interview Collection), p. 3.
12. Edward V. Schneier Jr., "Is Politics a Profession? A New School Says Yes," *PS: Political Science and Politics* 20 (1987): 889–895. In 1991, the Graduate School of Political Management moved to George Washington University.
13. DeVries, "American Campaign Consulting," 21.
14. "Publishers Perspective," *Campaigns & Elections*, April 1990, http://tinyurl.com/campaignselectionspublisher, accessed June 11, 2014, n.p.; Chris Meyer, "Ten Years in the Making," *Campaigns & Elections*, April 1990, http://tinyurl.com/campaignselectionstenyears, accessed June 11, 2014, n.p.
15. Rosenbloom reported that professional management firms worked on behalf of 150 candidates in 1970. Based on a figure of 372 contested races, this translates to around 20 percent of campaigns. See Rosenbloom, *The Election Men*, 53.
16. The 1978 figure uses FEC expenditure data coded by purpose from a representative sample of 163 major party candidates. See Edie Goldenberg

and Michael Traugott, *Congressional Campaign Study, 1978*, ICPSR Study 8431 (Ann Arbor, MI: Inter-university Consortium for Political and Social Research, 1985).

17. Medvic analyzed FEC data for 856 candidates in the 1992 election. See Stephen Medvic, *Political Consultants in U.S. Congressional Elections* (Columbus: Ohio State University Press, 2001), 74.

18. "Campaign Management Grows into National Industry," 706.

19. "Campaign Management Grows into National Industry," 707.

20. Bob Goodman, interview with Wayne C. Johnson (October 26, 1999), AAPC Interview Collection, p. 27.

21. Charlie Black, interview with Alfano Fremont-Smith (October 25, 1999), AAPC Interview Collection, p. 7.

22. "Campaign Management Grows into National Industry," 706.

23. Bob Goodman, AAPC Interview Collection, p. 28.

24. Joe Cerrell, interview with John Franzen (October 24, 1997), AAPC Interview Collection, p. 22.

25. Doug Bailey, interview with Larry Sabato (September 18, 1979), University of Virginia Center for Politics (hereafter Center for Politics Interview Collection), p. 2.

26. Doug Bailey, Center for Politics Interview Collection, p. 3; Stuart Spencer, interview with Larry Sabato (August 2, 1979), Center for Politics Interview Collection, p. 9; Chuck Winner, interview with Larry Sabato (August 7, 1979), Center for Politics Interview Collection, p. 20.

27. Joe Napolitan, AAPC Interview Collection, p. 15.

28. Peter Hart, interview with John Franzen (December 22, 1997), AAPC Interview Collection, p. 7.

29. General strategy consultants like Doug Bailey served eight or nine candidates in a season, whereas Lance Tarrance reported that his polling firms fielded surveys for upwards of fifty candidates. Doug Bailey, Center for Politics Interview Collection, p. 9; Lance Tarrance, interview with Larry Sabato (November 28, 1979), Center for Politics Interview Collection, p. 30.

30. Doug Bailey, Center for Politics Interview Collection, p. 12.

31. Doug Bailey, Center for Politics Interview Collection, p. 13.

32. Doug Bailey, Center for Politics Interview Collection, p. 13.

33. Doug Bailey, Center for Politics Interview Collection, p. 4.

34. Bob O'Dell, interview with Larry Sabato (October 19, 1979), Center for Politics Interview Collection, p. 15.

35. Ray Strother, interview with John Franzen (October 10, 1997), AAPC Interview Collection, p. 21.

36. Bob Goodman, AAPC Interview Collection, p. 28.

37. Jill Buckley, interview with John Franzen (August 25, 1997), AAPC Interview Collection, p. 6.

38. Jill Buckley, interview with John Franzen (August 25, 1997), AAPC Interview Collection, p. 6.

39. Matt Reese, interview with John Franzen (December 12, 1996), AAPC Interview Collection, p. 17.

40. Matt Reese, interview with John Franzen (December 12, 1996), AAPC Interview Collection, p. 17.

41. Data on TV airtime come from the *Statistical Abstract of the United States* series "Television—Estimated Time Charges for Spot Advertising," various years (deflated by population and GDP).

42. Bob Goodman, AAPC Interview Collection, p. 27.

43. Chuck Winner, interview with Larry Sabato (August 7, 1979), Center for Politics Interview Collection, p. 20.

44. Stu Spencer interview with unidentified individual, February 2, 1999, AAPC Interview Collection, p. 4.

45. For discussion of year-round work on behalf of parties, see Bob O'Dell, Center for Politics Interview Collection, p. 4, and Lance Tarrance, Center for Politics Interview Collection, p. 9.

46. Edward Walker, *Grassroots for Hire: Public Affairs Consultants in American Democracy* (New York: Cambridge University Press, 2014).

47. James Harding, *Alpha Dogs: The Americans Who Turned Political Spin into a Global Business* (New York: Farrar, Straus and Giroux, 2009).

48. Joe Cerrell, AAPC Interview Collection, p. 20.

49. Matt Reese, AAPC Interview Collection, p. 9. For Reese's place in the early development of voter targeting, see Sasha Issenberg, *The Victory Lab: The Secret Science of Winning Campaigns* (New York: Crown, 2012), 38–40, 124–125.

50. Matt Reese, AAPC Interview Collection, p. 10.

51. "Political Applications of the System," TSI Targeting Systems, Inc., 1980, Document T102170728, University of California, San Francisco Legacy Tobacco Documents Library, http://legacy.library.ucsf.edu/tid/utj19a00, accessed July 1, 2014.

52. Matt Reese, AAPC Interview Collection, p. 11.

53. Matt Reese, AAPC Interview Collection, p. 5.

54. Matt Reese to William O'Flaherty, Tobacco Tax Council, October 15, 1976, Document 03681379, University of California, San Francisco Legacy Tobacco Documents Library, http://legacy.library.ucsf.edu/tid/xgu00e00, accessed July 1, 2014.

55. Tabular Report, Nationwide TSI Survey, June 1980, Hamilton and Staff, Document T102170784 San Francisco Legacy Tobacco Documents Library, http://legacy.library.ucsf.edu/tid/htj19a00, accessed July 1, 2014.

56. Matt Reese, AAPC Interview Collection, pp. 15, 22.

57. Sarah Igo, *The Averaged American: Surveys, Citizens, and the Making of a Mass Public* (Cambridge, MA: Harvard University Press, 2007), 127–128.

58. John Hebert, "DP Works behind the Scenes at Firms Conducting Public Opinion Surveys," *Computerworld*, June 7, 1976, 18–19.

59. IBM 1130 Technical Press Release (February 11, 1965), http://www-03.ibm.com/ibm/history/exhibits/1130/1130_technical.html, accessed July 10, 2014.

An IBM 1442 punch card reader sold for $11,250, and an IBM 029 keypunch machine ran for $2,200. See classified ads, *Computerworld*, June 7, 1976, 109; *Computerworld*, May 3, 1972, 25. Adjusted for inflation, $45,000 is more than $400,000 in 2015; relative to GDP growth, it is more than $1.3 million in 2015 dollars.

60. "System/370 Announcement," IBM Data Processing Division Press Release (June 30, 1970), http://www-03.ibm.com/ibm/history/exhibits/mainframe/mainframe_PR370.html, accessed July 14, 2014.

61. Hebert, "DP Works behind the Scenes at Firms Conducting Public Opinion Surveys," 19.

62. Jean Converse, *Survey Research in the United States: Roots and Emergence 1890–1960* (Berkeley: University of California Press, 1987), 388–390.

63. Random digit dialing allowed pollsters to draw a probability sample stratified by geography using the area code and three-digit prefix of a telephone number, followed by a randomly generated four-digit suffix. On the use of telephone interviewing, see Bob Teeter, interview with Whit Ayres (February 16, 2011), AAPC Interview Collection, p. 7.

64. For the best in-depth treatment on the subject of telecommunication deregulation, see Martha Derthick and Paul Quirk, *The Politics of Deregulation* (Washington, DC: Brookings Institution Press, 1985), 174–201.

65. For telephone prices, see Robert Crandall, *After the Breakup: U.S. Telecommunications in a More Competitive Era* (Washington, DC: Brookings Institution Press, 1991), 71.

66. Data on computers come from Gavin Wright, "Purchases of computers, by type: 1955–1995," table Cg241-250 in *Historical Statistics of the United States, Earliest Times to the Present: Millennial Edition*, ed. Susan B. Carter, Scott Sigmund Gartner, Michael R. Haines, Alan L. Olmstead, Richard Sutch, and Gavin Wright (New York: Cambridge University Press, 2006).

67. Bob Teeter, AAPC Interview Collection, p. 9.

68. Tony Schwartz, the creator of the famed "Daisy Ad" for LBJ in 1964, put his costs at between $10,000 and $70,000 when interviewed in 1979. Walt DeVries, interviewed around the same time, put the upper bound of production costs at $100,000. Tony Schwartz, interview with Larry Sabato (September 7, 1979), Center for Politics Interview Collection, p. 19; Walt DeVries, interview with Larry Sabato (June 28, 1978), Center for Politics Interview Collection, p. 21.

69. Ray Strother, AAPC Interview Collection, p. 6.

70. Brian Matthew Conley, "Party People: Bliss, Brock, and the Rise of the Republican Party" (PhD diss., New School for Social Research, 2008), 187.

71. Jack Anderson, "Viguerie: A Modern Wizard of Oz," *Washington Post*, June 3, 1978, E43.

72. "Viguerie: Computer Arm of the Right," *Tuscaloosa News*, April 19, 1981, 27.

73. Rodney Smith, "The New Political Machine," *Computerworld*, July 16, 1984, ID/19–25.

74. Richard Keilbowicz and Linda Lawson, "Reduced-Rate Postage for Nonprofit Organizations: A Policy History, Critique, and Proposal," *Harvard Journal of Law and Public Policy* 11 (Spring 1998): 347–406.

75. Bill Peterson, "Direct Mail Writes New Chapter in How to Run a Political Campaign," *Washington Post*, November 17, 1982, A2.

76. Bob Teeter, AAPC Interview Collection, p. 27.

77. The 1974 legislation is technically a set of amendments to the 1971 Federal Election Campaign Act, which included measures for public financing of presidential campaigns and set limits on media spending by congressional candidates (this latter provision was repealed in 1974). For a discussion of campaign finance legislation, see Frank J. Sorauf, *Inside Campaign Finance: Myths and Realities* (New Haven, CT: Yale University Press, 1992), 7–12; Raymond J. La Raja, *Small Change: Money, Political Parties, and Campaign Finance Reform* (Ann Arbor: University of Michigan Press, 2008), 72–80.

78. Sorauf, *Inside Campaign Finance*, 100–106; La Raja, *Small Change*, 141–146.

79. *Citizens United v. Federal Election Commission*, 130 S. Ct. 876 (2010); *McCutcheon v. Federal Election Commission*, 133 S. Ct. 1747 (2013).

80. On early reform efforts, see Paula Baker, *Curbing Campaign Cash: Henry Ford, Truman Newberry, and the Politics of Progressive Reform* (Lawrence: University Press of Kansas, 2012).

81. Nelson Polsby, *Consequences of Party Reform* (Oxford: Oxford University Press, 1983).

82. *Buckley v. Valeo*, 424 US 1 (1976). On the aftermath of the decision, see Stephen Isaacs, "End Seen Near for Commission," *Washington Post*, January 31, 1976, A1.

83. Federal Election Commission, *Annual Report 1976* (Washington, DC: Federal Election Commission, 1976), 3, 15.

84. "Carter Campaign Penalized Again for Funds Misuse," *Washington Post*, October 14, 1978, A4; "Wallace Ordered by FEC to Repay $47,795 in Funds," *Washington Post*, March 24, 1978, A12; "$74,135 Sought from Udall's '76 Campaign," *Washington Post*, June 19, 1979, A11.

85. Jo Thomas, "Election Law Sets Ceilings But Ground Fog Remains," *New York Times*, June 10, 1979, E4.

86. "Election Panel Audits of Campaign Outlays Are Termed Too Slow," *New York Times*, September 14, 1979, A15.

87. Code of Federal Regulations, 11 CFR 1.1, Section 102.9 (May 1, 1977), p. 23; "Notice to All Candidates and Committees," September 29, 1976, Agenda Document 78-220, Federal Election Commission Regular Meeting, August 31, 1978.

88. "Notice to All Candidates and Committees," September 29, 1976, Agenda Document 78-220, Federal Election Commission Regular Meeting, August 31, 1978.

89. Elizabeth Beeker, "Suit Aims to End 'Walk-Around' Money," *Washington Post*, November 11, 1977, B4; telephone interview with Bradley Litchfield, former FEC director of policy, March 27, 2013.

90. Federal Election Commission, *Annual Report 1976*, 26.

91. Orlando Potter and William Oldaker, Memorandum Re: Resolution of Particulars, July 31, 1978, Agenda Document 78-213, Federal Election Commission Regular Meeting, August 31, 1978, p. 1.

92. Bob Costa, Memorandum Re: Recordkeeping and Reporting of Particulars for Expenditures, August 7, 1978, Agenda Document 78-220, Federal Election Commission Regular Meeting, August 31, 1978, p. 1.

93. Transcript of FEC Regular Meeting, August 31, 1978 (in possession of author); Federal Election Commission, *Annual Report 1978* (Washington, DC: Federal Election Commission, 1978), 20.

94. Costa, Memorandum Re: Recordkeeping and Reporting of Particulars for Expenditures, p. 5.

95. Fred Barbash and Bill Curry, "Campaign '80: In FEC Maze, Auditors Supplant 'Fat Cats,'" *Washington Post*, June 14, 1979, A9.

96. Barbash and Curry, "Campaign '80," A9.

97. Saurof, *Inside Campaign Finance*, 100–112. For data on PAC numbers, see "Number of Federal PACs Increases," Federal Election Commission News Release (March 9, 2009), http://www.fec.gov/press/press2009/20090309PACcount.shtml, accessed July 9, 2014.

98. Code of Federal Regulations, 11 CFR 1.1, Section 109.1 (May 1, 1977), p. 36.

99. Federal Election Commission, "Advisory Opinion 1979–80" (March 12, 1980), p. 4.

100. Federal Election Commission, "Advisory Opinion 1979–80," p. 5

101. Edward Walsh, "Conservative Unit Targets 20 Senators in '82," *Washington Post*, November 12, 1980, A10.

102. Sorauf, *Inside Campaign Finance*, 180.

103. Hank Parkinson, interview with Larry Sabato (July 23, 1979), Center for Politics Interview Collection, p. 16.

104. Roy Pfautch, interview with Larry Sabato (July 27, 1979), Center for Politics Interview Collection, p. 19.

105. Paul S. Herrnson, "Campaign Professionalism and Fundraising in Congressional Elections," *Journal of Politics* 54 (1992): 859–870.

106. Wally Clinton, interview with John Franzen (December 22, 1997), AAPC Interview Collection, p. 21.

107. On tracking polls, see Vince Breglio, interview with Larry Sabato (October 19, 1979), Center for Politics Interview Collection, p. 3.

108. Lance Tarrance, interview with Larry Sabato (November 28, 1979), Center for Politics Interview Collection, p. 25.

109. Peter Hart, AAPC Interview Collection, p. 15.

110. Vince Breglio, Center for Politics Interview Collection, p. 3.

111. Bob Goodman, AAPC Interview Collection, p. 11.
112. Walter DeVries, interview with Larry Sabato (June 28, 1978), Center for Politics Interview Collection, p. 23.
113. Data on political advertising for the period 1972–1992 come from the Television Bureau of Advertising as reported in Congressional Research Service, "Free and Reduced Rate Television Time for Political Candidates," *CRS Report for Congress*, 97-680 GOV (July 7, 1997), p. 5. Figures for total political expenditures come from Herbert Alexander, "Spending in the 1996 Elections," in *Financing the 1996 Elections*, ed. John Green (Armonk, NY: M. E. Sharpe, 1999), 15. Data on total television ad revenues come from Susan B. Carter, et al., eds., *Historical Statistics of the United States, Earliest Times to the Present: Millennial Edition* (New York: Cambridge University Press, 2006), Series De492. Following work by Stephen Ansolabehere and coauthors, I deflated figures by current GDP/2013 GDP to control for economic growth. See Stephen Ansolabehere, John de Figueiredo, and James Snyder, Jr., "Why Is There So Little Money in U.S. Politics?" NBER Working Paper 9409 (December 2002).
114. Walter DeVries, Center for Politics Interview Collection, p. 8.
115. Igo, *The Averaged American*, 287.
116. Lance Tarrance, Center for Politics Interview Collection, p. 28.
117. Matt Reese, AAPC Interview Collection, p. 9.
118. Wally Clinton, AAPC Interview Collection, p. 9.
119. Bill Lacy, interview with Larry Sabato (October 30, 1979), Center for Politics Interview Collection, 16.
120. Issenberg, *The Victory Lab*.
121. Four years later, Shapp ran again and won, serving two terms as governor of Pennsylvania. On Napolitan's work for Shapp, see Perry, *The New Politics*, 41–70.
122. "Campaign Management Grows into National Industry," 707. For evidence of the increased electoral competition in southern primaries, see Stephen Ansolabehere, John Mark Hansen, Shigeo Hirano, and James Snyder Jr., "More Democracy: The Direct Primary and Competition in U.S. Elections," *Studies in American Political Development* 24 (2010): 199.
123. Daniel Galvin, "The Transformation of Political Institutions: Investments in Institutional Resources and Gradual Change in the National Party Committees," *Studies in American Political Development* 26 (2012): 50–70.
124. "Sources and Uses of Funds Statement, January 1–October 31, 1980" and "National Republican Senatorial Committee, Proforma Source and Use of Funds Statement, January 1, 1979–December 31, 1980," both in GOP Series, Financial Records, Budget Summaries, H. John Heinz III Collection, Carnegie Mellon University.

125. Robin Kolodny and David Dulio, "Political Party Adaptation in US Congressional Campaigns: Why Political Parties Use Coordinated Expenditures to Hire Political Consultants," *Party Politics* 9 (2003): 729–746; David Dulio, "Party Crashers? The Relationship between Political Consultants and Political Parties," in *Handbook of Party Politics*, ed. Richard Katz and William Crotty (London: Sage, 2006), 348–358.

126. Charlie Black, AAPC Interview Collection, p. 3.

127. For survey evidence on consultants' motivations, see David Dulio, *For Better or Worse? How Political Consultants Are Changing Elections in the United States* (Albany: State University of New York Press, 2004), 56.

128. Bob O'Dell, Center for Politics Interview Collection, p. 3.

129. Matt Reese, AAPC Interview Collection, p. 26.

130. Joe Cerrell, AAPC Interview Collection, p. 3.

131. Matt Reese, AAPC Interview Collection, p. 1.

132. Bob O'Dell, Center for Politics Interview Collection, p. 1.

133. Lance Tarrance, Center for Politics Interview Collection, pp. 2, 9.

134. Doug Bailey, Center for Politics Interview Collection, p. 13.

135. For the role of consultants in partisan networks and the extended party, see Robin Kolodny, "Electoral Partnerships: Political Consultants and Political Parties," in *Campaign Warriors: Political Consultants in Elections*, ed. James A. Thurber and Candace J. Nelson (Washington, DC: Brookings Institutions Press, 2000); Paul Herrnson, "The Roles of Party Organizations, Party-Connected Committees, and Party Allies in Elections," *Journal of Politics* 71 (2009): 1207–1224; Jonathan Bernstein and Casey Dominguez, "Candidates and Candidacies in the Expanded Party," *PS: Political Science and Politics* 36 (2003): 165–169; Gregory Koger, Seth Masket, and Hans Noel, "Partisan Webs: Information Exchange and Party Networks," *British Journal of Political Science* 39 (2009): 633–653.

136. On the effects of consultants on campaigns, see Peter Francia and Paul Herrnson, "Keeping It Professional: The Influence of Political Consultants on Candidate Attitudes toward Negative Campaigning," *Politics & Policy* 35 (2007): 246–272; Sean Cain, "Political Consultants and Party-Centered Campaigning: Evidence from the 2010 US House Primary Election Campaigns," *Election Law Journal* 12 (2013): 3–17; Brendan Nyhan and Jacob Montgomery, "Connecting the Candidates: Consultant Networks and the Diffusion of Campaign Strategy in American Congressional Elections," *American Journal of Political Science* 59 (2015): 292–308.

137. Doug Bailey, Center for Politics Interview Collection, p. 7.

138. Doug Bailey, Center for Politics Interview Collection, p. 7.

139. Doug Bailey, Center for Politics Interview Collection, p. 7.

140. Matt Reese, AAPC Interview Collection, p. 17.

141. Ray Strother, AAPC Interview Collection, p. 19.

Chapter 8

1. Lynn Vavreck and John Sides, *The Gamble* (Princeton, NJ: Princeton University Press, 2013).

2. The number of candidates is much higher, but campaigns with less than $100,000 in contributions offer few opportunities for consultants to sell their wares. Data available from the National Institute on Money in State Politics, www.followthemoney.org, accessed November 1, 2014.

3. Most comparative explanations of political consulting focus on the media environment in the United States, as well as the diffusion of American campaign methods via US consultants who work overseas. On global diffusion, see Fritz Plasser, "American Campaign Techniques Worldwide," *International Journal of Press/Politics* 5 (September 2000): 433–454; David M. Farrell, Robin Kolodny, and Stephen Medvic, "Parties and Campaign Professionals in a Digital Age: Political Consultants in the United States and Their Counterparts Overseas," *International Journal of Press/Politics* 6 (Fall 2001): 11–30.

4. Daniel Kreiss, *Taking Our Country Back: The Crafting of Networked Politics from Howard Dean to Barack Obama* (Oxford: Oxford University Press, 2012).

5. Kreiss, *Taking Our Country Back*, 95, 198.

6. Sasha Issenberg, "Obama's White Whale," *Slate*, February 12, 2012, http://www.slate.com/articles/news_and_politics/victory_lab/2012/02/project_narwhal_how_a_top_secret_obama_campaign_program_could_change_the_2012_race_.single.html, accessed October 31, 2014.

7. Alexis Madrigal, "When the Nerds Go Marching In," *Atlantic*, November 16, 2012, http://www.theatlantic.com/technology/archive/2012/11/when-the-nerds-go-marching-in/265325/, accessed October 31, 2014.

8. See appendix table A2.

9. Author analysis of Center for Responsive Politics data on 2014 expenditures coded by purpose. Digital services include the categories of web ads, administrative data and technology, fundraising data and technology, and unclassifiable data and technology. Media costs include miscellaneous media, unspecified media buys, broadcast ads, media production, and media consulting. I am grateful to Andrew Mayersohn for making these data available.

10. Author's analysis of FEC data on campaign expenditures; see appendix for details.

11. Derek Willis, "Political TV Ads Can Be Wasteful. But That's Changing," *New York Times*, October 21, 2014, http://tinyurl.com/nytmespoliticaltvads, accessed March 27, 2015.

12. Kreiss, *Taking Our Country Back*, 194.

13. Kreiss, *Taking Our Country Back*; Matthew Hindman, "The Real Lessons of Howard Dean: Reflections on the First Digital Campaign," *Perspectives on Politics* 3 (March 2005): 121–128.

14. Rasmus Kleis Nielsen, *Ground Wars: Personalized Communication in Political Campaigns* (Princeton, NJ: Princeton University Press, 2012).

15. Nielsen, *Ground Wars*, 182–183.
16. Paul Waldman, "Political Consultants Have Never Been Richer, But Are They Endangered?," *American Prospect*, February 2014, http://prospect.org/article/political-consultants-have-never-been-richer-are-they-endangered, accessed April 4, 2014.
17. Matthew Hindman, *The Myth of Digital Democracy* (Princeton, NJ: Princeton University Press, 2009).
18. The quote is from Jim Gilliam, founder of NationBuilder. Andy Kroll, "The Evangelist," *American Prospect*, October 9, 2013, http://prospect.org/article/evangelist, accessed November 3, 2014.
19. Another important site of innovation was the online advocacy group MoveOn, which pioneered email solicitation during the impeachment of President Bill Clinton in 1998. David Karpf, *The MoveOn Effect: The Unexpected Transformation of American Advocacy* (New York: Oxford University Press, 2012).
20. Michael Silberman quoted in Kreiss, *Taking Our Country Back*, 87.
21. Kreiss, *Taking Our Country Back*, 89.
22. Jascha Franklin-Hodge quoted in Kreiss, *Taking Our Country Back*, 89.
23. Kreiss, *Taking Our Country Back*, 89–96.
24. Kreiss, *Taking Our Country Back*, 119–128.
25. Kreiss, *Taking Our Country Back*, 90.
26. Kreiss, *Taking Our Country Back*, 90–98, 119; Tom Lowry, "Obama's Secret Digital Weapon," *Bloomberg Business Week Magazine*, June 23, 2008, www.businessweek.com/stories/2008-06-23/obamas-secret-digital-weapon, accessed November 24, 2014.
27. Kreiss, *Taking Our Country Back*, 100–111. See also the account of VAN founder Mark Sullivan, "A New Model: VAN and the Challenge of the Voter-File Interface," in *Margin of Victory: How Technologists Help Politicians Win Elections*, ed. Nathaniel Pearlman (Santa Barbara, CA: Praeger, 2012), 133–146.
28. Kreiss, *Taking Our Country Back*, 175–180.
29. Kate Kaye, "New Wave of Post '08 Political Agencies Emerges," *ClickZ: Marketing News & Expert Advice*, April 26, 2010, www.clickz.com/clickz/news/1707319/new-wave-post-08-political-agencies-emerges, accessed November 24, 2014; Julie Bykowicz, "Tech Startups Making Millions Off the Presidential Race," *Bloomberg*, July 23, 2012, htwww.bloomberg.com/news/print/2012-07-23/tech-startups-making-millions-off-the-presidential-race.html, accessed November 11, 2014.
30. "Obama for America 2012 Campaign Organization," www.p2012.org/candidates/obamaorg.html#tech, accessed November 22, 2014; "Romney for President, Inc.—Organization, 2012 General Election," www.p2012.org/candidates/romneyorggen.html#comms, accessed November 22, 2014.

31. Figures include candidate committees (Obama for America and Romney for President, Inc.), as well as joint fundraising committees and allied PACs (Obama Victory Fund and Romney Victory, Inc.). Data retrieved from Center for Responsive Politics, http://www. opensecrets.org/expends/vendors.php?year=2012&type=cycle, accessed March 27, 2015.

32. Nathaniel Pearlman, "Bootstrapping an Enterprise: NGP and the Evolution of Campaign Software," in *Margin of Victory: How Technologists Help Politicians Win Elections*, ed. Nathaniel Pearlman (Santa Barbara, CA: Praeger, 2012), 199; Shane D'Aprile, "Judge Ends Aristotle Advertising Case," *Campaigns & Elections*, September 25, 2011, http://www.campaignsandelections.com/campaign-insider/811/judge-ends-aristotle-advertising-case, accessed November 21, 2014; Nancy Scola, "Field, Meet Fundraising: Inside the Merger of Two of the Left's Powerhouse Data Firms," *TechPresident*, November 11, 2010, http://techpresident.com/blog-entry/field-meet-fundraising-inside-merger-two-lefts-powerhouse-data-firms, accessed November 20, 2014.

33. Reed quoted in Kroll, "The Evangelist."

34. Moffatt quoted in Kate Kaye, "In Politics, Partisanship Pays Off for Some Tech Companies," *AdAge*, September 8, 2014, http://adage.com/article/campaign-trail/political-tech-picks-sides-stay-sidelines/294800/, accessed November 10, 2014.

35. Information on WPP, including a list of companies, is available at http://wpp.com/wpp/companies/, accessed November 26, 2014.

36. http://www.bsgco.com/about/team/leadership/joel-benenson; http://www.deweysquare.com/, accessed November 26, 2014. In the first six months of 2015, Benenson Strategy Group provided over $800,000 in polling services to Hillary Clinton. See http://www.fec.gov/data/CandidateSummary.do, accessed July 19, 2015. For speculation on the Clinton team, see Ruby Cramer, "Top Consulting Firm Emerges in Early Hillary Clinton Efforts," *BuzzFeedNews*, September 25, 2014, http://www.buzzfeed.com/rubycramer/top-consulting-firm-emerges-in-early-hillary-clinton-efforts, accessed November 26, 2014.

37. http://gpg.com/team/, accessed November 26, 2014.

38. http://www.prime-policy.com/talent/black, accessed November 26, 2014.

39. http://www.hkstrategies.com/leadership/mark-mckinnon, accessed November 26, 2014.

40. http://www.burson-marsteller.com/leaderships/donald-a-baer-world wide-chair-and-ceo-chair-penn-schoen-berland/, accessed November 26, 2014; http://www.wpp.com/wpp/investor/financialnews/2001/nov/16/wpp-acquires-penn-schoen-and-berland/, accessed November 26, 2014.

41. http://www.burson-marsteller.com/press-release/burson-marsteller-appoints-thomas-gensemer-as-u-s-chief-strategy-officer/, accessed November 26, 2014.

42. http://www.enhancedonlinenews.com/news/eon/20110104006352/en, accessed November 10, 2014.

43. Thomas Edsall has documented this development in "The Lobbyist in the Grey Flannel Suit," *New York Times*, May 14, 2012, http://campaignstops. blogs.nytimes.com/2012/05/14/the-lobbyist-in-the-gray-flannel-suit/, accessed March 27, 2015, and "The Shadow Lobbyist," *New York Times*, April 25, 2013, http://opinionator.blogs.nytimes.com/2013/04/25/ the-shadow-lobbyist/, accessed March 27, 2015.

44. Together, these four multinational holding companies control almost two-thirds of the revenue generated by the top fifty advertising agencies in the world. Rupal Parekh and Bradley Johnson, "Publicis Omnicom Group: All the Facts You Need to Know," *AdAge*, July 28, 2013, http:// adage.com/article/news/publicis-omnicom-group-facts/243346/, accessed November 26, 2014.

45. James Harding, *Alpha Dogs: The Americans Who Turned Political Spin into a Global Business* (New York: Farrar, Straus and Giroux, 2009).

46. http://www.webershandwick.com/who-we-are/bio/jack-leslie, accessed November 28, 2014.

47. "Publicis Group Expands U.S. Capabilities with Acquisition of Winner & Associates, Leading U.S. Public Affairs Firm," *PR Newswire*, March 28, 2000, http://tinyurl.com/publiciswinner, accessed November 28, 2014.

48. Stuart Elliott, "Fleishman-Hillard Buys Greer, Margolis," *New York Times*, December 26, 2000), http://www.nytimes.com/2000/12/26/business/the-m edia-business-advertising-addenda-fleishman-hillard-buys-greer-margolis. html, accessed March 27, 2015.

49. http://www.p2012.org/candidates/obamaorg.html#tech. GMMB data retrieved from Center for Responsive Politics, http://www.opensecrets. org/expends/vendor.php?year=2012&vendor=GMMB, accessed March 27, 2015.

50. Bradley Johnson, "Blue Chip Advertisers' Spending Hits Record $109B, Passing Pre-recession Peak," *Ad Age*, June 22, 2014, http:// adage.com/article/news/blue-chip-advertisers-spending- hits-record-109b/293819/, accessed April 25, 2015; http://www. businessinsider.com/12-biggest-advertising-spenders-in-2013-2014-6#proctor -and-gamble-spent-5-billion-on-ads-12, accessed April 25, 2015.

51. Mark Penn, "What Companies Can Learn from Political Campaigns," *Harvard Business Review*, December 21, 2011, https://hbr.org/2011/12/ what-companies-can-learn-from, accessed March 27, 2014.

52. Jack Martin, "Public Relations and Public Affairs," *WPP Annual Report & Accounts, 2013*, p. 74, www.wpp.com/annualreports/2013/, accessed November 24, 2014.

53. Martin Sorell, "Why We Exist," *WPP Annual Report & Accounts, 2013*, p. 14, www.wpp.com/annualreports/2013/, accessed November 24, 2014.

54. Emily Schulthies, "Obama Techies Sell Startup to NGP VAN," *Politico*, November 14, 2013, http://www.politico.com/story/2013/11/ obama-techies-sell-startup-to-ngp-van-99866.html, accessed March 27, 2015.

55. Karsten Strauss, "The Democratic Campaign Machine Gets a Shot in the Arm: NGP VAN Buys NationalField," *Forbes*, November 14, 2013, http://www.forbes.com/sites/karstenstrauss/2013/11/14/ the-democratic-campaign-machine-gets-a-shot-in- the-arm-ngp-van-buys-nationalfield/, accessed May 1, 2015.

56. Totals calculated by author; see appendix for a description of method. Figures include expenditures by the candidate committees as well as allied PACs (Romney Victory Inc. and Obama Victory Fund 2012).

57. See appendix table A6.

58. See appendix table A7.

59. http://www.bpimedia.com/about/, accessed March 27, 2015.

60. http://www.prnewswire.com/news-releases/andrew-bleeker-founder-of- bully-pulpit-interactive-joins-hill-knowlton-113603389.html, accessed November 10, 2014.

Chapter 9

1. Sasha Issenberg, *The Victory Lab: The Secret Science of Winning Campaigns* (New York: Crown, 2012).

2. Mordecai Lee, "Government Is Different: A History of Public Relations in American Public Administration," in *Pathways to Public Relations: Histories of Practice and Profession*, ed. Burton St. John III, Margot Opdycke Lamme, and Jacquie L'Etang (London: Routledge, 2014).

3. Joe Klein, *Politics Lost: How American Democracy Was Trivialized by People Who Think You're Stupid* (New York: Doubleday, 2006).

4. Harold D. Lasswell, "The Theory of Political Propaganda," *American Political Science Review* 21 (August 1927): 631.

5. See, for example, John Geer, *In Defense of Negativity: Attack Ads in Presidential Campaigns* (Chicago: University of Chicago Press, 2006).

6. Pollsters with academic backgrounds include Richard Wirthlin (a former economics professor), Bob Teeter, Bill Hamilton, Mark Mellman, and Stanley Greenberg.

7. Issenberg, *The Victory Lab*.

8. Lawrence Jacobs and Robert Shapiro, *Politicians Don't Pander: Political Manipulation and the Loss of Democratic Responsiveness* (Chicago: University of Chicago Press, 2000).

9. These spots are available at "The Living Room Candidate: Presidential Campaign Commercials, 1952–2012," http://www.livingroomcandidate.org/ commercials/1952, accessed October 3, 2014.

10. Edie Goldenberg and Michael Traugott, *Campaigning for Congress* (Washington, DC: Congressional Quarterly, 1984), 116.

11. See, for example, Robert Salisbury and Kenneth Shepsle, "U.S. Congressman as Enterprise," *Legislative Studies Quarterly* 6 (November 1981): 559–576; John Aldrich, *Why Parties? A Second Look* (Chicago: University of Chicago Press, 2011).

12. Lee, "Government Is Different." See also Mordecai Lee, *Promoting the War Effort: Robert Horton and Federal Propaganda, 1938–1946* (Baton Rouge: Louisiana State University Press, 2012).

13. Theodore Lowi, *The Personal President: Power Invested, Promise Unfulfilled* (Ithaca, NY: Cornell University Press, 1986).

14. Edward Walker, *Grassroots for Hire: Public Affairs Consultants in American Democracy* (New York: Cambridge University Press, 2014).

15. Larry Sabato, *The Rise of Political Consultants: New Ways of Winning Elections* (New York: Basic Books, 1983).

16. See, for example, Robin Kolodny and Angela Logan, "Political Consultants and the Extension of Party Goals," *PS: Political Science and Politics* 31 (1998): 155–159.

17. John Aldrich, *Why Parties? A Second Look* (Chicago: University of Chicago Press, 2011), 284-290.

18. Klein, *Politics Lost.*

19. Michael McGerr, *The Decline of Popular Politics: The American North, 1865–1928* (Oxford: Oxford University Press, 1986).

20. Sarah Igo, *The Averaged American: Surveys, Citizens, and the Making of a Mass Public* (Cambridge, MA: Harvard University Press, 2007).

21. Robert Westbrook, "Politics as Consumption: Managing the Modern Election," in *The Culture of Consumption: Critical Essays in American History, 1880–1980*, ed. Richard W. Fox and T. J. Jackson Lears (New York: Pantheon, 1983), 145–173.

22. Matt Grossmann, "Campaigning as an Industry: Consulting Business Models and Intra-party Competition," *Business and Politics* 11.2 (2009): article 2, p. 10.

23. Henry Brady, Richard Johnston, and John Sides, "The Study of Political Campaigns," in *Capturing Campaign Effects*, ed. Henry Brady and Richard Johnston (Ann Arbor: University of Michigan Press, 2006).

24. Paul Herrnson, "Campaign Professionalism and Fundraising in Congressional Elections," *Journal of Politics* 54 (1992): 859–870; Sean Cain, "An Elite Theory of Political Consulting and Its Implications for U.S. House Election Competition," *Political Behavior* 33 (2011): 375–405.

25. Grossmann, "Campaigning as an Industry."

26. Matt Grossmann, "What (or Who) Makes Campaigns Negative?" (paper presented at the annual meeting of the American Political Science Association, Chicago, Illinois, September, 2009); Brendan Nyhan and Jacob Montgomery, "Connecting the Candidates: Consultant Networks and the Diffusion of Campaign Strategy in American Congressional Elections," *American Journal of Political Science* 59 (2015): 292–308.

27. Gregory Martin and Zachary Peskowitz, "Parties and Electoral Performance in the Market for Political Consultants," *Legislative Studies Quarterly*, 40 (2015): 441–470.
28. Adam Sheingate, "The Terrain of the Political Entrepreneur," in *Formative Acts: American Politics in the Making*, ed. Stephen Skowronek and Matthew Glassman (Philadelphia: University of Pennsylvania Press, 2007), 13–31.
29. Rasmus Kleis Nielsen, *Ground Wars: Personalized Communication in Political Campaigns* (Princeton, NJ: Princeton University Press, 2012).

Appendix
1. For information on OpenRefine, see http://openrefine.org/.
2. This was the minimum threshold within each data set, rather than a minimum across all five data sets.

INDEX